P9-CRW-939

BLACK ENTERPRISE
GUIDE TO
BUILDING YOUR CAREER

MAYWOOD PUBLIC LIBRARY
121 SOUTH 5TH AVE.
MAYWOOD, IL 60153

Black Enterprise books provide useful information on a broad spectrum of business and general-interest topics, including entrepreneurship, personal and business finance, and career development. They are designed to meet the needs of the vital and growing African-American business market and to provide the information and resources that will help African-Americans achieve their goals. The books are written by and about African-American professionals and entrepreneurs, and they have been developed with the assistance of the staff of *Black Enterprise,* the premier African-American business magazine.

The series currently includes the following books:

Titans of the B.E. 100s: Black CEOs Who Redefined and Conquered American Business
by Derek T. Dingle

Black Enterprise Guide to Starting Your Own Business
by Wendy Beech

The Millionaires' Club: How to Start and Run Your Own Investment Club—and Make Your Money Grow!
by Caroline M. Brown

The Black Enterprise Guide to Investing
by James A. Anderson

Against All Odds: Ten Inspiring Stories of Successful African-American Entrepreneurs
by Wendy Harris

Take a Lesson: Contemporary Achievers on How They Made It and What They Learned Along the Way
by Caroline Clarke

Forthcoming:

In the Black: A History of African Americans on Wall Street
by Gregory S. Bell

Bridging the Digital Divide: Technology Strategies for African American Entrepreneurs
by Bernadette Williams

Wealth Building Journal: A Day-by-Day Journey to a Brighter Future, a Better You
by the Editors of *Black Enterprise* Magazine

BLACK ENTERPRISE GUIDE TO BUILDING YOUR CAREER

Cassandra Hayes

John Wiley & Sons, Inc.

Copyright © 2002 by Cassandra Hayes. All rights reserved.

Published by John Wiley & Sons, Inc., New York.
Published simultaneously in Canada.

No part of this publication may be reproduced, stored in a retrieval system or
transmitted in any form or by any means, electronic, mechanical, photocopying,
recording, scanning or otherwise, except as permitted under Section 107 or 108 of
the 1976 United States Copyright Act, without either the prior written permission
of the Publisher, or authorization through payment of the appropriate per-copy fee
to the Copyright Clearance Center, 222 Rosewood Drive, Danvers, MA 01923,
(978) 750-8400, fax (978) 750-4744. Requests to the Publisher for permission should
be addressed to the Permissions Department, John Wiley & Sons, Inc., 605 Third
Avenue, New York, NY 10158-0012, (212) 850-6011, fax (212) 850-6008, E-Mail:
PERMREQ@WILEY.COM.

This publication is designed to provide accurate and authoritative information in
regard to the subject matter covered. It is sold with the understanding that the
publisher is not engaged in rendering professional services. If professional advice or
other expert assistance is required, the services of a competent professional person
should be sought.

Library of Congress Cataloging-in-Publication Data:

Hayes, Cassandra
    Black enterprise guide to building your career / Cassandra Hayes.
       p. cm.—(Black enterprise books)
    Includes index.
    ISBN 0-471-41710-6 (pbk. : alk. paper)
    1. New business enterprises.   2. Black business enterprises.   I. Title.   II. Series.
    HD62.5 H384 2002
    650.14'089'96073—dc21

                                                                            2001045646

Printed in the United States of America.

10   9   8   7   6   5   4   3   2   1

To Eric and Max

ACKNOWLEDGMENTS

I want to thank *Black Enterprise* magazine and Caroline Clarke for the opportunity to write my first book. Special thanks to Donna Ladson, Jeannine Carter, Nancy Rubenstein, M.D., Aaron Dekar Lawson, Terrence Alan Reese, Barbara Easterling, Elizabeth Janice, Darryl S. Hollar, James A. Anderson, Dr. Maryalice Mazzara, Dr. Alexander J. Motyl, Regina McCannelly, Gary Brown, Stefanie Solomon, Phyllis Peterson, J. J., Dr. Elizabeth Stone, Dr. Philomena Essed, Dr. Teun Van Dijk, Eric Bowman, Esq., my mother Violet Hayes, my sister Jennifer Hayes-Bowman, and most of all God for all the love, guidance, and support they have bestowed upon me.

CONTENTS

INTRODUCTION

Work . . . it shapes our lives, pays our bills, and defines who we are to the rest of the world. It's a preoccupation and an occupation. Work is unarguably an important dynamic; it influences everything else we do. If you want a rewarding career instead of just a job, the value and importance of your work can increase tenfold. Yet, despite the importance of a career, many people aren't armed with the knowledge of where to begin choosing or finding one.

In grade school, you may have fantasized about being an astronaut or a doctor. When you were in high school, your parents may have extolled the virtues of teaching, or practicing law. They may even be your role models for those professions. As you contemplated college, you may have investigated the possibility of being an engineer or a fashion designer. You may have applied to schools that concentrated on those disciplines. Despite all of this soul-searching and investigation, you may still have walked across the stage on graduation day, accepted your college diploma, and asked yourself, "What do I do now?"

The *Black Enterprise Guide to Building Your Career* will help you to separate the wheat from the chaff in the job scene, dispel some of the job-search myths, and move you closer to linking the factors that can make a successful career happen. This book can guide you, whether you're just starting out or are already working but are considering making a switch and "starting over." The advice here can help you find fulfillment in an area of your life that can encompass virtually half of your waking hours. The road to career discovery should be challenging, intriguing, entertaining, and, ultimately, rewarding.

Launching a successful career means understanding where you fit into the larger picture of the world of work. Let's begin by looking at where African Americans are in the workplace today.

THE LANDSCAPE

There are more than 250 million people in the United States. According to the Bureau of Labor Statistics,[1] almost 150 million of them work—whether part-time, full-time, or on a contract or temporary basis. The U.S. Census Bureau[2] estimates that, in 2000, among employed African Americans age 16 and over, 25 percent of women and 18 percent of men worked in managerial and professional specialties (e.g., as engineers, dentists, teachers, lawyers, and journalists). Similarly, a higher proportion of women than men worked in service jobs (27 percent versus 17 percent) and in technical, sales, and administrative support jobs (38 percent versus 20 percent).

Among African Americans age 25 and over, 79 percent had earned at least a high school diploma, and 17 percent had attained a bachelor's degree by March 2000. Both percentages represented record levels of educational attainment. This increase is projected to continue well into the new century if African Americans are armed with the right skills and resources to make informed career decisions.

What skills do you need? In scanning today's employment horizon, certain things become clear. No longer will any of the three employment sectors—public, private, or nonprofit—bloat their payrolls with employees who cannot produce 110 percent. Those who stand to reap rewards are individuals with technical, marketing, and, above all, interpersonal skills. Don't look for this to be ending any time soon. Those who heed the call will thrive; those who don't will be left behind.

The unemployment rate hovered around 4 percent for seven years. Only in the early part of 2001 did that flurry begin to subside as the economy started to tighten its belt.

Human resources managers aren't hitting the brakes yet, but they're easing up on the accelerator as they move ahead, says Eric Rolfe Greenberg,[3] director of management studies at the American Management Association in New York. Broadly speaking, companies are hiring from the line and firing from the staff, says Greenberg.

Companies are creating jobs where people design, make, sell, and service their products; at the same time, they are eliminating administrative functions and squeezing whole levels out of the management pyramid. The only support functions showing strong hiring patterns are in information technology (IT) and production technologies. Hence, in some companies, job creation may be happening concurrently with job elimination.

It's important for African Americans to get into line jobs [those that contribute to the bottom line, such as in sales or research and development (R&D)], and to make themselves indispensable, according to Wesley Poriotis,[4] CEO at Wesley, Brown & Bartle Co., Inc., a New York executive search firm. "Multiple skills will be your bulletproof vest," he adds.

So, as you chart out your career plans, keep in mind that diversified skills and multitask ability will be essential. In fact, as you plan for your ultimate career, you might have at least three careers along the way: a pharmaceutical salesperson for your first five years of full-time work, a brand manager for a consumer goods company during your thirties, and possibly a college professor of marketing 10 years later. Experience will be key. Earlier generations stayed on one job until they received the perennial gold watch. For you, getting experience from different areas will be the norm. Many people work 15 years but get only one year's worth of experience because they concentrate on just one department. They then become prime targets for layoffs. "It's not about moving up; it's about moving across," adds Poriotis. "You must break down the glass walls and not just focus on the glass ceiling."

WORKFORCE 2020

In 1987, the *Workforce 2000*[5] study by the Hudson Institute (based in Indianapolis) set American employers on their heads with the news—backed by proven research—that the workplace, nationwide, would be increasingly peppered with more shades of black, brown, red, and yellow than the customary white. In response, companies launched elaborate diversity management programs to accommodate the cultural and ethnical evolution that would take place. Eleven years later, the Indianapolis think tank revisited the critically acclaimed study and issued *Workforce 2020*. Armed with new data, the report not only reinforces its original research, which asserted that more women and minorities would be entering the workforce, but also counters some serious misconceptions about the earlier landmark study.

When *Workforce 2000* was first released, a flurry of media-generated "myths and half-truths" abounded: jobs in manufacturing would disappear; technology would be dumbed down and would destroy current jobs; wages would decrease and the middle class would shrink; the majority of tomorrow's workforce would be nonwhites and women; and global trade would harm American workers. Yet, in the throes of this "Information Age," the revised study tells today's workers and businesses to heed the following warnings:

- Manufacturing jobs won't totally disappear; the demand for U.S. exports remains strong in emerging countries. But workers will have to compete globally for their jobs and should upgrade their technological skills in order to survive.
- Successful workers will be those who acquire the technological skills necessary for advancement. Many will transfer into the service industry, where jobs will be fueled by aging baby

---

THE FUTURE OF WORK

"Quality of life at work and home will continue to grow in importance and people will change jobs more frequently. Workers will choose their employers based on flexibility and family-friendly programs."—*Joyce L. Gioia, strategic business futurist, president of The Herman Group in Greensboro, North Carolina, and co-author of* Lean & Meaningful: A New Culture for Corporate America *(Oakhill Press)*[6]

"Companies will come to better understand the importance of 'environment' where team spirit, values, ethics and mission statements will become increasingly important to employees."—*Joyce L. Gioia*

boomers, who will represent a large majority of the consumer market.

- Whites will continue to replace other whites in the workforce. Representing 76 percent of the workforce today, they will still hold 68 percent of the jobs in 2020. Minorities will constitute little more than half of new workforce entrants and only one-third over the next decade. African Americans will continue to represent only 11 percent of the workforce. Hispanic workers will increase from 10 percent in the year 2000 to 14 percent in 2020.

WHERE THE JOBS ARE

Key Industries

Alas, as the average American tries to keep up with the latest PC technology, the high-tech arena is reinventing itself for the next frontier. "Silicon Valley is still strong and going biotech," says Michael Reid,[7] founder and managing director of Michael James Reid & Co., a San Francisco-based executive search firm. Reid adds that venture capitalists of the Valley are looking at research areas such as Triangle Park, North Carolina, in order to team together science and technology. This is a booming area for African Americans, and it's important for those with science and tech backgrounds to be in front of this wave and ride it, says Reid.

Another area of job creation is what Reid terms the "adversity opportunity." This trend is evident in what has occurred in the past decade with companies such as Denny's and Texaco. Companies that were in the midst of those controversies will open the greatest number of opportunities for midlevel and senior jobs and board appointments, says Reid. Companies that have been accused of unfair employment practices will be scrutinized for the next five to 10 years. In an effort to shed the stigma, they have made huge employment turnarounds, he says. This has led and will continue to lead other companies to follow suit.

In addition to information technology (IT), sales, marketing, health care and engineering, other industries will experience dramatic growth. "The big comeback could very well be the area of finance and accounting," says Ken Abosch,[8] principal and motivation content

Occupations with the fast growth and high pay that have the largest numerical growth, projected 1998–2008

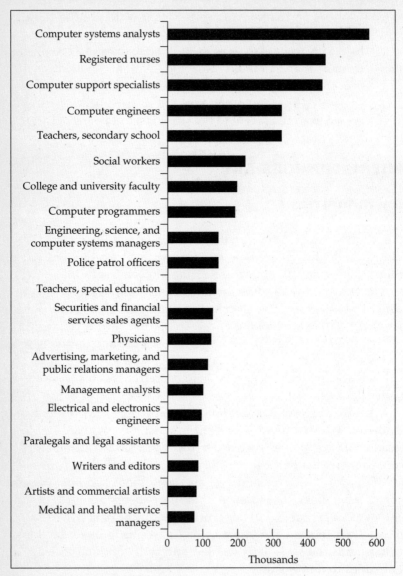

Source: U.S. Bureau of Labor Statistics.

Occupations with the largest numerical decrease in employment, projected 1998–2008

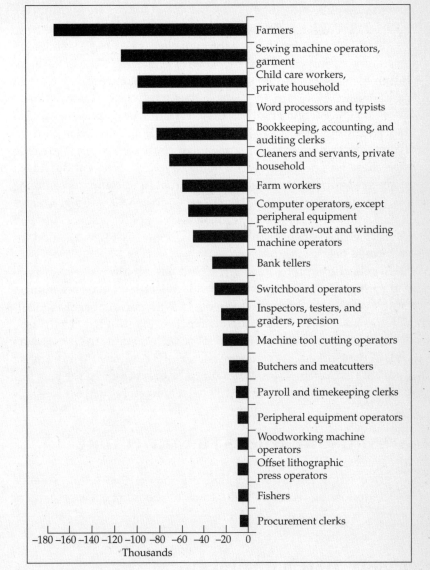

Source: U.S. Bureau of Labor Statistics.

leader at Hewitt Associates in Lincolnshire, Illinois. Like many corporate functions, these areas had cut staff and now there appears to be a shortage of these professionals.

Another sleeper industry is risk management. Individuals who can determine creditworthiness through the use of high technology and data crunching can write their own paychecks. "Those with co-branding and smart card experience who can manage every facet of the credit card cycle are in highest demand," says Susan Allard,[9] founder and CEO at San Francisco-based Allard Associates Inc., an executive recruiting firm specializing in the banking and credit card industry. Allard states that, as companies continue to target diverse groups, there will be an increased demand for minority candidates at e-commerce, insurance, mortgage, and mutual fund companies, among others. Starting salaries range from $50,000 to $65,000. Top graduates with backgrounds in statistics, economics, computer science, applied mathematics, and other technical fields will qualify to get the nod for these coveted posts.

For collections professionals, the path has not always been as pristine. Long regarded as a career wasteland, collections is fast becoming a hot training ground for top executive posts. With personal debt at an all-time high, and with soaring delinquencies and bankruptcy filings, banks and creditors are looking for folks with quantitative skills who can call in the markers. As company charge-offs continue their dramatic rise, so will the average top salaries for these executives. In the past few years, their annual pay has jumped 50 percent to more than $165,000.

FASTEST GROWING JOBS FOR THE FUTURE

There are exciting paths to take that you may not have even considered. The following list represents some of the most exciting careers of the future.

Computer System Analysts, Engineers, and Scientists

High-tech—the mother of all job creation industries—will continue to woo more workers into its fold. Significant increases in these jobs reflect the growth in consulting and systems integration and the development of technologies that create new areas for computer use. The rapid spread of computers and information technology has generated a need for highly trained workers to design and develop new hardware and software systems and to incorporate new technologies. Computer systems analysts, engineers, and scientists, including about 114,000 who were self-employed, held about 1.5 million jobs in 1998, according to the U.S. Bureau of Labor Statistics. Their employment was distributed among the following detailed occupations*:

Computer systems analysts	617,000
Computer support specialists	429,000
Computer engineers	299,000
Database administrators	87,000
All other computer scientists	97,000

Requirements: Relevant work experience and a B.S. degree in computer science are prerequisites for many jobs; for more complex jobs, a graduate degree is necessary or preferred. Computer systems analysts, engineers, and scientists must be able to think logically and have good communication skills. They often deal with a number of tasks simultaneously; therefore, an ability to concentrate and pay close attention to detail is necessary. Although computer specialists sometimes work independently, they often work in teams assigned to large projects. They must be able to communicate effectively with computer personnel, such as programmers and managers, as well as with users or other staff who may have no technical computer background.

Salary: Median annual earnings of computer systems analysts were $52,180 in 1998. The middle 50 percent earned between $40,570 and $74,180 a year. The lowest 10 percent earned less than $32,470, and the highest 10 percent earned more than $87,810.[†]

Organization: Black Data Processing Associates (BDPA), Thought Leaders, 1111 14th Street N.W., Suite 700, Washington, DC 20005; 800-727-BDPA; www.bdpa.org

---

*Source: *Occupational Outlook Handbook, 2000–2001 edition.*
[†] U.S. Bureau of Labor Statistics.

Special Education Teachers

As the school-age population increases, there will also be a rise in the number of students with special needs. More acute attention to and understanding of developmental issues in children will require professionals who can address these needs. Special education teachers held about 406,000 jobs in 1998, according to the U.S. Bureau of Statistics. The majority of special education teachers were employed in elementary, middle, and secondary public schools. The remainder worked in separate educational or residential facilities, or in homebound or hospital environments.

Requirements: Bachelor's degree in special education, plus state exam and licensing. A master's degree may be required in some states. Special education teachers must be patient and able to motivate these students and understand their special needs. Teachers must be creative and ready to apply different types of teaching methods when necessary. They must also communicate well; a great deal of their time will be spent interacting with students, parents, and school faculty and administrators.

Salary: Median annual earnings of special education teachers in 1998 were $37,850. The middle 50 percent earned between $30,410 and $48,390. The lowest 10 percent earned less than $25,450; the highest 10 percent, more than $78,030.*

Organization: National Clearinghouse on Careers and Professions Related to Early Intervention and Education for Children with Disabilities, 1920 Association Drive, Reston, VA 20191-1589, www.special-ed-careers.org

Pharmacists

As the general population ages, the increase in cures and treatments for different diseases, and in drug advancements, will fuel the demand for more pharmacists. Pharmacists mix and dispense medications ordered by physicians or other health care prescribers, and are fast becoming more involved in drug therapy decision making and patient counseling. Earnings are very high, but some pharmacists work long hours, nights, weekends, and holidays. Pharmacists held about 185,000

---

*U.S. Bureau of Labor Statistics.

jobs in 1998, according to the Bureau of Labor Statistics. Most worked in community pharmacies, grocery or department stores, or for mass merchandisers. Others worked in hospitals or clinics, at mail-order pharmacies, pharmaceutical wholesalers, and home health care agencies, or for the federal government.

Requirements: B.S. degree in pharmacy (five years of study plus licensing and registering). All pharmacists must pass a rigorous examination in the state in which they plan to practice. Prospective pharmacists should have scientific aptitude, good communication skills, and a desire to help others. They must also be conscientious and pay close attention to detail, because the decisions they make affect human lives.

Salary: Median annual earnings of pharmacists in 1998 were $66,220. The middle 50 percent earned between $52,310 and $80,250 a year. The lowest 10 percent earned less than $42,550 and the highest 10 percent more than $88,670 a year.*

Organization: National Pharmaceutical Association, 107 Kilmayne Drive, Suite C, Cary, NC 27511; 919-469-5858

Speech Pathologists and Audiologists

These specialists provide speech and hearing services, evaluate speech and language abilities, and help improve communication skills. Managed health care has increased the demand for speech pathologists and audiologists in sync with the expansion of outpatient rehabilitation services. About half work in schools; most others are employed at health care facilities. An aging population is fueling the demand for audiologists, due to the probability of increased hearing loss. In addition, baby boomers are now entering middle age—the years when the possibility of neurological disorders and associated speech, language, and hearing impairment increases. Medical advances are also improving the survival rate of premature infants and trauma and stroke victims, who then need assessment and possible treatment.

Speech-language pathologists and audiologists held about 105,000 jobs in 1998, according to the U.S. Bureau of Labor Statistics. About one-half provided services at preschool, elementary, and secondary school levels, or at colleges and universities. Others worked in offices of speech-language pathologists and audiologists; hospitals; offices of

---

*U.S. Bureau of Labor Statistics.

physicians; speech, language, and hearing centers; home health agencies; or other facilities. Some speech-language pathologists and audiologists are self-employed in private practice, according to the U.S. Bureau of Labor Statistics.

Requirements: Bachelor's degree—and preferably, a master's degree—state licensing and certification, as well as teaching credentials. A master's degree in speech-language pathology or audiology is the standard credential. Other requirements are 300 to 375 hours of supervised clinical experience, a passing score on a national examination, and nine months of postgraduate professional clinical experience.

Salary: Median annual earnings of speech-language pathologists and audiologists were $43,080 in 1998. The middle 50 percent earned between $34,580 and $55,260 a year. The lowest 10 percent earned less than $27,460, and the highest 10 percent earned more than $80,720 a year.*

Organization: National Black Association for Speech-Language and Hearing, 3605 Collier Road, Beltsville, MD; 202-274-6162

Accountants

Demand for these professionals will continue to increase because of the ongoing complexity of financial transactions, tax laws, accounting procedures and reporting requirements, and a low rate of turnover in the profession. Major growth areas include management consulting; international business; internal auditing; investigative, environmental, and cost accounting; and estate planning. Accountants and auditors held over 1,080,000 jobs in 1998, according to the U.S. Bureau of Labor Statistics. They worked throughout private industry and government, but about one out of four worked for accounting, auditing, and bookkeeping firms. Approximately one out of 10 accountants or auditors were self-employed. Most states have adopted uniform licensing legislation that will become effective in the future. Many schools have altered their curricula accordingly, and prospective accounting majors should carefully research accounting curricula and the requirements for any states in which they hope to become licensed.

Requirements: Most jobs require at least a bachelor's degree in accounting or in a related field. However, more lucrative opportunities exist for certified public accountants (CPAs), certified management

---

* U.S. Bureau of Labor Statistics.

accountants (CMAs), and certified internal auditors (CIAs), who are required to obtain additional experience and pass a four-part examination. Based on recommendations made by the American Institute of Certified Public Accountants (AICPA), 17 states currently require CPA candidates to complete 150 semester hours of college coursework—30 hours more than for the usual four-year bachelor's degree. Job seekers who obtain professional recognition through certification or licensure, a master's degree, proficiency in accounting and auditing computer software, or specialized expertise will have an advantage in the job market. Accountants should have an aptitude for mathematics and be able to analyze, compare, and interpret facts and figures quickly.

Salary: In 1998, the median annual earnings of accountants and auditors were $37,860. The middle half of the occupation earned between $29,840 and $49,460. The top 10 percent of accountants and auditors earned more than $76,160, and the entry level earned less than $23,800. Accountants and auditors earn slightly more in urban areas.*

Organization: National Association of Black Accountants Inc. (NABA), 7249-A Hanover Parkway, Greenbelt, MD 20770; 301-474-NABA, www.nabainc.org

Advertising, Marketing, and Public Relations Managers

Employment is projected to increase rapidly, but competition for jobs is expected to be intense. Advertising, marketing, and public relations managers coordinate the market research, marketing strategy, sales, advertising, promotion, pricing, product development, and public relations activities for a firm or corporation that wants to market its products and services profitably.

- *Advertising managers* in small firms may serve as liaisons between the firm and the advertiser or promotion agency/client. In larger firms, advertising managers oversee in-house account services, creative services, and media services departments.
- *Marketing managers* develop the firms' detailed marketing strategy. In addition, they identify potential markets—for example, business firms, wholesalers, retailers, various levels of

---

* U.S. Bureau of Labor Statistics.

government, or the general public. Marketing managers develop pricing strategy with an eye toward maximizing the firm's share of the market and its profits while ensuring that the firm's customers are satisfied.

- *Public relations managers* direct publicity programs to a targeted public. They often specialize in a particular area, such as crisis management, or in a specific industry, such as health care. Advertising, marketing, and public relations managers held about 485,000 jobs in 1998, according to the U.S. Bureau of Labor Statistics. They work in almost every industry, particularly wholesale trade, manufacturing firms, advertising, computer and data processing services, and management and public relations. College graduates with extensive experience, a high level of creativity, and strong communication skills will find ideal job opportunities. Those with new media and interactive marketing skills will also be in high demand.

Requirements: A wide range of educational backgrounds is acceptable for advertising, marketing, and public relations managerial jobs, but many employers prefer a broad liberal arts background. However, requirements vary, depending on the particular job. For marketing, sales, and promotion management positions, some employers prefer a bachelor's or master's degree in business administration with an emphasis on marketing. For advertising management positions, a bachelor's degree in advertising or journalism is preferred. For public relations management positions, a bachelor's or master's degree in public relations or journalism is preferred.

Salary: Median annual earnings of advertising, marketing, promotions, public relations, and sales managers in 1998 were $57,300. The middle 50 percent earned between $38,230 and $84,950 a year. The lowest 10 percent earned less than $28,190, and the highest 10 percent earned more than $116,160 a year.*

Organizations: National Association of Market Developers, P.O. Box 2936, Grand Central Station, New York, NY 10163; www.namdnt .org; Public Relations Society of America, 33 Irving Place, New York, NY 10003-2376; www.prsa.org; National Black Public Relations Society, 6565 Sunset Boulevard, #301, Los Angeles, CA 90028; 213-466-8221; Sales

---

*U.S. Bureau of Labor Statistics.

and Marketing Executives International, 5500 Interstate North Parkway, No. 545, Atlanta, GA 30328-4662; www.smei.org

Paralegals

In our increasingly litigious society, the need for law professionals will grow. In some states, paralegals serve as mediators, in lieu of costly attorneys. Paralegals help lawyers prepare for closings, hearings, trials, and corporate meetings. They investigate the facts of cases and ensure that all relevant information is considered. They also identify appropriate laws, judicial decisions, legal articles, and other materials that are relevant to assigned cases. Paralegals may also prepare written reports that attorneys use in determining how cases should be handled. Paralegals are projected to rank among the fastest growing occupations in the economy; increasingly, they are performing many legal tasks formerly carried out by lawyers. Paralegals held about 136,000 jobs in 1998, according to the U.S. Bureau of Labor Statistics. Most worked at private law firms; the remainder worked for corporate legal departments and various levels of government. A small number of paralegals own their own businesses and work as freelance legal assistants.

Requirements: Paralegal training is obtained through associate or bachelor's degree programs, or through a certification program. However, more and more employers want graduates of four-year paralegal programs, or college graduates who have completed paralegal certificate programs.

Salaries: In 1998, full-time, wage-and-salary paralegals had median annual earnings of $32,760. The middle 50 percent earned between $26,240 and $40,960. The top 10 percent earned more than $50,290, and the bottom 10 percent earned less than $21,770.*

Organization: National Association of Legal Assistants, Inc., 1516 South Boston Street, Suite 200, Tulsa, OK 74119; www.nala.org

Registered Nurses

This is the largest health care occupation (over 2 million jobs), according to the Bureau of Labor Statistics. There is an increasing demand for

---

* U.S. Bureau of Labor Statistics.

all health services, as well as a trend, among hospitals, to replace licensed practical nurses with fully registered nurses. The growth of the elderly population, especially those over age 85, will increase the demand for nursing homes, skilled-care nursing facilities, and geriatric nurses. There will always be a need for traditional hospital nurses, but a large number of new nurses will be employed in home health, long-term, and ambulatory care. Registered nurses held about 2.1 million jobs in 1998, according to the Bureau of Labor Statistics. Most jobs were in hospitals. Others were mostly in doctors' offices, clinics, nursing homes, temporary help agencies, and schools, or with home health care agencies and government agencies. The remainder worked in residential care facilities, social service agencies, religious organizations, research facilities, management and public relations firms, insurance agencies, and private households.

Requirements: A B.S. degree in nursing is preferred. However, there are three major educational paths to nursing: (1) associate degree in nursing (A.D.N.), (2) Bachelor of Science degree in nursing (B.S.N.), and (3) diploma. A.D.N. programs, offered by community and junior colleges, take about two years. State licensing is required. Nurses should be caring and sympathetic. They must be able to accept responsibility, direct or supervise others, follow orders precisely, and determine when consultation is required.

Salary: Median annual earnings of registered nurses were $40,690 in 1998. The middle 50 percent earned between $34,430 and $49,070 a year. The lowest 10 percent earned less than $29,480, and the highest 10 percent earned more than $69,300 a year.*

Organization: National Black Nurses Association, 8630 Fenton Street, Suite 330, Silver Spring, MD 20910; 301-589-3200; www.nbna.org

It won't always be easy, but to compete in today's workplace, you must devise a career or life plan. Being indecisive will only slow you down. You may not know what you want to do immediately, but acquiring the skills that employers want today will eventually prepare you for the job you will want tomorrow.

This book begins with the basics. Chapter 1 addresses how you decide on and then plan your future. Questions to ask are: What do you want to be doing X years from now, and what do you have to do to achieve that goal? A plan has to be developed during your college, or

---

*U.S. Bureau of Labor Statistics.

even your high school years, to eventually make your later years fulfilling. What does it take to devise a plan?

If you have followed your plan, you've gotten the fundamental training or education. Now you have to go forward. The first step is preparing your *resume.* Chapter 2 addresses this integral job search tool. I have seen a lot of resumes in my time, and I am always disappointed that, with so many career books available, so many resumes are lacking. I don't just mean style; I mean presentation, grammar, punctuation, phrasing, and so on. This chapter will give you the basics for a crisp hard-copy resume (and the online option) and will also provide some advice on how to make the best presentation via font size and style.

In Chapter 3, learn the finer points of *networking* and work hard at building your network of contacts—people who will help you in your job search and research. Chapter 4 will provide all the information you need for taking your *job search* on the road and online. Learn how and where to research companies, and make the most of everything from career fairs to temporary employment to land the job of your dreams. Before you can punch a clock, you have to have the all-important *interview.* Many people look good on paper, but when you talk to them, things are different. Chapter 5 details the dos and don'ts of job interviews: how to dress, what to say, and how to bolster what the screener sees on paper. This is your chance to shine; however, you shouldn't overshine or be too demure. This is when companies evaluate whether you "fit" and how you will work within the corporate culture. Hiring is not just about qualifications anymore. Qualifications probably got you into the reception area, but how you apply those achievements will be integral, and that's what companies are looking for. Your communication style, presentation, temperament, confidence, and appearance are all evaluated.

Is more education what you need? Then Chapter 6 will fill you in on *graduate school, internships, and studying abroad*—tools that may enrich your career and life experiences and make you even more attractive to employers. Before, during, and after you receive a job offer, employers are finding out more about you than you know. The job is almost yours, but is the salary what you expected? In Chapter 7, learn how to research *salary* surveys and how to negotiate to get paid what you're worth. There were many *African American corporate mavericks* who paved the way for many of the opportunities available today. Chapter 8 tells what it was like for those who were fortunate enough to climb the crystal staircase to the top. Find out how to get the most out of a relationship with an *executive recruiter,* and the dos and don'ts of being headhunted, in Chapter 9. Once you've gotten a job, you have to learn how to keep it. Chapter 10 provides information for midcareer professionals and offers tips on how to make career transitions. Chapter 11 introduces you to corporate culture, the workplace, and what it's like *on the job.* Chapter 12 will round out your career portfolio with a quick lesson in business *etiquette.*

Your career is what you make it. With a lot of motivation and skill, and a little good fortune, you should be able to make your career dreams come true. Good luck!

1

PLANNING YOUR CAREER

Career planning is a rewarding process. *You* explore and determine *your* ideal career direction based on *your* interests, personality, values, style of work, aptitudes, and skills. Life is fast-paced today. Years could go by before you explored your potential and determined what you would truly enjoy doing for a living. Many businesspeople can attest to the financial and social pitfalls associated with choosing the wrong major or changing to another major midway through college. In a survey of college-educated workers between the ages of 30 and 55, almost half of the 400 people polled said they would choose a different major if they had a chance to redo their college curriculum. The survey, conducted for George Mason University and the Potomac Knowledge Way,[1] in Fairfax, Virginia, contends that the majority of college graduates have switched careers at least once, and about one in five expects to switch in the future.

Call it her luck or her skill, career coach Nancy Friedberg[2] is a miracle worker. When she met one of her clients—a librarian—he was stuck in a career rut. However, two years and eight counseling sessions later, with Friedberg's help, he switched from the public sector and library science to the private sector and technology consulting.

How did an English literature major end up as an SAP consultant for a Big Five accounting firm? Through Friedberg's career coaching, he realized that his ability to learn and communicate new skills far outweighed his lack of technological expertise. He parlayed those skills during interviews and performance appraisals. He became focused, confident, and motivated, and Friedberg helped him find a career he was passionate about. But it wasn't by chance. Friedberg advises: "It is so important to plan your career and not drift wherever the wind blows. You must do some careful long-term strategic planning, make a commitment, and accept the fact that there will be some trade-off. Too often, people try to fit themselves into a job instead of finding a job that fits."

Weary of the travel demands of the consulting profession, Friedberg's client recently joined a New Jersey pharmaceutical company. The move is a step up but may be only temporary. The next stage of his life plan includes maintaining regular hours so that he can be home with his wife and new baby, as well as pursue an MBA degree. In five years, Friedberg's client not only found fulfilling work and a successful career path, but also quadrupled his salary, catapulting him into the six-digit range.

WHY PLAN?

When you love the work you do, you do it well. You're more motivated, confident, and successful. Opportunities seem to always come your way, and those around you see a difference in you. Work becomes fun. People tend to be far more productive, go farther in their career, and enjoy life more fully when they are happy in their job and their work environment. Surveys often bear out that many working adults do not like their work. Fortunately, the resources available today are allowing more workers to make optimum career choices.

It is cheaper to do your homework up front than to stay in the wrong job too long or change your major halfway through college. With your career plan in hand, you can become successful much sooner and can sidestep some irreversible career decision mistakes.

Staying in the wrong job will cost you a lot in terms of money, health, happiness, and your well-being. Individuals often enter a less-than-fulfilling career without fully exploring other, more rewarding options. They may choose their career based on how much money they can make or because of peer or family influence. Think about how often you have heard someone say, "I fell into the job and really didn't know what I was getting into." Unfortunately, these same people may have spent more time making far less important decisions in other areas of their lives. Successful career planning involves reaching inside yourself and gaining some insight into the fundamental nature of various careers. Only then can you find out what elements make up your ideal career, and why certain other careers are dead wrong for you.

CAREER AT A GLANCE— SMOOTH SAILING

Occupation: Cruise director

Job description: Oversees all passenger activities and entertainment.

Salary range: $40,000 to $80,000

Training: Minimum of three years' cruise ship experience in assignments such as social activities coordinator, youth counselor, sports director, or purser. Background in travel, customer service, or hospitality is a plus.

An average day at work: Be prepared to work from Sunday to Sunday, 16 hours a day, and to always have a smile ready for the hundreds of passengers on your ship. Coordinating musicians and performers, managing a staff ranging from 25 to 100 people, and overseeing onboard adult and children activities are just some of your duties.

For more information on opportunities in this field, contact Keiser Career Institute, 1926 10th Avenue N., Lake Worth, FL 33461; 561-547-5472; www.Keisercareer.com.

TO BE OR NOT TO BE COUNSELED?
THAT IS THE QUESTION

Whether they want a first career or a career change, many people have sought out the services of career counselors. Referrals can be found at colleges and universities, or from career planning organizations such as the Five O'Clock Club (a national career networking organization that has chapters throughout the country), or through word of mouth.

Find someone, locally, who understands your area's job market and is experienced in helping people develop career plans. You can also locate career counselors or coaches through schools, online, or word of mouth. Their job is to help people implement work plans, or to act as job buddies who can help to remove career blocks. The greatest benefit of having a counselor, coach, or buddy, is the perspective that other person can provide. You might be able to tune up your car, but a mechanic can probably do it faster and better. Keep in mind that there are no set national criteria for qualification as a career counselor. Some counselors must undergo rigorous state licensing requirements and have advanced degrees in counseling or social work; others draw on years of job experience and merely hang out a shingle. Fees can range anywhere from $100 to $200 an hour, depending on the experience of the counselor.

The optimal career planning process involves the use of various types of career tests (also known as assessments or instruments), such as the Myers-Briggs Type Indicator® (see pages 23–26) and the Campbell Inventory, to help you better understand your career interests, motivation, work style, personality, values, skills, and aptitudes. These tests are also as close as your computer and can be taken online for nominal fees. Consider these online sources:

- *Careers By Design*® (www.careers-by-design.com). This site offers fee-based personalized assessments, using popular personality tests such as the Myers-Briggs Type Indicator®.
- *Organizational Diagnostics Online* (www.od-online.com). The Personality Profiler you'll find here is geared to help you target the perfect job or to enhance your current work situation at any stage of your professional life.
- *The Career Key* (www.ncsu.edu/careerkey). A free psychologist-developed personality and job-preference test is available here.

MYERS-BRIGGS TYPE INDICATOR® (MBTI®)

Through a battery of 93 questions, the Myers-Briggs Type Indicator® (MBTI®), published by the Consulting Psychologists Press, Inc. (www.cpp.com), and administered by a career counseling professional, can determine which of 16 types you fit. Clients are given a list of the best and worst occupational rankings for their type. Here is a sample. (The full report is more detailed.)

Sample Career Report for John Switch

This report is designed to help you understand your results on the Myers-Briggs Type Indicator® (MBTI®) and how they can be applied to your career. Your answers to the MBTI questions indicate that your four-letter type is ISTJ. This is also known as Introverted Sensing with Thinking and Judging. Your results can help you:

- Choose a career.
- Change your career.
- Increase your job satisfaction.
- Plan your career development.

Part 1: Summary of Your MBTI Results

Below is a graph of your preference clarity indexes (pci) on the four preference scales. The length of each bar is based on a formula that compares the two choices for each preference. "Very clear" means that you chose the preference consistently; "Slight" means that your choices were more evenly divided. Below the graph is a short explanation of each preference. Do your choices seem to fit you?

MYERS-BRIGGS TYPE INDICATOR® (MBTI®) *(continued)*

REPORTED TYPE: ISTJ   Pci: INTROVERSION   I   10
                                        SENSING   S   17
                                        THINKING   T   9
                                        JUDGING   J   4

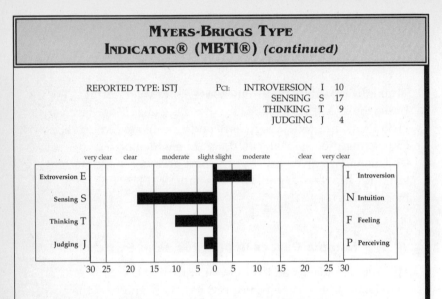

- Where a person focuses his or her attention

  E **Extraversion:** People who prefer Extraversion tend to focus on the outer world of people and things.

  I **Introversion:** People who prefer Introversion tend to focus on the inner world of ideas and impressions.

- The way a person gathers information

  S **Sensing:** People who prefer Sensing tend to focus on the present and on concrete information gained from their senses.

  N **Intuition:** People who prefer Intuition tend to focus on the future, with a view towards patterns and possibilities.

- The way a person makes decisions

  T **Thinking:** People who prefer Thinking tend to base their decisions primarily on logic and on objective analysis of cause and effect.

  F **Feeling:** People who prefer Feeling tend to base their decisions primarily on values and on subjective evaluation of person-centered concerns.

MYERS-BRIGGS TYPE INDICATOR® (MBTI®) *(continued)*

- How a person deals with the outer world

  J **Judging:** People who prefer Judging tend to like a planned and organized approach to life and prefer to have things settled.

  P **Perceiving:** People who prefer Perceiving tend to like a flexible and spontaneous approach to life and prefer to keep their options open.

The Most Popular Occupations for ISTJs

In the list below, the top 10 most popular occupations for ISTJs are rank-ordered. Many occupations offer management or administrative positions. These are attractive to ISTJs because these employees tend to be task-oriented and decisive, and they base their decisions on facts and experience. Other careers on this list require a high degree of precision or technical knowledge.

1. Operator/Technician: water pollution control
2. Steelworker
3. Police Officer: manager
4. Manager: regional telephone company
5. Manager: top level in government
6. Manager: small business
7. Corrections Sergeant
8. Certified Public Accountant
9. Manager: public
10. Manager: retail store

MYERS-BRIGGS TYPE INDICATOR® (MBTI®) *(continued)*

The Least Popular Occupations for ISTJs

Below is a ranking of the top five least popular occupations for ISTJs. ISTJs are found in these occupations, but in relatively low numbers. If you are considering one of these occupations, it may be for reasons other than your type preferences.

1. Dental Hygienist
2. Fine Artist
3. Counselor: runaway youth
4. Clergy: all denominations (except priests)
5. Musician or Composer

Keep in mind that this is only one "menu" for determining your career path. The results should be interpreted by you and your counselor or test administrator. You must evaluate your skills and abilities, your work and personal interests, and your goals and values. You must also weigh your career choice based on detailed research of the respective careers that interest you.

If years of agonizing standardized tests and college exams have left you apprehensive about test taking, just consider the benefits. It is a short-term inconvenience for long-term gain, and it allows you to:

- Discover your career-related interests and abilities.
- Identify occupations that match your interests, competencies, and personality.
- Pinpoint corresponding fields of study for further education.
- Understand how you adjust to circumstances, people, and demands in your work environment, and evaluate whether these adjustments result in stress or satisfaction.

- Identify your communications and leadership style.
- Determine transferable skills and accomplishments.
- Find out who you are.

Other things to consider while charting your career path include determining your needs and desires regarding salary and quality of life. Ask yourself:

- How much money do I want to make?
- Do I want to work with people or isolated from people? With my hands or my mind—or both?
- What contribution do I want to make, and where? To society or to a company's bottom line?
- Do I need to be in control, or part of a team, or following the pack?
- Where do I want to be in five, 10, or 20 years?

These are important questions. Peers and family may be very influential, but you have to do what *you* want to do. Let's face it: It's one thing to have a goal in your head; it's another to commit it to paper, name it, and devise a plan for getting it done. Goals are powerful tools that help determine success, vision, and focus. They also further ensure exceptional results. Not only must you determine your goals, but you must also recommit to them regularly, acknowledge and celebrate your accomplishments, and, probably most important, reevaluate your goals periodically, to see whether they still fit.

WHAT TYPE ARE YOU?

Career success is not simply determined by your interests and aptitudes. By the time you have taken your high school SAT (Student Aptitude Test) you've pretty much determined whether your aptitude is analytical or creative. What is a little bit more obscure, usually overlooked, harder to determine, and equally important is determining the work environment for which you are best suited and in which you would best perform. For employees to perform optimally on their job, their work environment must nurture their specific personality type. Take the following self-assessment test to determine your personality type and career options. In each A–B pair, circle the letter that applies to your answer:

1. *Do you often:*
   A. Accept things the way they are
   B. Question why things are a certain way
2. *Do you prefer to:*
   A. Be given the correct answer or solution
   B. Figure things out on your own
3. *If paid the same wage, would you prefer working with your:*
   A. Hands
   B. Mind
4. *Which do you prefer:*
   A. To organize
   B. To analyze
5. *Are you a:*
   A. Doer
   B. Thinker
6. *Are you inclined to be:*
   A. Easy to approach
   B. Somewhat reserved
7. *Do you think of yourself as:*
   A. An outgoing person
   B. A private person
8. *Do you find interacting with strangers:*
   A. Invigorating
   B. Taxing
9. *At a party, do you:*
   A. Interact with almost everyone
   B. Interact with a few friends
10. *Which would you prefer:*
    A. Attend a function with friends and family
    B. Go to a movie
11. *On the job, would you prefer your activities to be:*
    A. Scheduled
    B. Unscheduled

12. *Which would you prefer:*
   A. Having regular consistent work assignments
   B. Being assigned different tasks or jobs

13. *In your place of employment, would you prefer to wear:*
   A. One hat
   B. Many hats

14. *Would you rather have:*
   A. A job where you never left your office
   B. A job that required travel

15. *Which is better:*
   A. A lot of structure
   B. Frequent change

Questions 1–5
If you selected more As than Bs, you are a (**D**) type or **Doer** and do not require a lot of intellectual stimulation, on your job or in your career, to perform well. If you selected more Bs than As, you are a (**T**) type or **Thinker,** and ample intellectual stimulation on your job is necessary for you to remain interested and productive.

Questions 6–10
If you chose more As than Bs, you are an (**S**) type or **Social** individual and work best in environments where you are socially stimulated. If you selected more Bs than As, you are an (**R**) type or **Reserved** individual who requires little social stimulation to function optimally in your workplace.

Questions 11–15
If you chose more As than Bs, you are a (**C**) type who prefers **Consistency** and likes to always know what is expected of you. If you chose more Bs than As, you are a (**V**) type. You prefer **Variability** and you work best with a lot of environmental stimulation.

   Group your three letters together to get your personality type, and consider, in the list below, the careers that are most appealing to people with that personality type. Does one of those possible career options seem right for you?

DSC   Physical, occupational, and speech therapists, athletic coach, mortician, dentist, hotel manager.

DRC   Lab technician, pharmacist, librarian, paralegal.

DSV   Actor, executive recruiter, human resource executive, musician, real estate agent, caterer.

DRV   Construction worker, park ranger, military officer, executive chef, graphic designer.

TSC   College professor, bank branch manager, engineer technician, loan officer.

TSV   Physician, lawyer, marketing executive, public relations manager, psychologist, film producer, detective.

TRC   Biologist, chemist, accountant, physicist, geologist, actuary, aerospace engineer.

CAREER AT A GLANCE— FLYING ANGELS

Occupation: Flight nurse

Job description: Accompany a flight paramedic and a pilot on air medical missions aboard Medivac helicopters. Duties include assessing injuries and administering critical care to rescued victims, en route to emergency care facilities. Par for the course: on-call assignments and rough terrains.

Salary range: $35,000 to $70,000

Training: An RN degree and minimum of three years' critical care experience. Depending on the institution, certification in pediatric advanced life support (PALS) and advanced cardiac life support (ACLS) are mandatory.

An average day at work: After receiving a call, you have five minutes to get ready to fly to a farm, highway, or backyard with absolutely no idea of what the emergency is until you get there. Then you have one hour (commonly referred to as the "golden hour") to assess, treat, stabilize, and transport a patient to a hospital.

For more information about flight nurses, contact the Air & Surface Transport Nurses Association, 9101 E. Kenyon Ave., Suite 3000, Denver, CO 80237, 800-897-NFNA, www.astna.org; or the National Flight Paramedics Association, 383 F Street, Salt Lake City, Utah 84103, 800-381-NFPA, www.nfpa.rotor.com.

TRV   Computer programmer, air traffic controller, auto mechanic, fashion designer, archaeologist.

HOW TOP EXECUTIVES MADE IT TO THE TOP IN CORPORATE AMERICA

Answering the Call

Bruce Gordon,[3] president of retail markets for Verizon Communications in New York, stands calm, smack dab in the middle of one of the most volatile industries during one of its most tumultuous times. His steadfast demeanor was honed in Camden, New Jersey, in a close-knit family of five, headed by two educators. Bell of Pennsylvania seemed as good a choice as any for this college-football wide receiver and "liberal arts kid" who graduated from Gettysburg College in Pennsylvania in 1968.

Early in his career, Gordon chose a company that, he says, "offered the most money and would allow me to get back to Philly." Like many other who joined the company as management trainees he planned to stay in his job only a few years and then move on. His cavalier attitude didn't last long. Soon after he joined the Bell system, there were talks about converting the monopoly into a competitive business and the company's energy level increased. What stood out most for Gordon was the fact that, of the 850 people in the company, only one black person was in a director position. Surely, he reasoned, there was room for him at the top. If not, then he would make room.

"I wasn't a traditional person. Being a child of the '60s, I had a natural resistance to the status quo," says Gordon (1998 *Black Enterprise* Executive of the Year). In 1970, he had already established a reputation as being outspoken, even militant. A weekly column in a suburban Philadelphia paper, *Today's Post*, became his bully pulpit for speaking out on race relations and other controversial subjects.

Watching Gordon from the sidelines was a sales general manager named Carl Nurick, who liked Gordon's intrepid spirit. They connected on those terms. When the buzz around Bell of Pennsylvania was to fire Gordon, by then a business office manager, Nurick said, "Send him to me," and Gordon was moved from customer service into sales. Under Nurick, Gordon's unconventional wisdom and bravado were nurtured.

But he would eventually consider leaving, at least for a moment. Bitten by the academia bug in 1971, Gordon turned in his resignation one Friday to take a job as director of a Philadelphia urban school for academically challenged students. Over that weekend, Gordon had second thoughts. He didn't want to bump heads with his father, who was working on a similar project as dean at a local community college. That Sunday, Gordon called his boss and asked to come back.

After regrouping, Gordon sailed through management assignments in operations, personnel, sales, and marketing. All the while, he was making a name for himself with a winning marketing philosophy focused on three things: (1) what the customer wants, (2) what the competition thinks, and (3) what will distinguish the company from the rest of the pack.

Then, in 1985, on the heels of deregulation, the AT&T behemoth crumbled into seven regional Bells. Gordon was appointed vice president of sales at what then became the Bell Atlantic Corporation. As a Regional Bell Operating Company (RBOC), Bell Atlantic provided local telephone service for 12 million customers in Delaware, New Jersey, Maryland, Pennsylvania, Virginia, West Virginia, and the District of Columbia. But the company had to find ways to keep its head above water.

In 1988, after a year as an Alfred Sloan Fellow at Massachusetts Institute of Technology (MIT), and with a freshly minted master's degree in management, he took hold of the 100-year-old corporation and turned it "upside down and inside out" as a vice president of sales and marketing. In the recent merger of Bell Atlantic and Verizon, Gordon was named president of retail markets.

Gordon admits he can be impatient, compulsive, and intense. Hermann Hesse's novel *Siddhartha,* about an East Indian merchant in search of the answers of life, has helped him harness those emotions. However, as he moved through the business, taking on more responsibility, the book taught him that having balance in his life would make him a better person and enhance his career. Having learned to summon patience and tranquility when under fire, Gordon also learned that even positive things in excess are a problem.

Sweet Prospects

Corporate mavericks like Gordon are rare, and although other success stories are similar, the path to the top may have different curves and turns. Arnold Donald[4] determined his career track early. By his junior year in high school, the present chairman and chief executive officer at

Merisant Company, in St. Louis, Missouri, the maker of Equal® sweetener, had his career track mapped out—and marked by duality. "I wanted to be general manager at a science-based company whose products would make a difference in the world," he recalls. It was the perfect resolution for a young man interested in science and business.

His plan included dual degrees in economics and mechanical engineering, and an MBA from a top business school. In 1972, Donald turned down offers from Yale, Stanford, and West Point, and chose the intimate educational environment of Carleton College. While earning his engineering degree at Washington University, in St. Louis, he was vice president and a founding member of the National Society of Black Engineers. In 1977, with both undergraduate degrees in hand and at least 20 job offers on the table, Donald opted for a senior market analyst position at Monsanto. At the same time, he was earning an MBA in finance and international business at the University of Chicago Graduate School of Business. His strategy was to always maximize the probabilities. Although he had no desire to work in finance, he knew that the MBA would be important for a general management offer, and he immersed himself in it. The strategy worked.

Prior to joining the start-up Merisant in March 2000, Donald (1997 *Black Enterprise* Executive of the Year) was a corporate senior vice president at Monsanto, having moved up, in 1998, from being copresident of the company's Nutrition and Consumer Sector. Prior, he was copresident of the $4-billion-plus agriculture sector. Named the 1997 Agri-Marketer of the Year by the National Agri-Marketing Association, Donald also served on the management team of Monsanto's pharmaceutical unit, Searle, maker of anti-arthritis drugs and oral contraceptives. Donald's four-pronged philosophy for business success is: (1) aim to fulfill the company's mission, (2) know your customers' needs, (3) bring in diverse and talented people, and (4) deliver results.

Getting "A Piece of the Rock"

When Chuck Chaplin[5] joined the Prudential Mortgage Capital Company in 1983, he planned to stay a few years, learn the ropes, and move on. Having worked three years as a city planner with the New Jersey Department of Community Affairs and the New Jersey Economic Development Authority, Chaplin saw a limited, yet rewarding opportunity to succeed in real estate investment with the industry leader, Prudential.

At the time, the Philadelphia native didn't realize how a little technical know-how and a lot of perseverance would fuel the engine for his rise to become vice president and treasurer of the nation's largest life insurance company. When famed retailer R. H. Macy approached Prudential in 1986 for mortgage financing for a $3.7 billion leveraged buyout, the 29-year-old Chaplin was asked to work out the details of the deal.

An associate at the time, he was one of the few loan officers who was adept at computers and available to work on the project over the Christmas holiday. He was willing to crunch the numbers for a deal that looked—to his superiors—like a lot of work for little payout. "I worked on it over the weekend," says Chaplin. He analyzed the stakes for Prudential, weighed the store's image, and determined what would be the alternative for the real estate if Macy's went belly-up. In one of the largest private financing deals ever put together, Newark (New Jersey) based Prudential agreed to loan Macy's $800 million—most of the real estate financing needed for the transaction.

The successful deal kicked Chaplin's career into overdrive. The 15-year term loan was repaid in eight years when Macy's was acquired by Federated Department Stores in 1994. Prudential walked away with a 10 percent average return. His handling of this monumental event catapulted Chaplin from the rank of associate to director, and then to regional vice president. In time, Chaplin grew out of his job. "I discussed with my bosses the best ways for me to become a well-rounded executive," says Chaplin.

He was directed toward the treasurer's department, an area in which he had little expertise. But he has a master's degree in city and regional planning from Harvard, and a BA in psychology from Rutgers University—and, he learned fast. In 1992, he took the position as vice president and assistant treasurer at the parent company, where he gained accounting and finance experience.

Today, as senior vice president and treasurer at Prudential Financial, Chaplin is entrusted with managing assets of one of the nation's largest insurance and financial companies. He's the first African American in Prudential's history to hold the post that is traditionally reserved for individuals being groomed for senior positions. Over the past 20 years, Prudential treasurers have completed three- to five-year terms and then gone on to head one of the insurance and finance giant's business units. There's no reason why that tradition should stop now.

FOLLOW YOUR HEART

Often, people don't take the time to look back on what they were good at or what interested them in high school or even in grade school. Too often, people limit themselves by not assessing their inherent skills and interests and then researching the careers that would be an ideal fit.

As a child, Javetta Robinson[6] knew she wanted to have an impact on education and she loved numbers. When she put the two together, she chose a career in school finance. After getting a BS in accounting from California State University at Sacramento in 1987, Robinson set her sights on becoming a school district CFO (certified financial officer).

Many advisers tried to steer Robinson toward the corporate sector or public financing, but to no avail. "I had many job offers in those areas, but I didn't even consider them," recalls Robinson. Her choice was not the most glamorous of accounting careers, and not one that many colleges prepare young people for, but Robinson's career plan included garnering as much on-the-job experience as possible. That meant getting hired by the education unit of the California State Controllers Office.

Sometimes, in life, you have to be uncomfortable before you can be comfortable. Robinson was turned down for the first two auditing positions she applied for at the Controllers Office. Undaunted, the Long Beach, California, resident switched gears, took a cloverleaf turn away from her dream job, and landed a job with the Department of Health.

But her opportunity would come sooner than she thought. During her first day of work at the Health Department, she got a call that a position had opened in the coveted Controllers Office and she immediately transferred. The auditor's position in the Women, Infants, and Children's (WIC) unit of the Controllers Office wasn't her dream job, but it got her closer to the education unit.

For a year and a half, she begged the education unit manager to hire her, but no positions were available. In the meantime, Robinson shored up her auditing experience—a requirement for a higher level position—and became a certified public accountant (CPA). In 1995, when the WIC unit funding was in jeopardy, she was moved into the education unit. However, Robinson's plan was just getting started.

"I set a goal to be promoted every two to three years. If I wasn't promoted, I asked why or began looking for opportunities elsewhere." Robinson learned everything she could as she chalked up the 1,000 hours of auditing experience required to advance. "I would even do other people's work. I wanted to get all the experience I could get," says the present president of the western region of the National Association of Black Accountants.

Robinson befriended CFOs of other districts. In 1997, after reading a newspaper article quoting the woman touted to be the best Associate Superintendent of Business in the state, Robinson vowed to work for her one day. She called the woman and asked her to be her mentor. When a position opened in her mentor's district, Robinson was chosen.

In 2000, with five promotions in 12 years and unparalleled auditing, personnel management, and fiscal skills tightly under her belt, Robinson was promoted to chief financial officer at the Compton Unified School District. Reporting directly to the state administrator, she controls a budget of $327 million and has 100 employees and 23 schools under her financial management. "Specializing helped my career tremendously. I knew there was a market and need for my skills, and moving around from company to company would not have gotten me to this point," says Robinson. "I am much further along in my career than my peers at public accounting firms."

KNOW ALL THERE IS TO KNOW

Robinson learned all she could for a career within her organization. That same rule applies even more when you're making a move outside. Regardless of where you are in your career, it's important to do informational interviews with people in the field (or company) you want to enter. Also, expand your research to libraries and the Internet. Then set your goals and devise a job search strategy.

If you ask average persons to name the number of career opportunities available, most can only list about three dozen. However, there are more than 250 job titles, according to the Bureau of Labor Statistics. You must expose yourself to other opportunities. Then you can plan your work and work your plan.

THE OCCUPATIONAL OUTLOOK HANDBOOK (OOH)

Compiled by the Bureau of Labor Statistics of the U.S. Department of Labor, *OOH* is the government's premier career guidance publication. It provides detailed information on over 250 occupations that account for over 120 million jobs. For each occupation, *OOH* discusses the nature of the work, the typical working conditions, details on the requirements for entry and the opportunities for advancement, and the projected job growth relative to the entire economy over the next decade. In some cases, the ease or difficulty of finding a job is also described.

Users also will find current data on earnings, employment of salaried and self-employed workers, related occupations, and sources of additional information. Each statement begins with a section that highlights key occupational characteristics. For more than 50 years, this versatile volume has proven useful to career counselors, students, and other job seekers. Completely revised every two years, the *Occupational Outlook Handbook* is a comprehensive, up-to-date, and reliable source of career information.

Just as a map takes you where you're traveling on a highway, so your goals are a map for the road you're traveling in life. We all have set goals at one time, but perhaps failed to bring them into focus and achieve them. Each person's success is uniquely different. As a result, your goals should be personal and reflect *you*, and they will inevitably change over time.

DEEDS OVER DOLLARS

Just because Greenpeace and the Urban League don't frequent job fairs doesn't mean they're not looking. There are more than 1 million nonprofit, or not-for-profit, organizations in the United States that need capable workers to execute their missions. Despite the altruistic nature of these groups, they're not only for idealists. Corporate and government downsizing has sent many professionals scurrying to the nonprofit arena. Those entering must bring not only a sense of moral leadership but formidable technical and management skills as well. A caveat: Expect long hours, low pay, and limited resources. The dearth of African Americans in upper management has also been a stumbling block. However, for some, the nonprofit sector is a rewarding and creative career alternative that offers variety, autonomy, and flexibility.

As the number of nonprofit groups continues to increase, so will job opportunities. If you've always dreamed of helping the homeless, teaching school in Kenya, or working in a museum, the avenues of entry are many. They include educative, environmental, health, and legal services. Foundations, trade associations, and many civic, social, religious, fraternal, and international organizations are included in the nonprofit category. Arts and cultural centers also qualify.

As the former executive director of LEAP (Leadership, Education and Athletics in Partnership), a nonprofit organization in New London, Connecticut, Henry Fernandez[7] guided 700 children, ranging in age from seven to 14, through an intense year-round educational program. He was helped by 200 full- and part-time staffers. Each summer, Connecticut college students move into eight low-income and disadvantaged neighborhoods. Their mission: to provide daily academic skill building and mentoring to local children.

Higher corporate salaries and expense accounts couldn't lure the Harvard University and Yale Law School graduate to the fold. "There's an appreciation given to people who make a lot of money, but here, we value the struggle," he said of LEAP. Fernandez could have opted for the big bucks, "but it would not have been as intellectually challenging as motivating people." Still, the nonprofit sector is not without its rewards. Fernandez earned $32,500 his first year—the most money he had ever made in a year until that time.

HARD WORK REAPS HIGH REWARDS

The nonprofit sector gives many people the chance to do what they couldn't do in corporate America. With over a $3 million budget, Fernandez ran the equivalent of a small-to-midsize firm. He had the authority to determine the direction of the organization. Fernandez, who interned as a fixed-income researcher at First Boston Corporation while at Harvard, says that the for-profit sector would have given him an opportunity to spend and invest other people's money, but not to implement policy.

The training for his job was arduous. Fernandez, plowed a way through various grass roots and civil rights organizations. Besides serving as a press liaison during the campaign of Ken Reeves, the first African American mayor of Cambridge, Massachusetts, Fernandez also taught school in Zimbabwe.

Organizing community support, developing funding strategies, supervising personnel, and "functioning in the political diaspora of New England politics" are the tasks that filled Fernandez's 12-hour workdays. In the first three years after he co-founded LEAP, the program grew exponentially. The organization received over $1 million in government grants, and actor Paul Newman paid the rent for LEAP's New Haven headquarters.

People who are considering the plunge into the nonprofit sector should first decide on the type of organization they want to target, and why. Job seekers should be clear on their values and determine whether the organization's mission matches theirs. Burnout can happen, so you need to be employed doing what you love.

Even though the nonprofit sector is 70 percent female, few women make it to the top. Audrey R. Peeples' entree into the nonprofit sector came in 1973.[8] After she returned to work from maternity leave, her position as a trust administrator at Continental Bank in Chicago (now Bank of America, Illinois) changed. After 10 years with the bank, Peeples thought she was on the fast track in her career, but after several rotations in different areas, she was no longer happy with the job. Having been encouraged by her employer to sit on several nonprofit boards, Peeples jumped ship. She became associate regional director at the National Girl Scouts Association.

Weary of the travel the position required, she soon took over the post of assistant director and eventually executive director at Girl Scouts of Chicago. She had finally had an opportunity to be in charge. "I had hit the glass ceiling and could never have been a CEO in corporate America," reflects Peeples. "Back in the '70s, companies didn't take career women seriously." Peeples then moved to the YWCA of Greater Chicago where she served as executive director and eventually took over as CEO. Having retired in June 2001, Peeples now serves as a consultant to nonprofits specializing in board development and management issues.

For those not ready to plunge head first into the arena, she encourages private sector professionals to seek out volunteer nonprofit opportunities through their employer. Companies view "loaning" their executives to nonprofits as another way to help the organization and to showcase their employees. For the employees, serving on a nonprofit committee or board not only offers exposure to challenging issues that work may not provide, but they gain a resume builder as well.

THE DIVERSITY MYTH

One misconception of the nonprofit sector is that it's the benchmark of diversity, dominated by people of color.

The low number of minorities in top management at "mainstream" nonprofit organizations has prompted growing concern about racial and ethnic diversity in a sector that serves so many people of color. To reverse this trend, universities are trying to recruit more minorities for their nonprofit management graduate degree programs. Nonprofits are also making attempts to improve their board and staff diversity.

CAREER FORECAST

The nonprofit sector is no longer considered a dumping ground for corporate outcasts. In fact, nonprofit organizations are competing with other industries for quality personnel.

Government budget cuts have set the stage for strategic alliances among many compatible nonprofit organizations. As a result, the need for experienced managers is high. Accountants and lawyers will be challenged in a sector that must deal with liability and be more accountable to its donors, the IRS, and the general public.

As the nation leans toward managed health care, hospitals, nursing homes, and counseling centers will need health care professionals who can guide them through the transition. Those skilled in government relations will fare well as community block grants take center stage. Human resources professionals should come prepared to recruit and retain not only paid employees but volunteers as well. Fund raising, marketing, grant writing, program development, and communications are other critical areas to consider.

A key challenge for nonprofit groups is their adoption of a more corporate-like structure without sacrificing the uniqueness that separates them from the government and corporate sectors. One shaky area

DID YOU KNOW?

Calvin Darden began his career 30 years ago working part-time unloading packages at United Parcel Service while in college. He was thrilled to be earning twice the minimum wage and never thought that, today, he'd be one of the company's two senior vice presidents of U.S. operations.—*Black Enterprise*, February 2000

is salaries. Currently, salaries in the nonprofit sector are, on average, 15 percent lower than in the private sector. But that's changing as nonprofit groups look for innovative ways to make the sector attractive. Incentive and performance pay, bonuses, gainsharing and retirement plans—staples of the private sector—are gaining ground. Perquisites such as tuition reimbursement, flexible hours, and day care provisions are also finding their way into compensation packages.

According to Unifi Survey of Not-for-Profit Compensation: 2000[9] CEOs averaged $148,000 a year. Top government affairs executives earned $100,000, and top financial officers averaged $84,374. The top human resources professionals earned $76,003.

Organizations based in the Northeast generally pay more than those in other regions. Because of the high cost of living there, salaries in New York rank among the highest in the nation.

In paid or volunteer positions, on the board of directors or heading a committee, African Americans should look toward making strides in the nonprofit arena. Not every individual is going to be a chairman or CEO of a Fortune 500 company, but other professionals with a great desire can take their business acumen and share it in their neighborhoods and communities.

WHEN WORKING MEANS WORKING FOR YOURSELF

Working for someone else, even if it means an expense account and a key to the executive washroom, is not the be-all and end-all for many employees. Some independent souls choose to embark on their own adventure and craft their own "manifest destiny." Owning your own business means hard work and determination in the face of not just outside adversity but even personal doubt at times. Some businesses can grow while you hold down a full-time job, but others will take all of your focus and wherewithal to make them happen. This option can mean immeasurable risk. Remember the old gambling adage: You can't play with scared money.

STRIKING OUT AS AN ENTREPRENEUR: JUST WHAT THE DOCTOR ORDERED

Entrepreneurs have confidence and determination that are not necessarily learned, but are inherent. Take Heather Boatman.[10] When she graduated from college with a degree in biochemistry, she followed the route prescribed for her by her parents—a route in medicine. She loved the challenge associated with solving the most complex of mathematical problems and took delight in her biology practicals and the internships that had her researching cures for cancer, but she entered the ivy-covered doors at Georgetown University School of Medicine content in the knowledge that by learning medicine, she would soon have her own practice and call all the shots.

By the time she reached her second year, the heavy hand of managed health care and the diminishing role of doctors as the ultimate arbiters of medical treatment weighed heavily on her. She questioned whether she could endure the intrusion of insurance companies' questioning, even refusing, her analysis of and treatment for patients. The thought daunted her dream of becoming an internist. Unfortunately, at the same time, her own health challenges were too much to handle, and she was forced to take a leave from medical school. During the semester that she sat out, she had time to examine how important the profession of medicine was for her. When the time came for her to go before the school's board to request permission to reenter, Boatman chose not to. The dream of running her own business far outweighed her desire to fight the system of managed health care. She found an alternative career in which she would be the captain of her ship. "Even if I had to work for someone initially, I always knew that I would work for myself and not retire waiting for a gold watch and a 401(k) to mature," says Boatman.

She entered a one-year training program to be a cytotechnologist—an analyst of cancer cells at local laboratories and for oncologists at various hospitals. At up to $50 an hour, the field proved to be lucrative. Boatman not only set her own hours, but was also able to start her own business and review cancer cell slides for civil court cases and independent clients. Despite her newfound career, Boatman still craved having her own freestanding business—working one-on-one with individuals and helping them.

She found that calling after she and her husband moved to Palm Springs, California, a city known for its golf courses, resorts, and spas. Boatman set her sights on owning her own spa. That opportunity would allow her to control the shots *and* provide services to people. She enrolled in a five-month aesthetician program where, enhanced by her medical background, she learned everything about skin—from facials to skin-peels. "When I decided to open a spa, I didn't want to depend on someone else's knowledge. I took two months to develop a business plan," says Boatman. "I tried to learn as much as I could on my own, and then paid people for their knowledge—such as real estate and insurance attorneys, an accountant, and an architect. I became a nail technician and an aesthetician, met with a lot of top consultants in the spa industry, attended conferences, bought tapes and books."

She and her husband, an attorney, raised the $200,000 needed to open the salon and spa. Within a year, Boatman opened her salon to rave reviews. Her small staff includes hairstylists, nail technicians, and aestheticians. She anticipates $1 million in revenues within the spa's first three years. "I think I've always been an entrepreneur. I've always had that spirit. I don't believe one chooses to be an entrepreneur, it is something innate," says Boatman. "It was my personality type, and today I am happy living my dream."

DRESSED FOR SUCCESS

Most people don't start out as entrepreneurs; they often work in a chosen career or position before they realize they want to embark on their own venture. Amsale Aberra[11] started her business on sheer gut instinct and necessity. While planning her 1985 wedding, Aberra surveyed all the rhinestone, bead, and lace-laden gowns that abounded and saw nothing that whetted her appetite for a minimalist bridal gown. This prompted the Ethiopian native to design her own. A year later, she turned something old into something new.

By shunning the overly ornate wedding gown designs of the past and bringing forth classic, clean, and sophisticated versions, she fulfilled the wedding dress dreams of many women. "There were questions in my mind about whether there was a demand for such a dress. I thought: Was I the only one who wanted a simple gown?" says Aberra. "I took no formal surveys, but asked married people and those in the bridal industry who showed an interest." It all began with a $13,000 full-page ad in *Bride's* magazine, featuring only a photo of one of her dresses, and her name and phone number. The phones rang off the hook during the week the magazine hit the stands. In 1986, Aberra—with the business insight of her Harvard MBA/JD husband and $50,000 of their own money—launched Amsale.

Aberra developed her penchant for stylish clothes as a child growing up in Addis Ababa, Ethiopia. She and her sister regularly made their own clothes. The daughter of an Ethiopian government minister, Aberra left home in 1973 to study political science at Green Mountain Junior College in Vermont. When the Ethiopian government was toppled only months after her arrival in the United States, her father was imprisoned, abruptly ending her flow of funds.

She moved to Boston, which has a large Ethiopian population, and worked several odd jobs to raise money to continue her education. In 1981, she completed her studies at Boston State College and then pursued her love of fashion by enrolling in New York's Fashion Institute of Technology. After graduating in 1982 with a degree in fashion design, Aberra became a design assistant at Harve Bernard before going out on her own.

Her defining moment came in 1990, when she gained her first account with the country's largest wedding dress retailer, Kleinfeld's, in Brooklyn, New York. Her business strategy, like her gowns, is simple: steady growth and exclusivity. "We don't want to grow beyond our means," states Aberra. On average, no more than two retailers in a big city can carry her dresses; hence, the Amsale brand maintains its quality and cachet. Her advice for fledgling entrepreneurs: "You must be committed and do it with passion. If you don't enjoy it, get out."

A GREAT RIDE TO THE TOP

Other entrepreneurs have built their multimillion-dollar businesses over time. Growing up on a farm in Greenville, Kentucky, Cornelius Martin[12] (1997 *Black Enterprise* Auto Dealer of the Year) learned that hard work pays. When he was 14 years old, his father made a deal with him and one of his brothers: grow and sell the family's tobacco crop and they could use the money to buy a car. They brought in and sold the crop and later bought a 1957 Ford, which they tinkered with, drove for miles, and finally wrecked a year later. But the beauty, speed, and complexity of automobiles intrigued Martin for years to come. It became a fascination that would spawn an enterprise.

Today, Martin, CEO of Martin Automotive Group and owner of Oldsmobile/Cadillac, Dodge/Jeep/Eagle, Chevrolet/Geo, and four Saturn dealerships, has many more cars to choose from. Operating seven stores in four states requires quick and easy access—a difficult task with at least four-hour drives from store to store. But the two pilots who command Martin's seven-seat Beechjet 400 can transport him between offices within an hour. From his two-story office complex and headquarters in Bowling Green, Kentucky, Martin has built an organization made of more than just cars. Nestled under the watchful eye of Martin Management Group are also lucrative insurance, real estate, and aviation concerns.

Contributing to this success is Martin's astute knowledge of the automobile business. Unlike many car dealers today, Martin doesn't just depend solely on showroom salesmanship. He's gotten oil under his fingernails. "When I was younger, I planned to own a garage or repair facility. As a black person, I thought that I would never be able to own a dealership," he recalls. With that in mind, Martin attended West Kentucky State Vocational School in 1969, where he learned auto maintenance and management. A year later, he worked as an auto technician while majoring in business at Wright State University in Dayton, Ohio. After a year in college, Martin left to work full-time.

In 1978, with his reputation as a technician known throughout Dayton, Martin was recruited by Bob Shannon, of the former Dayton Shannon Buick Company. Then 29, Martin agreed to come on board only if Shannon would help him acquire a dealership. Back then, says Martin, you just didn't go and set up your own franchise, especially as a minority. You needed someone who could take you under his or her wing and sponsor you. Under Shannon, Martin worked his way up from shop foreman to sales representative. In 1982, Martin entered the grueling two-year General Motors Minority Academy Dealer Program. He alternated months between GM's campus in Flint, Michigan, and Shannon's dealership, studying the machinations of the business.

After graduation, Martin scoured the country for a store. He looked at dealerships in Poughkeepsie (New York), Philadelphia, and

St. Louis. Studying the five-year growth trends of various cities, Martin was impressed with Bowling Green, Kentucky. Its attractions were that its unemployment was low and it was one of the fastest growing areas in the state, says Martin, who could have tried to enter a large metro market. "Most prospective dealers want to be in big markets, but the way I see it is that if you're not making any money, it doesn't matter where you are." Looking back over the past years, Martin recognizes that the relationships he has built, combined with his management skills and perseverance, have helped him to avoid many of the potholes in the industry and to build a thriving operation. Overflowing with the confidence of his success, he says, "It's been a great ride."

GET READY FOR THE LONG HAUL

You need to have a plan in place and a strategy mapped out. This is the hard part: You have to remember that implementing your career plan is a full-time job in itself. You can't get discouraged. You must stick to your timetable. Plans may change in specifics, but they should remain the same structurally—they should get you from one place to the next. You must also be prepared for changes in your plan. Life's episodes have a way of changing outcomes and forcing you to go in different directions. The key is: Don't founder too long; get back on track. Don't get caught in a depressing cycle of jumping from one dissatisfying job to the next.

2

FINE-TUNING YOUR RESUME

SELL YOURSELF!

Forget about those childhood adages and proverbs about humility and discretion—at least for now. Silence isn't golden, and the meek might find it incredibly hard to inherit a plum job, much less the earth, unless they can prove their mettle. In the job search arena, it's more like "The squeaky wheel gets the grease"—and the job. There is no one better to tout your virtues, skills, and competencies than you. And your first curtain call onto the job search stage is your resume.

Admittedly, a resume alone, no matter how good, will not get you a job. However, a *good* resume will attract the attention of the hiring manager and perhaps secure a job interview. Many job candidates who didn't secure a job due to lack of experience or because the position was already filled have been told later by the hiring manager, "I can't hire you at this time, but your resume was exceptional!" Your goal at this point is to make your resume supreme.

Let's keep in mind its purpose. A resume demonstrates your accomplishments and qualifications to a potential employer. If the employer likes what he or she sees, you will be contacted for a face-to-face meeting. Your strategy should be to emphasize the experience and skills that employers are in the market for. You must view yourself as a business and your resume as a promotional brochure about you—"the company"—that must prove to a potential employer—"the client/customer"—what you have accomplished, your work experience, and, ultimately, your ability to provide the services the employer seeks. Your resume is also an example of your communication and organizational skills. A well-done resume provides insight into your value as an employee. A sloppily produced resume is a terrific way to get taken out of the running before the race even begins. Understand that recruiters and hiring authorities often use the resume to rule people "out" rather than "in," so, it behooves you to have a sharp, concise, action-worded resume that catches the attention of the reader.

A lot of information is available on resumes and resume writing. Some of it is contradictory, but most of it is useful. Find a good book devoted solely to resumes, and learn the fundamentals of resume writing. Try to stay with the most current material you can find; resume advice follows trends. The Internet is home to plenty of free advice and information, but most of that information will be less detailed than a good resume guide. There are some tried-and-true strategies that you need to put in place before you even think about soliciting potential employers.

Human resource professionals or screeners are deluged with resumes each day, for myriad jobs. When they have so many resumes to review, you've got about 20 seconds for yours to grab their attention. A resume is merely a flash card of your accomplishments. Before you can get an interview, you must stir the interest of the recruiter or hiring manager, and that means meeting certain demands on paper first. A resume advertises you and your skills. It must scream out, "This is who I am. This is what I want to do in my career." It must intrigue the employer and convince him or her that you are worth investigation.

What determines whether your resume will make the cut or end up in the trash? In a job market that is precarious, that depends. Today's job market has gone back and forth quickly between being a buyer's market (the employer receives a stack of competitive resumes) and a seller's market (applicants offer needed hard-to-find skills) and back to a buyer's market. During these ebbs and flows, some people have become "professional students"—they are afraid to leave college because the recruiters are not interviewing as widely as they have in the past. Those already in jobs are afraid to leave—or even to interview—for fear that no other jobs are to be had.

However, that should only remind you that if you hope to even turn the heads of employers, then your resume must deliver. That very important document you will be sending puts your career on the line. Once received, it must stand alone, on its own, and sell you and your skills to a very busy reader. Don't worry if some, or maybe all, of your past work is not related to the job for which you are applying. If you're knocking on an entry-level door, the employer expects that you have worked at Burger King or Circle K sometime in your past! Just remember that while you'd like your talents to stand out, there are some distinct rules to abide by, in order to make your resume shine.

THE FINER POINTS OF A GOOD RESUME

- Make sure you use a standard type font like Times New Roman or Helvetica—one that has as few "extras" (like bullets, italics, and so on) as possible. Unless you are in the graphic design field, few employers take kindly to resumes that are "works of art" or experiments with the fonts of ancient Sanskrit. The reason for this: Many companies now are scanning resumes into computers rather than reading them. Use off-white, ivory, or buff-colored good-quality, medium-weight bond paper. Under office fluorescent lights, these choices are easier on the eyes of someone who looks at hundreds of resumes each week.

- Avoid large paragraphs (over six or seven lines). If you provide small, digestible pieces of information, you stand a better chance of having your resume actually read. Keep it to one, or no more than two, pages.

- Now you have a new enemy: the electronic scanner. Anything the scanner can't read is lost. Scanners seek out the key words and phrases that fit the job description. Use action verbs that will give a kick to your resume—"supervise," "manage," "revenues," "saved," "implement," and "develop," just to name a few. These words should relate to the available job and emphasize your skills and, accomplishments, such as, "C++," or "HTML" if you are in technology. Don't use full sentences. Instead, begin each line with an action word such as "accomplished," "compiled," "diagnosed," "established," "implemented," "obtained," or any number of similar proactive words that are as close as your thesaurus.

- Include high school information only if you are a recent grad or did not attend college or a relevant training program.
- Don't use declarative sentences like "I developed the . . ." or "I assisted in . . . ." Granted, the resume is "all about you," but leave out the "I."
- Avoid passive constructions, such as "was responsible for supervising." It's not only more efficient to just say, "supervised," it's stronger and more succinct, and it connotes action.
- Make the most of your experience. To form an idea of what you can do for them, potential employers need to know what you have accomplished.
- Don't be vague. Describe things that can be measured objectively. Telling someone that you "improved customer service call times" doesn't say much. Stating that you "cut call answer times by 10 percent, saving the company $2,000 a month in overtime pay" does. Employers will feel more comfortable hiring you if they can verify your accomplishments.
- Be honest. There is a difference between making the most of your experience and exaggerating or downright lying about it. A trained human resources manager can easily spot a falsified resume. You might get a job now, but lying can cost you a better job later on, when deeper background checks and verifications show that you duped your most recent or current employer.
- As you craft your resume, make sure you include your name, address (including apartment number), and phone number at the top. E-mail addresses are also good.
- Don't neglect appearance. Your resume must be neat. Today, many resumes are sent online or by fax, but that shouldn't stop you from making sure that the original is attractively laser-printed on good stock. Even though you may have landed the interview via a faxed or e-mailed version, a crisp copy will be expected when you show up for the interview. Above all, proofread and let someone else proof it. It must be free of typos!

Many human resource professionals say that more than half the resumes they receive are not read because they are so poorly written. It took the pros too long to determine:

1. Where the applicant was career-wise.
2. What relevant experience, skills, education, and aptitudes were being brought to the position.
3. Any reason for expending the time needed to interview the applicant.

GETTING STARTED

You may have in your head a distinct picture of how you see yourself, but it's not easy to get that image down on paper. Faced with that dilemma, many job seekers resort to the professional services of a resume writer or follow formatted templates found in books and online. These are all perfectly good alternatives. However, most people still craft their own resumes. The determining factor is: You must know yourself so that you can market yourself better. You'll have to gather or recall information about your:

- Employment, internship, or fellowship experience.
- Education (high school, undergraduate, and graduate school; exchange student; semester overseas).
- Volunteer or co-curriculum experience (worked at a soup kitchen; was captain of the debate team, and so on).
- Special training (seminars, certifications, licensing, and so on).
- Skills (computer, second language, artistic achievement).
- Military experience (ROTC, Armed Forces).
- Awards and honors (Valedictorian, Dean's List, Phi Beta Kappa).
- Memberships and activities (both professional and social).

Work Experience

Write down the most important details of every job or internship you've held. No job is too small, so don't discount anything. That camp counselor position you had in college is no less important than the management trainee position you may hold now. If you've been in the workforce several years or more, concentrate on your most recent jobs, but don't disregard part-time work or your first few jobs. Focus on these areas:

- The name, address, and telephone number of each employer.
- The exact dates worked at each firm.
- Names of supervisors or immediate managers.
- Approximate number of hours worked weekly or monthly.
- Duties and responsibilities.
- Awards and recognition.

It's important to relay your accomplishments. Did you contribute to the success of a new project? Did you get a promotion or special merit pay because of a job well done? Your job descriptions should contain phrases such as: "Developed new standards for filing, which led to increased office efficiency" or "Enhanced a computer software design that helped the company process expense reports quicker." Be sure to state the benefits you helped to provide. Use numbers or dollar amounts when you can—they drive up the credibility volumes. If you won an award, highlight why it was significant. Maybe you were the first new-hire or the only one of 40 in your department to receive it. These facts should all find their way into your resume.

Education

If you are a recent college graduate, include the name and address (city and state) of all your schools, beginning with your most recent one. List the years you attended, the degree earned, your major field of study (and minor, if any), honors, and important courses. Include the years you were there, the degree or diploma you earned, your major and minor as well as your GPA (if it is impressive), and any honors you may have received. Pertinent co-curricular activities (such as working on a special research project with a renowned professor) and internships should also be included.

Volunteer Work

Don't underestimate the value of your volunteer experience just because you didn't get paid. Some volunteer experience actually boosts a resume, particularly for applicants with limited work experience. Were you a coach of a Little League team, an instructor at the local Police League or "Y," a counselor at a crisis help line? All these experiences transfer into the workplace in the form of leadership and people skills. Your volunteer experience also shows that while you were (or were not) employed full-time, you still had the initiative to stay busy, get involved, gain valuable experience on your own time, and contribute your talent to a worthy cause.

Be sure to include each organization's name and the name of the director or other authority figure you worked with; the exact dates and number of hours per week you worked; the specific skills required; your duties and responsibilities; and any awards you and/or the organization received while you were there.

Special Training or Special Skills

Have you had on-the-job training from your employer? Did you take management courses outside your job? Perhaps you speak a foreign language. If you've been in the armed forces, list your rank, tour of duty, and accomplishments or assignments. Detail your computer skills or any other skills, and your level of expertise.

YOUR RESUME: CHRONOLOGICAL, FUNCTIONAL, OR A COMBINATION?

There are three types of formats to choose from: (1) the chronological, (2) the functional, and (3) the combination or hybrid. A job objection below your contact information is an option. It helps screeners determine the job you desire, instead of trying to figure out where you belong—all within those 20 seconds of resume face time.

There's a saying that one can reveal too much information. That is something you don't want to do here. Provide the reader with all the pertinent information about your skills and abilities; however, steer clear of listing your personal references, personal statistics, personality profiles, and photographs. You never know who may read your resume; don't provide information such as marital status, height, weight, testimonials, nationality, or pictures that may encourage a more biased approach to your resume because of the reader's own personal biases.

Chronological

This is the most common resume style, and the one that employers prefer. In the chronological format, the emphasis is placed on employment experience. The applicant's job history is presented in reverse chronological order; the most recent jobs are placed at the top of the list. Executive search and human resources professionals want to see clear-cut dates and make sure that the candidate isn't hiding something. It is a good format because it is easy to follow and little work is required to put it together.

Caveat: Not everyone has a perfect job history with no gaps along the way. Despite its popularity, there are some reasons why the chronological format may not be right for you. If you are just entering the workforce from school, a chronological resume may actually highlight your lack of experience. You may have held jobs recently that have no relevance to the position you're applying for. If you are reentering the workforce after a substantial absence, this resume approach will highlight your recent inactivity. Any large gaps in your recent employment history will be evident, and you may be asked about them.

EXAMPLE: CHRONOLOGICAL RESUME

LINDA HARROLD
12733 Chatom Way, #2F
Chicago, Illinois 33217
(312) 388-4256
Lharrold@det.com

EXPERIENCE

10/1996–Present: Marketing Manager, Ardent Inc., Chicago, IL

An effective team player and cross-functional manager who manages a $28 MM Personal Care product launch through the development of sales plans and market strategy that help meet a profit plan objective. Experience includes:

- Developing, presenting and executing the new product positioning and pricing strategy that resulted in a 5% sale increase vs. initial launch.
- Creating and managing the sales launch event, which included producing a video and managing live hair demonstrations.
- Creating new promotions and merchandising that meets quarterly sales performance objectives.
- Developing new products for seasonal sales energy.
- Routine sales and competitive trend analysis.
- Supervision of all consumer and sales communication pieces, including print media.

2/1995–9/1996: Associate Manager, Forge Company, Nashville, TN

- Managed a $12MM P&L of the Personal Care business through the development of quarterly sales plans and routine monitoring of sales and margin impact of various product mixes.
- Assisted in the development of the Skincare categories through the merchandising and management of all field and consumer communication, sku management.

12/1994–2/1995: Assistant Marketing Manager

Developed and executed marketing promotions for Ever-Young brand with over $24MM in annual sales, through:

- Design and implementation of marketing communications plan for Dual User strategy, reaching 60% of target.
- Analysis of Ever-Young and competitive businesses for implementation of defensive marketing plan
- Supervision and execution of product production and promotions for new product launch of Pro-Vitagen.
- Developed and executed Hispanic market test for successful trial and repeat use of Elysium skincare product.
- Management of $1.5MM advertising and promotion budget.
- Assisting in the development of teen Web site, which generated 30% audience growth per month.

1/1994–12/1994: Assistant Promotions Manager, Selectect Foods, New York, NY

- Strategic development and implementation of promotion and media events that met marketing objectives for frozen foods category.
- Competitive analysis of brand categories through market research, sales data and tracking of promotion events, which resulted in the implementation of enhanced pricing strategy.
- Effective communication and management of new product sales launch which included developing sales materials, incentives, and sales video production.

7/1990–12/1993: Promotions Assistant, Forest, May and Cole, New York, NY

- Assisted Promotions Manager with advertising and PR executions.

EDUCATION:	12/1996	**Fordham University, New York, NY**
		Master's Degree: M.S. Marketing Communications
	6/1990	**Marymount College, Tarrytown, NY**
		Bachelor's Degree: B.A., Political Science
AFFILIATIONS:		National Black MBA Association
ADDITIONAL SKILLS:		Fluent in French
TECHNICAL SKILLS:		Microsoft Word, Excel, PowerPoint, QuarkXPress

Functional

This type of resume highlights job experience by job title, and group accomplishments according to a functional area or overall job objective. It is an expanded summary of qualifications and devotes most space to the duties and responsibilities of all the jobs an applicant has held over the course of a career. Skills and previous relevant experience (including educational experience) are presented at the beginning of this resume. They are organized so the employer can see how the applicant's skills relate to the available position. It may take more effort to write a functional resume, but you are free to highlight your talents instead of your recent job experience.

This resume is best for career changers or people who have been out of the workforce for some time—those who need to concentrate on functional rather than specialized skills. This format highlights what they can do rather than where their earlier activities were done.

Caveat: A functional resume may raise concerns in some employers' minds as to whether you are withholding information. This doesn't mean that functional resumes are ignored or that they can't be effective. But an employer looking for a clear job history may be put off by the functional format, especially if you've used a functional resume to hide your inexperience or a long gap in your employment history. If you send this resume to a screener who is wary about functional resumes, you might risk being rejected. Individuals not adept at synthesizing data in this way can find this style challenging. In categories such as "Sales/Marketing" or "Financial Management," it takes some creativity to group your duties and responsibilities into such clusters.

EXAMPLE: FUNCTIONAL RESUME

MICHAEL WILLIAMS
224 Bolder Road, White Plains, NY
Tel: (914) 234-7588; Work: (523) 864-8726
Email: MIA446@compuserve.com

Account Management professional with eight years of business-to-business experience developing accounts with a background in the transportation and chemical industries in the areas of sales and procurement. Demonstrated ability in developing strong international relationships coupled with sourcing new business and controlling expenses.

SELECTED ACCOMPLISHMENTS

- Negotiate annual contracts for Conner Oil exports to the Latin American region, resulting in a savings of nearly $300,000.
- Designing new process to accommodate $400 million in Conner Oil global tanker movements worldwide, to ensure a smooth transition for the SAP environment and the year 2000.
- Recommend alternative packaging modes to customers in order to unseat competitor, yielding cost reductions for the customer and new business for Time Shipping.
- Developed strong relationships with overseas affiliates in order to engage in push-pull activities to increase sales, especially in the face of changing governmental regulations in Eastern Europe, affecting imports and exports.
- Increased revenue of the territory for exports and imports in the trans-Atlantic trade lane from $9 MM to over $18 MM by identifying new business opportunities and acquiring new accounts.
- Endorsement of Export Enhancement Program (for the Middle East) within Time Shipping resulted in new business for Time Shipping and the primary vendor position with the client.
- Successfully targeted previously unexplored foreign-to-foreign trade (Europe to Asia) opportunities which became a new source of revenue for Time Shipping.
- Over $1.5 million revenue gained from new business due to strong focus on the small shipper arena, especially with exports to the former Soviet Union.
- Recipient of President's Outstanding Salesperson Award.

COMPANY AFFILIATIONS

Conner Oil, Westport, CT   1996–Present
Account Representative
Planning Through Development
Latin American Trade Lane Manager
Bell Atlantic, New York, NY   1994–1996
Account Manager
Time Shipping, Jersey City, NJ   1992–1994
Account Executive
Sales Associate

EDUCATION

NEW YORK UNIVERSITY, STERN SCHOOL, New York—MBA
SUNY ALBANY, New York—MS Transportation Management
CUNY City University, New York—BBA INTERNATIONAL BUSINESS

Combination

This resume, sometimes referred to as the "hybrid," uses the best features of both the chronological and functional formats. You can begin your resume in a functional style, listing relevant skills and accomplishments, and then launch into detailed work histories. Skills and accomplishments are still listed first; the employment history follows. You need to reveal where you worked, when you worked, and what your job position was. This will allay a prospective employer's worries about your experience, and it still allows you to emphasize your talents and how you would use them if you get the job you are applying for. Most employers might still prefer a chronological resume, but this format is a good alternative to the functional resume. It concentrates on achievements rather than titles, and it is great for career changers and those with work history gaps.

Caveat: Resume purists will still favor the chronological style. Because the dates and titles won't be in the places where they expect them, you may not get the proverbial 20 seconds that screeners devote to resumes.

EXAMPLE: COMBINATION RESUME

Terrence Ramsey
12 Rumson Place
Coltsneck, NJ 07013

Phone: (856) 862-4396
Cellular Phone: (856) 689-3481
Email: TRamsey23@altavista.com

OBJECTIVE: Management opportunity requiring a strong professional background with a proven track record in corporate market development.

PROFILE

- Six years Management and Sales experience.
- Highly skilled in managing large employee groups and departments within high-volume customer service environments.
- Adept in quality management processes; selecting, training, and motivating personnel; management team building and coaching employees.
- Successful results with new system implementations relating to preferred customer programs and employee efficiency.
- Strong background in monitoring daily financial reporting for revenue generation and long-range strategic planning functions.
- Proven record as a troubleshooter in resolving customer relations and sub-quality issues and in turning around potentially troubled situations into profitable opportunities.
- Comprehensive background in business negotiations at multiple levels of management and decision making.

WORK HISTORY
1999–Present   Fantasy Island Amusement Park   Beach Haven, NJ
Director of Operations

- Supervise theater operations with the goal of optimizing guest satisfaction by providing leadership and communicating the expectations and vision of the company.
- Develop plans and systems to recruit and train management personnel to maintain company standards and goals.

- Execution of corporate marketing programs.
- Effectively budget and maximize financial profitability of a site generating annual revenue of $3 million.

1997–1999   Shawnee Place   **Fremont. CA**
General Manager

- Provide leadership and guidance to all levels of amusement park personnel.
- Coordinate the efforts of Senior Managers, Managers, and staff personnel to achieve optimum park operations.
- Enforce the Company's policies and standards in all areas of operations.
- Develop management personnel through guidance and training to achieve increasing levels of responsibility.

Senior Manager
AMC24 @ First Colony, 1999   Sacramento, CA
AMC24 @ Deerbrook, 1998–1999   Pasadena, CA

- Directly oversee department heads including: Human Resources, Food Service, Marketing, Facilities, Administration, Financial, and Daily Operations.
- Prepare short-/long-term projection for Sales and Expenses, and implement effective cost control procedures.
- Implementation and coordination of systems to ensure the highest standard of customer service and efficiency.
- Monitor Operating Expenses and Revenue Generation.

Facilities Manager
AMC16 @ Crossroads, 1997 Arlington, VA

- Oversee the design and fixtures of the building.
- Implement and coordinate systems with Senior Manager to reduce Operating Expenses.
- Manage maintenance team to ensure a pristine and safe complex.

EDUCATION
BA, Marketing, Howard University, Washington, DC, 1997
Minor in Business Management

TITLE IT RIGHT

The government, corporate, and nonprofit sectors have different ways to describe their occupations, but they don't always translate well. It is one thing to say "I was the careers editor," but the industry needs to know that "I was an *associate editor*," the universal title that all those in the industry could relate to. A G 15 title has to be translated to the corporate nomenclature so that the screener knows where you would fit within a company, as a manager or an assistant manager. You have to be as clear as you can *before* they get to your job description: "I managed, evaluated, and directed three to five employees."

The most common challenge when people are trying to shift to another industry is translating their titles and responsibilities for potential employers. For example, people in banking, oil, insurance, and government have a difficult time moving over to consumer goods and services companies because their titles don't translate accurately. "Assistant vice president" in a bank may only be equal to a branch or niche marketing manager; the same title in a consumer goods company may apply to a product director who controls the entire marketing of a product.

Human resource professionals take the path of least resistance: They won't try to do the translation. They don't know what the hierarchy was at your former company or what factors govern those titles, so, if you can, use a generic version of your title and, above all, focus on your responsibilities.

Every employer, no matter how obvious, should be identified with a one-line tagline, for example, leading aircraft engine maker; major N.E. ad firm; mid-size printing company. These details give employers the scope of what you've done and where you fit into the scheme of the company. You may have been the director of communications; however, if it was a three-person company, your job was not the same as that of a director at a Fortune 500 company. Employers need to know, not guess, whether you fit what they're looking for. That knowledge can get you just that much closer to the job.

Do try to keep the details as relevant as possible. You should target no more than two different industries, and tailor a resume for each. Do some research and visit each company's Web site to find out about its hiring practices, job openings, and titles you can cross-reference.

Keep in mind that what looks good to you on paper isn't always appropriate for electronic transmission, storage, retrieval, keyword searching, and/or forwarding. Although some templates may be less than aesthetic, that is the format the job site has selected for the efficient review of the thousands of submissions the company may have to deal with. Have pity on the poor people who have to sort through and select *your* resume. Chances are that they will not want to bother with a nonstandard resume if they can't find the information where they expect to see it.

REFERENCES: CHOOSING YOUR ALLIES

The last line of most resumes reads: "References furnished upon request." Are your references up to par? References play a major role in your job-hunting campaign and must be able to provide testimonials to the quality of your work. That generally rules out family members and close friends. Employers know that those people are too close for comfort and may not be as objective as someone you know through a work relationship.

Professional references very often are people you've worked for or with. They may be people whom you know through social or professional organizations. You may be a project manager for a volunteer organization or a fund raiser. The person you choose should be able to state how you contributed to the organization.

Find someone who can describe your work ethic and is able to provide an example or two of the caliber of your work. It's important to choose an individual who is able to credit you with something that helped the department or organization to be more successful. If your reference is an employer, the fact that the company would hire you again speaks volumes.

Some employers may request a candidate's last three performance appraisals, in lieu of references. For others, letters of reference may do, but only from individuals who won't mind being contacted. Here's how to get the most out of your reference pool:

- *Be prepared:* Have the names, addresses, phone numbers, and, if available, e-mail addresses of three to five individuals when you go to the interview. Some interviewers may want to do advance checks.
- *Be discriminating:* Choose references who can add value to the type of job you're interviewing for. For example, your former

employer can speak about projects that proved your work ethic and your contribution to the bottom line; your minister can speak about the role you played in a recent fund-raising effort. Note: Don't overload your references. They may be contacted too often if you put the same names on every application.

- *Refresh their memories:* It doesn't look good if a prospective employer contacts a reference who displays a case of amnesia when it comes to you. Call the references, request permission to use their names, and then give them some talking points or areas you wish them to mention or concentrate on.

- *The bigger the better:* Potential employers may not be compelled to contact your former coworkers; they may be more interested in hearing what your superiors have to say about you. The higher up the food chain the individual is, the more credible the reference is viewed.

- *New questions:* Some references may be asked whether a potential job candidate "was moody" or "often angry," to determine whether the individual fits their corporate culture. Yet, many references shy away from such questions for fear of being sued by you later. Often, a reference, particularly if it is a former employer, will only provide "name, rank, and serial number" or just the dates of your employment and your title—factual

---

THINGS THAT MAKE YOU GO HMMM . . .

Typos are major flaws and can make a hire–don't-hire difference, so always have someone look over your resume. Search for any telltale goofs that you might not have noticed before. Can any organizations you belong to provide more info than you want known? Your age may come through in your graduation dates; your nationality may come through in where you live or in other companies you have worked for or organizations you're a member of. Employers are evaluating you on different fronts. Are you providing clues that you might regret or that you cannot help revealing?

information that can easily be verified rather than subjective information that can be a determining factor in whether you land the job.

- *Be honest:* Many employers conduct background checks. Tell the truth now and avoid the shame and career suicide of being terminated later.

FIVE WAYS TO GET YOUR RESUME NOTICED

1. *Keep it short and sweet.* The more succinct your resume, the greater its impact. Focus on your work over the past five years; spotlight only relevant information and accomplishments.
2. *Avoid the unique.* Stay away from colored paper or fancy typefaces. Stick to high-quality laser copies printed on high-quality bond.
3. *Save the grocery list.* Companies want to see results. Don't offer only your title and duties. Provide tangible evidence showing how you saved the company money, increased sales, or enhanced productivity.
4. *Tell the truth.* Conventional wisdom has it that more than half of the resumes submitted for jobs contain some form of fabrication. Avoid exaggerating your education or other credentials. Most employers do extensive background checks before—and sometimes after—you've been given the nod.
5. *No form resumes, please.* You are applying to different companies that require different skills. Tailor your skills, actions, and results for each position you're applying for. Don't make a reviewer work to see where you'll fit. Point the way to a spot up front.

THE OFTEN MISUNDERSTOOD AND UNDERESTIMATED COVER LETTER

You put all your energy and soul into making sure your resume reflects all your skills and accomplishments in a professional manner.

However, you're frozen in your tracks when you have to craft the letter that will introduce the resume to employers. There aren't enough pennies in the fountain at Trafalgar Square to account for all the great opportunities that qualified and talented individuals pass up just because they can't or won't write the cover letter. Countless job seekers send out polished resumes without including this all-important feature.

Three brief paragraphs have the power to make or break a career chance by either never being written or being written incorrectly. The cover letter sets the tone for your presentation to the employer. If you can't be there to present your resume, the cover letter acts on your behalf. Your voice, and the tone and clarity of that voice, will determine whether the employer moves on or takes a closer look.

Paragraph one states your interest in the company and mentions a recent development at the firm (e.g., a recent acquisition, a new product it has introduced) or, if it is a new company, a round of funding it may have received to further its business. This kind of attention shows your knowledge of the organization and prompts the screener to read on.

Paragraph two provides specific examples of why the organization should be interested in you—your experience and qualifications. Include career landmarks and especially accomplishments at your current job. You don't need to go into a long dissertation. Choose an area on your resume that can apply to the prospective company's needs, and expand on that area.

Paragraph three mentions that you will follow up with a phone call to confirm that your resume has arrived and to check its status. Be sure to double-check the spelling of names and titles, and the company name. A well-written letter is free of typos and grammatical errors.

Don't make the major cover-letter mistake of "mass mailing"— sending the same letter to all the employers you're targeting. Screeners know a generic cover letter when they see one. Make sure you include some reference to how your skills will transfer to the needs of the company and the responsibilities of the position you're applying for.

Blind resume mailings seldom hit. You may know people who have mailed out 100 resumes and heard nothing. If you are not applying for a specific job, try to find out the name of the human resource professional or hiring manager, and address your letter accordingly. Companies receive hundreds of resumes. If yours is not directed to a particular individual, it may never be seen.

ALL YOU EVER WANTED TO
KNOW ABOUT RESUMES

- *The Wall Street Journal and National Business Employment Weekly Resumes* by Taunee Besson (John Wiley & Sons), offers a step-by-step outline for crafting your resume, real sample resumes, and proven advice from successful career counselors and human resource professionals.

- *Resumes, Resumes, Resumes: Top Career Experts Show You the Job-Landing Resumes That Sold Them* by the editors of Career Press (Career Press). This book has worksheets that will help you detail all the information about your career and get you started toward writing a winning resume.

- *Electronic Resumes: A Complete Guide to Putting Your Resume Online* by James C. Gonyea and Wayne M. Gonyea (McGraw-Hill). This book-and-disk package helps you create resumes online, using Microsoft software programs. The steps in creating and posting online resumes are explained in simple, nontechnical terms.

SHOULD YOU OMIT SOME JOBS FROM YOUR RESUME?

Generally, people do so because they were fired or they performed unsatisfactorily. The pitfall is that some companies do extensive background checks; they may find your omitted job on something as unlikely as your credit report.

It's best to put all your cards on the table in the beginning. Here are the key points to remember:

- The easiest thing to remember is the truth. Do your explaining up front in your resume, so you don't have to explain later.

- In a few rare circumstances, you can omit a job from your resume—for example, if the position was in an unrelated field and its omission will leave only a one- or two-month gap. If the gap is three months or longer, keep the job in.
- If the employer calls you on the gap in jobs, try to turn a negative into a positive. Provided you have not lied or been evasive about anything else on your resume, give the real reason why you left the job out. Your explanation won't promise you a job, but at least it will allow you to clarify things—and dilute any bad taste you may have left in the employer's mouth.

INTERNET RESUMES

Technology is affecting not only where people are employed but also how they land jobs. Online job and resume banks are fast becoming time-saving and efficient resources for job seekers. Databases that list resumes are an emerging segment on the Internet. Through them, prospective employers are contacting needed workers, instead of the other way around, and this reversal adds strength to the skills you bring to the marketplace.

Whether you surf the Net or subscribe to any of the numerous online service providers, you can find scores of databases, resume banks, and job-matching services (see Chapter 4). Online job searching isn't a substitute for tried and true networking, hard-copy resumes, and the classifieds, but it certainly has increased job seekers' playing field. Note: The convenience of the Internet has lead some employers to limit the number of resumes it accepts, so you must keep up with ads and act quickly.

A traditional, hard-copy resume must be visually appealing; an electronic resume must be formatted so that it can be read by an employer *and* be acceptable to scanners that search for the key words that will get your resume noticed. Posting your resume online will get it to the right people quickly and efficiently. On most sites, posting a resume is as easy as filling in a few fields for your name, address, and phone number, and then pasting the body of your resume into a text box. ASCII (American Standard Code for Information Interchange) sites require you to paste only plain text. Others allow you to use HTML (hypertext markup language).

FYI

Keep in mind that your current employer, who does not know about your efforts to transfer out, may also be looking for a job candidate online. If he or she happens upon your resume, your gig will be up. Monitor your resume and remove it when you get a job.

You've been told to use action verbs for your resume. Discard that rule for online resumes. Nouns are the stars, and you should use the words intrinsic to your industry. For example, if you're interested in journalism, make sure you include words like "news," "editor," "writer," and other words that will make your resume stand out.

OTHER EXTRAS: CAREER PORTFOLIO

With competition for jobs at an all-time high, job seekers need more than a resume. A career portfolio—a bound collection of your work samples and credentials—may be the tool that sets you apart from the rest. Traditionally used by early-/mid-career job seekers, portfolios are being created today by college students, to showcase their achievements to a potential employer. Although portfolios can be organized for many purposes and audiences, yours should show the skills employers want, and prove that you're capable of moving to the next stage in your career or making a specific career shift.

To package your portfolio, first gather your credentials. These include a resume; copies of diplomas, certificates, licenses, and letters of recommendation; evidence of special talents such as computer skills or foreign languages; sales ranking reports, community involvement documents, and any audio or visual artifacts (e.g., tapes or photographs) that support your abilities.

Unlike a resume, the elements of a portfolio can help an individual who has had limited work experience prove his or her ability to handle greater responsibility. For job-seekers who have had numerous jobs, portfolios can highlight their accomplishments or even rationalize their many moves.

How you package your portfolio depends on what's included; for most job applicants, a 9-by-12-inch leather-bound "photographer's portfolio" is conservative, sleek, and impressive. Present your portfolio during the initial interview so that the potential employer can see your skills and talents up front. Some career counselors suggest bringing it to the second interview, when your qualifications are more closely examined.

THE PERSONALIZED WEB SITE

Freshly minted college and graduate-school graduates are making use of their own Web sites. These sites detail the individual's work experience and personal information, and allow employers to find out more data about a candidate before the initial interview. Be careful about giving your personal Web site address to every prospective employer. As much as the Internet has helped minority candidates by making employers look at "blind" credentials before skin tone, Web sites chock full of personal information and photos can contribute to ruling out otherwise qualified candidates because of visitors' personal biases.

Your resume has to sell you in short order. Put in the time and effort necessary to craft a stellar resume and you've at least gotten your foot in the employer's door. While you may have all the requirements for a particular position, your resume is a failure if the employer does not instantly come to the conclusion that you "have what it takes." View yourself as a business and your skills as the product you're selling. If your resume is a good advertisement of your offerings, then you're guaranteed to make the sale.

3

BUILDING A NETWORK

A search firm may be able to place you in a job, or you might find one through a newspaper's classified ads, but, according to many career experts, the most productive and powerful source of jobs is networking. Most human resource professionals say that approximately seven out of 10 jobs are gleaned through networking, and the chances of finding a job are probably better with networking than with any other source.

Networking is just that—work. It is labor-intensive. It requires gathering, classifying, working, and reworking long lists of names and addresses, plus hosting lunches and dinners, and making brief visits to your contacts. While it seems easy ("Just make a list and make some calls"), networking isn't a pushover. Only recently has it acquired a name and been proven to be a great method of attaining a job. The frustration comes because unless you are a natural at schmoozing and are willing to pursue it wholeheartedly, networking is hard work.

It requires conversation and a keen eye for possibilities and opportunity, but it's not as far-reaching as you think. When a friend suggests an accountant or a dry cleaner, or when you strike up a conversation with the person sitting next to you on an airplane—that's networking. You are finding out information about a possible service you need or an

72

interest you have. It's the same process that kicks in when someone recommends you to an employer because you have made a good impression on him or her.

Networking translates to building relationships based on trust. When you tell someone something about yourself, he or she assumes that it is the truth and may later put his or her reputation on the line by passing along your name, goals, or accomplishments to someone else who is in a position to help you. Therefore, *never* misrepresent yourself.

The process of networking has three basic elements:

1. *Creating the network:* Amassing a valuable list of names of people who can help you. Remember that this list is not static. It fluctuates with every move, relocation, or life change of you or one of the individuals listed. You must keep this list up-to-date and build on it constantly.

2. *Working the network:* Calling your contacts, making appointments, and visiting them with a distinct purpose in mind.

3. *Following-up:* Keeping the flow of information going; checking with your network contacts and reminding them of your career and job-search efforts. Networking is not a one-way street. You must be able to give back to the network and provide any knowledge and leads you have, if you expect to have such information come to you.

BUILD YOUR NETWORK

You may think that because you have a pile of business cards, have made initial contacts with some key people at companies you're interested in working at, and know a friend who has a friend who works at Company X, your networking strategy is on target. But ask yourself: "Why am I still not in the job I want to be in?"

Many people underestimate the power of networking and miss good opportunities because they don't really understand and prepare for the process. To begin, you must first make a list of all the people who will form your network. Networking is about reaching out to and building relationships and rapport with people who can hire, mentor, or support you. They're usually family members, friends and acquaintances, professional contacts, and people you meet by chance.

To gain the most from these connections, you must have a polished presentation. The initial contact is usually verbal. Remember, you are marketing yourself. In your presentation, include information about your current work situation and responsibilities, as well as your goals. Highlight your job skills, work history, and interests. Next, rate the individuals on your list according to how you believe they can help you advance.

Because networking is so informal—casual meetings, lunches, introductions of one friend to another, flanked by the thread of conversation and human contact—it is easy to take it for granted. By applying yourself to the process, you expose yourself to leads and inside information that can reveal industry trends, facts, and more networking contacts. Each contact can reap two or three more. A journalist worth his or her mettle is nothing without sources. To build those sources, he or she leaves each interview with the names of two or three other people who can provide the same or similar information. For the average job seeker, the strategy should be no different. Adding to your list keeps your network healthy until you achieve your goal. One very well known national news anchor goes through his card file each day and calls someone to catch up. He has done this every day for years. When he exhausts the file, he starts all over again.

The best people to include in your network are insiders who work in the job, industry, or company you wish to enter. You may not have this hot list out of the box, but you can hone it over time. Start scheduling informal meetings with the people on your contact list. The telephone is a good link, but face-to-face meetings are always better. Your aim is to get the word out, to as many people as possible, that you are looking for a job. Tell them the type of job you're seeking, and persuade them to keep their eyes open and spread the word. Don't expect the network to go on automatic pilot. If someone promises to walk your resume into his company's human resources office, follow up in a timely manner. Check the status and get the name of the person you should contact for more information.

It might sound like a cliché, but networking is still an important key to getting the job you want. No college senior knows that better that Lydia Cutrer.[1] Keen on making her mark as an investment banker, the 20-year-old Temple University senior has already made career strides that many seasoned professionals only talk about. "For me, it's been about relationships," say Cutrer, who was a participant in Sponsors for

Educational Opportunity (SEO), one of New York City's first mentoring programs for high school students. SEO also provides, to college undergraduates of color, orientation, training, coaching, and substantive internships in various careers. "When I began college, I had heard about accounting and thought it would be a great foundation for business. During my freshman year, I joined the student chapter of NABA [National Association of Black Accountants] my first week, in order to find out more about the career and get involved. I also update mentors and my supporters on my progress, sending out notes and e-mail regularly."

Not content with just one affiliation, the New Orleans native is also a member of the National Black MBA Association and has done internships at AT&T and Chase. As the youngest member of the Next Generation Network, one of the many career programs offered by the Executive Leadership Council in Washington, DC, Cutrer has positioned herself beneath a tree of low-lying fruit, and she already has her pick of the harvest. She has an analyst job offer from Chase—an invitation to enter the two-year investment banking program after graduation. Early in her career, Cutrer hopes to pursue an MBA degree and maybe enter the field of venture capital or urban revitalization.

TAKE IT SLOW

The worst networking is done at networking parties. People walk around and do five-minute "get-to-know-you" conversations with everyone in the room. At the end of the evening, they might have a fistful of business cards, but they are no further in their job search because they don't know how to use networking, or they didn't target just a few people with whom they can realistically follow up.

Each personal meeting provides an opportunity for your contact to get to know you better, to like you a bit more, to become interested in your well-being, and to decide whether to help you. It is easier to remember someone you have met than someone you have only spoken to on the telephone. Being able to link a name with a face—or some other distinguishing characteristic—is a good start for a new relationship.

Don't get your contact's guard up by delivering a bum's-rush list of your requests and needs. Don't run up and ask for a job. If a contact has warmed up to you and knows of a job opening, he or she will mention it.

Don't expect news of a job; in fact, make it clear that you are not asking for a job, but only for advice and some recommendations on how to proceed in your job search efforts.

After each personal meeting, send the contact a short note of thanks. Thoughtfulness and gratitude go far, and a postcard or note card will be appreciated. Granted, it is easier these days to shoot off a quick e-mail, but a letter or note lasts longer and says that you thought enough about the meeting and the person to sit down and write.

NETWORK YOUR WAY INTO COVETED CAREERS

Quentin Williams[2] says that a combination of persistent and appropriate networking landed him dream jobs at the FBI, the NFL, and the NBA. "Appropriate" networking here means doing a good job *always*. Over his career, his high work ethic was communicated by word of mouth, and when opportunities became available, his name was the first on everyone's lips. "There are many people who have the skills, but don't have the motivation and assertiveness. It's more of me selling myself to other people, by being diligent in displaying my skills," says Williams, who is team president for North Charleston's National Basketball Development League and is helping to lay the groundwork for the NBA's new development league.

With his sights always set on being an FBI agent, Williams worked six months at a private law firm after graduating from St. John's University School of Law, in Brooklyn, New York, while his FBI application was pending. "It gave me the opportunity to gain legal experience and helped me rule out medical malpractice litigation as a career." A year and a half passed before Williams completed the FBI's arduous application process (background investigation, physical test, written exam, psychological evaluation, and panel interview) and was off to the academy in Quantico, VA.

After four years as a special agent in New York, investigating bank robberies, hijackings, drug cases, and white-collar and organized crime, recognition for his work came from more than the FBI. "I put my heart and soul in the job and showed other agencies, such as the U.S. Prosecutor's Office, U.S. Attorney's Office, and local police agencies, that I was able to do the job," he adds.

Although Williams had no intention of leaving the FBI, an offer to join the U.S. Attorney's office in Connecticut was enticing. "I slept on the offer for six months before taking it. I knew that it was one of the best legal positions to have, and I wanted to learn how lawyers tried cases." After Williams had spent a few years as an Assistant U.S. Attorney, his former FBI boss, who was moving to the NFL headquarters in New York, invited Williams to come with him. Recommendations from others in law enforcement helped him to land the position of NFL Senior Manager/Player Liaison. His primary responsibilities included prevention of player off-field misconduct by creating league policies and communicating them to players and club personnel. "I had been networking and didn't even know it," recalls Williams.

One afternoon, while at the NFL Pro Bowl in Hawaii, Williams began networking. "I saw Michael Huyghuye, senior vice president of Football Operations for the Jacksonville Jaguars, eating lunch with his wife. I said hello and they invited me to join them. During the course of that lunch, we talked informally, and I weaved into the conversation information about my background and goals, careful not to be too aggressive," Williams recalls. A year later, Huyghuye called Williams and offered him the position of Director of Player Development and Staff Counsel for the Jacksonville Jaguars.

He later took on the role of Director of Player Administration and Community Affairs, with responsibility for negotiating player contracts and complying with NFL salary-cap rules while overseeing the player development and community affairs departments. Williams also served as Legal Counsel for the club on both football and non-football-related matters. Under his guidance, the team won the award for the NFL's Most Outstanding Player Development Program in 2000. Huyghuye later confided to Williams that their informal lunch together convinced him that he needed Williams on his team.

"What people forget to do is to work. Instead, they focus solely on networking. Networking for me is doing a good job, and not just when people are watching. People get into work behavior patterns, slack off, leave early," says Williams. "People should work as though they are accountable. I've always taken pride in what I've done, and I've been given opportunities because people see that."

But how does one get into the coveted arena of sports—a field where retirement is the only way that positions open up? "If you want to get into sports and entertainment, an MBA or law degree is a must," says Williams. "A degree in sports management is so career-specific that if you can't get into sports immediately, what are you going to do? You have more diversity with the MBA or law degree. You must also do internships and if you're good, you will be offered a position. The combination of the internship and the postgraduate degree gives you the best tools."

QUID PRO QUO

Networking is a two-way street. You don't have to pay back in kind, but the little things you do could make a difference. For example, there might be no way that you can help a senior executive make a job contact, but perhaps you can help tutor her son in math. As you scan the newspapers and industry trades, you may want to clip out an article that pertains to your contacts' industry or company and mail it to them for their reference. Of course, what you have to offer may be something that individuals can do on their own, but your initiative and your recognition and respect of the rules of networking will give you credibility and persuade people to help you again and again.

Don't rule out any contact, no matter how humble. Your objective is to let the whole world know that you're looking for a job except for your current boss. As you make the rounds, you will realize that not only are you making many useful contacts, but you are increasing your knowledge of your industry and becoming known to many people.

REAP COLLEGE REWARDS FOR LIFE VIA UNIVERSITY CONFERENCES

You planned to go, but something came up. You wanted to go, but thought you had to be an alumnus to attend. Wrong! University conferences are great networking venues. And, best of all, they offer valuable opportunities for you to launch or advance your education and career. They shouldn't be passed over lightly.

Alumni groups from colleges and universities across the country sponsor annual conferences where members can meet and share information. But these gatherings typically aren't limited to alumni members. Everyone, from the mildly curious to go-getter professionals, can take advantage of the lectures, seminars, and job fairs they offer.

Whether you go for one day or one week, these conferences can offer you a way to meet people in your field—or in an area you're hoping to enter.

If your school doesn't specialize in a particular area, you can gain leverage from another school's strength and get a better handle on industry trends and job opportunities.

Conferences offer a double benefit. Corporations have a chance to actively recruit talented candidates, and job seekers have one-stop shopping for interviews with a host of companies in one day. Surprisingly, not many students take advantage of these fairs. They assume that jobs will be waiting for them, and they miss out on wonderful opportunities.

CAREER AT A GLANCE— APPEALING TO THE PALATE

Occupation: Executive chef

Job description: Responsible for the day-to-day restaurant operations in fine restaurants, hotels, or corporate dining rooms. Duties include menu development, supervision of culinary staff, and catering and vendor negotiations.

Salary range: $50,000 to $80,000. Bonuses are the norm, and some chefs also receive 1 to 2 percent of the establishment's food profits.

Training: Five to 10 years of experience, which can include a degree in culinary arts and/or apprenticeships in various restaurants (preferably in Europe) or under the auspices of another executive chef.

An average day at work: Preparing for the dinner crowd; negotiating with vendors; coordinating deliveries. Depending on the size of the restaurant, you could be supervising various other chefs and staff and serving upward of 100 entrees a day. Each order must live up to the menu.

For more information on executive chefs, write to: The Black Culinarian Alliance, P.O. Box 2044, North Babylon, NY 11703, www.blackculinarians.com.

In addition to providing networking avenues, many conference seminars offer information to help overcome social hurdles. Before entering Howard University College of Medicine, Tanya Savage[3] attended conferences at schools like Emory University and Morehouse College. As a student at a predominantly white women's college in Georgia, the Pensacola, Florida, native found she had to face daily bouts with racism, classism, and even sexism from male professors. "There were no black professors," she says. "I was not exposed to any black leadership at all." Savage, who was recruited by the college and awarded scholarships, says she needed desperately to find an outlet.

The college was not filling her social needs, so Savage, then president of the black students association, persuaded the dean to pay her way to some conferences. By going to conferences that focused on race and class issues, she was able to implement, on her own campus, changes that ultimately helped her and her fellow black students.

Most school-based conferences take place during the spring. Trade associations and corporations often cooperate with alumni groups in sponsoring conferences. Costs vary, depending on the length of the conference and the accommodations for visitors. To find out more, contact the alumni association of the college or university you're interested in.

MENTORS AND AVENUES TO NETWORKING: HOW TO CHOOSE AND GET THE MOST OUT OF THEM

Finding the right mentor is key because the right one will open doors to other executives, activities, and projects that might otherwise be out of your reach. But how do you find a mentor? Professional organizations and your own job are good places to start. According to the Society for Human Resource Management,[4] mentors should have at least five to 10 years more experience than their protégés. They should also be:

- Well positioned within the company, influential, assigned sizable responsibilities, and well respected.
- Genuinely interested in your career development.
- Someone whom you trust and with whom you have rapport.

You may have a formal mentoring relationship available within your company, or an informal relationship may develop with someone you admire—a former professor, a member of the clergy, or someone outside the realm of your professional or personal life with whom you have formed a bond. You would benefit greatly from finding a mentor who has similar interests and experiences. A good mentoring relationship is not one-sided. As a protégé or mentee, you must be proactive, stay dedicated to maintaining the relationship, and display a willingness to learn. Goals and expectations should be determined from the outset.

Mentoring is important because when you are coming into a new company you don't know the dynamics. "Many people don't realize how important it is they should do their very best from the start and a mentor can help you do this," says Dexter Bridgeman,[5] president of Diversified Communications Group, a New York-based diversity management-consulting firm that also provides executive search services to corporations. Mentoring is important because, when you are coming into a new company, you don't know its dynamics. Work is different from college. As an employee, you can't be late or skip work altogether on some days. If you tend to have these bad habits in the workplace, a mentor can explain the value of maintaining a good work ethic, and can evaluate the quality of your work, adds Bridgeman, who was also the publisher of *Mentoring* and *Minority MBA* magazine.

By showing you the ropes and explaining the company culture, a mentor adds to your professional development and helps you move up the corporate ladder. Work isn't just about doing the job; it's about doing the job well. "You must find a mentor who is also on the ball. The worst thing is to have a mentor who is not respected or doesn't have it on the ball because that can sink you through association. Often, people think that a mentor has got to be culturally or racially the same. That is the furthest thing from the truth," says Bridgeman. "Culturally, it might be easy because there is a comfort level when you have an African American mentor . . . , but essentially you want someone you can learn from, who is going to make your transition into the company as smooth as possible."

MISTAKES WITH MENTORS

- *Don't get too involved from a personal perspective.* "This is the biggest mistake in a mentor–mentee partnership," says Bridgeman. "You want to keep the relationship on a professional level. Everyone has 'drama' in his or her life, and the mentor doesn't need the additional burden of dealing with an argument you might be having with a friend, or with your financial difficulties. Drawing the mentor into your personal life can cause him or her to distance you, and you will sacrifice the learning experience—the very reason for your entering into the partnership."

- *Apply what you've learned.* Mentors get personal satisfaction from knowing that they are helping you and seeing that the time and effort they're giving you are paying off. If every other Wednesday you meet your mentor for dinner, but you are not developing professionally, or an ongoing problem at work is not being resolved, your mentor may advise you to find another job or move into another area.

- *Don't resist constructive criticism.* Your mentor is there to guide you, so be prepared to hear the naked truth. Even if you don't agree with the advice offered, at least be open to the possibilities and discuss your concerns so that you both arrive at a resolution and agree on your development.

IS ONE MENTOR ENOUGH?

With companies downsizing and rightsizing, anyone networking a career around one person might now find that person more concerned about his or her own career, says Stephen L. Buckner,[6] president of Buckner and Associates, an executive search firm in Oakland, California.

Many companies have "flattened out" by shedding much of the hierarchical middle- and upper-management structure of the past. As a result, the number of positions in the $65,000 to $100,000 range—from which most mentors emerge—has declined, according to Buckner.

To compensate, you should seek out, as mentors, three or four people with diverse backgrounds. They need not come from within your company. One mentor should be focused toward advising you if and when it is time for you to move to another organization or industry, or even to try entrepreneurialism, adds Buckner.

It is also important to seek out people who are familiar with new technology, and to establish a support group of people from different cultural groups. With the organizational process becoming more team-oriented, Buckner suggests that employees concentrate more on self-development and not depend on others to guide their career. In the future, formal mentorship will disappear for people of color, Buckner predicts, so employees must take more responsibility for their own career development.

DID YOU KNOW?

While a student at Harvard, Franklin D. Raines, Chairman and CEO of Fannie Mae, and a Rhodes Scholar, took a bullhorn and urged students to launch a campus-wide strike protesting the Vietnam War.—*Black Enterprise,* February 2000

IT TAKES TWO

Often, the people being mentored view the mentor relationship as one-sided. It isn't. You must enter the relationship with thoughts about how your initiative can motivate your mentor to give you the best advice, and not just about what the mentor can do for you.

Show your mentor that you value his or her expertise and experience. Be prompt for appointments, send thank-you notes, and give timely feedback about how you used and benefited from his or her advice. Inform your mentor of your career aspirations and your business strengths and weaknesses. Being open and honest can help to continuously expand the relationship.

You must create value for your mentor. Ask what he or she hopes to get from the relationship, and do your part to achieve those goals. Also, small things do count. If you come across something that would appeal to your mentor, like an article in a newspaper or trade journal, share it with him or her.

If you've done all of these things and the relationship has still stalled, have a heart-to-heart talk with your mentor about what needs to be done mutually to improve it. If things still don't improve, then you must find another mentor who can provide the resources you need.

AFRICAN AMERICAN ORGANIZATIONS FOR BUILDING NETWORKS

Hundreds of African American organizations address almost every career interest or professional endeavor. The following list samples just a few. However, you can find others, as well as convention dates and places, in the *Black Enterprise* Calendar of Events, published each month in the "Powerplay" section. You may also call a particular organization, or log on to its Web site, to find the chapter or affiliate nearest you.

Association of Black Psychologists was established in 1968 and has 27 chapters nationwide, with some 1,200 members. It is dedicated to the psychological well-being of African Americans. It holds an annual conference and offers psychological testing, community health projects, education, licensing, and certification. It publishes a journal 10 times a year and issues a monthly newsletter.

> 821 Kennedy Street, NW
> Washington, DC 20040
> 202-722-0808
> www.abpsi.org

BDPA Information Technology Thought Leaders represents professionals in the field of information technology. The organization conducts IT programs, projects, seminars, and workshops in more than 40 cities. It conducts educational programs for high school students and holds an annual conference.

> 9315 Largo Drive West, Suite 275
> Largo, MD 20774
> 800-727-2372
> www.bdpa.org

Black Retail Action Group, Inc. (BRAG) was formed in 1970 to get more African Americans involved in the retail industry. The group holds workshops, seminars, and networking sessions as well as career guidance seminars with high school and college students. BRAG members keep current on employment and career opportunities in retail, and make referrals when appropriate. Each year, BRAG holds an awards dinner and publishes a newsletter.

> P.O. Box 1192
> Rockefeller Center Station
> New York, NY 10185
> 212-308-6017

Blacks In Government (BIG) has represented the interest of African American professionals in federal, state, and local governments since 1975. The organization has more than 300 chapters throughout the nation and monitors the hiring practices, quality of training programs, and promotion policies of government agencies.

> 1820 11th Street, NW
> Washington, DC 20001-5015
> 800-433-3280
> www.bignet.org

National Alliance of Black School Educators (NABSE) was founded in 1970. Its membership of more than 5,000 educators throughout North America includes teachers, superintendents, school board members, higher education faculty, and policy makers. The organization is committed to increasing the academic achievements of African American students by providing training and support opportunities for educators. It holds an annual conference and publishes a quarterly newsletter.

> 310 Pennsylvania Avenue, SE
> Washington, DC 20004
> 202-608-6310
> www.nabse.org

National Association of Black Accountants Inc. (NABA) was formed in 1964 to address the dearth of African Americans in the accounting profession, particularly as CPAs. There are more than 130 chapters across the country, and the association's mission is to enable minorities to maximize their career potential in accounting. It also awards student scholarships, holds regional student conferences and an annual convention, and offers job placement service to its members.

> 7249-A Hanover Parkway
> Greenbelt, MD 20770
> 301-474-6222
> www.nabainc.org

National Association of Black Journalists (NABJ) represents journalists at the nation's major newspapers, magazines, and radio and television stations and networks. The association was founded in 1975 to expand and balance media coverage of the African American community and to recruit and educate students. Educational programs are offered by the more than 61 chapters to assist journalists in upgrading their professional skills and to encourage entry into management positions. NABJ holds an annual convention and publishes a journal six times a year.

> 8701-A Adelphi Road
> Adelphi, MD 20783
> 301-445-7100
> www.nabj.org

National Association of Market Developers Inc. represents professionals in marketing, sales, public relations, and other related fields that cater to the delivery of goods and services to the African American consumer market. The group offers seminars and career information for students. It holds a national convention annually.

P.O. Box 4446
Rockefeller Center Station
New York, NY 10185
212-994-6982
www.namdnt.org

National Association of Minority Media Executives (NAMME) represents media managers and executives of color working in newspapers, magazines, radio, television, cable, and new media. The organization provides executive development, management training, and mentoring to new managers. It also provide opportunities for members to network and share experiences through meetings, newsletters, and technology.

1921 Gallows Road, Suite 600
Vienna, VA 22182
888-968-7658
www.namme.org

National Association of Urban Bankers: Urban Financial Services Coalition is an organization of some 3,000 minority professionals in the banking, finance, and insurance industry. It provides educational, technical, and advisory assistance to minority businesses and students, and awards student scholarships.

1300 L Street, NW, Suite 825
Washington, DC 20005
202-289-8335
www.naub.org

National Bar Association Inc., founded in 1925, represents more than 17,000 lawyers, judges, educators, and law students. It offers legislative advocacy, seminar development, and technical assistance to members in specific legal areas. It holds an annual meeting and publishes a bi-weekly newsletter and a bimonthly magazine.

1225 11th Street, NW
Washington, DC 20001
202-842-3900
www.nationalbar.org

National Black Association for Speech-Language and Hearing was developed to meet the needs and aspirations of African American speech-language pathologists, audiologists, and students, and the black community. Founded in 1978, the association offers educational seminars, hosts a biannual review course for the national exam, and organizes conferences on recruitment and retention of African American students in higher education. It offers scholarships and holds an annual convention.

> 3605 Collier Road
> Beltsville, MD
> 202-274-6162
> www.nbaslh.org

National Black Nurses Association has 70 chapters across the country. It works to recruit nurses into the field, and serves as a job bank. Membership is open to all registered and licensed practical nurses, as well as to students. It publishes a quarterly newsletter and holds an annual conference.

> 8630 Fenton Street, Suite 330
> Silver Spring, MD 20910
> 301-589-3200
> www.nbna.org

National Black Police Association Inc. has more than 100 member associations representing more than 35,000 members. The organization holds an annual conference, serves as an advocate for minority police officers, and has a national network for the training and education of police and others interested in law enforcement.

> 3251 Mount Pleasant Street, NW
> Washington, DC 20010
> 202-986-2070
> www.blackpolice.org

National Black Public Relations Society was formed in 1982 to promote and expand opportunities for minorities in public relations. The organization conducts seminars, provides speakers for community groups and students, and awards student scholarships. It also has a skills bank for public relations practitioners and publishes a quarterly newsletter.

> 6565 Sunset Boulevard, #301
> Los Angeles, CA 90028
> 213-466-8221

National Brotherhood of Skiers Inc. holds its annual ski Summit in February and promotes both recreational and competitive skiing among minorities. More than 7,000 skiers, from more than 48 ski clubs, are affiliated with the group. The organization is also instrumental in developing and financing the training of future U.S. ski team members and Olympic athletes.

> 1525 East 53rd Street, Suite 418
> Chicago, IL 60615
> 773-955-4100
> www.nbs.org

National Coalition of Black Meeting Planners (NCBMP) was formed to improve the planning and execution of minority meetings, conferences, and exhibitions, as well as to promote the role of African Americans in the hospitality industry. The coalition provides career forums and publishes a quarterly newsletter.

> 8630 Fenton Street, Suite 126
> Silver Spring, MD 20910
> 202-628-3952
> www.ncbmp.com

National Coalition of 100 Black Women seeks to empower African American women and is dedicated to community service, leadership, and development. It is also committed to promoting career opportunities through networking. The organization holds biannual conventions and publishes a newsletter.

> 38 West 32nd Street, #1610
> New York, NY 10001
> 212-947-2196
> www.ncbw.org

National Dental Association, founded in 1913, promotes the professional development of African American dentists and supports health care programs for minority communities. There are more than 45 chapters; membership includes some 2,500 dentists. An annual convention is held.

> 3517 16th Street, NW
> Washington, DC 20010
> 202-588-1697
> www.ndaonline.org

National Forum for Black Public Administrators (NFBPA) is a network of 3,000 members, in more than 50 chapters across the country, devoted to the advancement of African American public administrative leadership. The Forum offers programs and seminars in executive leadership development, and mentors students and young professionals.

> 777 North Capitol Street, NE, Suite 807
> Washington, DC 20002
> 202-408-9300
> www.nfbpa.org

National Optometric Association is an organization of minority optometrists devoted to developing the skills of professional optometrists and delivering quality eye care to minority communities. It holds an annual convention and publishes a newsletter.

> 3723 Main Street, P.O. Box F
> E. Chicago, IN 46312
> 877-394-2020
> www.natoptassoc.org

National Pharmaceutical Association was founded in 1947 for the development of African American pharmacists. The group holds a national convention, offers student scholarships, and publishes a quarterly newsletter.

> The Courtyard's Office Complex
> 107 Kilmayne Drive, Suite C
> Cary, NC 27511
> 919-469-5858

National Sales Network is composed of sales professionals and entrepreneurs from all industries. The network encourages the pursuit of careers in sales and sales management professions. Local chapters conduct seminars on selling and negotiating skills, the job search, and more. The network holds an annual conference and distributes a quarterly newsletter.

> 225 DeMott Lane, Suite #2
> Somerset, NJ 08873
> 732-246-5236
> www.salesnetwork.org

National Society of Black Engineers (NSBE) develops intensive programs for increasing the participation of African Americans and other minorities in the fields of engineering and engineering technologies. The organization produces three publications annually and holds its convention in March. It boasts some 10,000 student and professional members nationwide.

1454 Duke Street
Alexandria, VA 22314
703-549-2207
www.nsbe.org

National Urban League Inc. is the premier social service and civil rights organization in the United States. Its mission is to help African Americans attain social and economic equality. It has affiliates in 115 cities in 34 states and the District of Columbia, and it holds an annual conference.

120 Wall Street
New York, NY 10005
212-558-5300
www.nul.org

100 Black Men of America Inc. was formed in 1986 to bring together progressive men across the nation who could contribute their skills and experience to helping the African American community. The group focuses its efforts on education, jobs, health, and housing issues. It holds an annual convention and publishes a newsletter.

141 Auburn Avenue
Atlanta, GA 30303
404-688-5100
www.100blackmen.org

Student National Medical Association was established in 1964 by students at Howard University and Meharry Medical Schools and the National Medical Association. The organization has a membership of more than 2,500 medical school students and physicians in more than 130 chapters nationwide. It helps recruit minority high school students for medical careers, holds an annual medical education conference, and publishes two quarterly publications.

1012 10th Street, NW
Washington, DC 20001
202-371-1616
www.snma.org

Don't rule out sororities and fraternities. If you aren't a member, there are graduate chapters that you can join.

OTHER RESOURCES

- *The African American Network: Get Connected to More Than 5,000 Prominent People and Organizations in the African American Community,* by Crawford B. Bunkley (Plume).
- *National Directory of African American Organizations 2000–2002* (Philip Morris Companies; 212-880-5000). This book offers a wealth of contact information for black professional organizations, plus references and related publications.
- *Black Enterprise Entrepreneurs Conference and Strategic Summit.* Network with hundreds of entrepreneurs. B.E. 100s CEOs, top executives, decision makers from corporate America, and industry vendors attend this four-day event held in May, in Nashville, Tennessee. Its seminars and special events, such as the golf outing and awards dinner, offer prime networking opportunities as well as ways to glean proven advice that can help you advance your business.
- *Black Enterprise Pepsi Golf & Tennis Challenge.* This is an opportunity to experience the ultimate in power networking while enjoying only the finest in leisure pursuits. The Labor Day weekend event is held at the world-class Doral Golf Resort and Spa, in Miami, Florida, and hosts over 1,300 guests. Professionals interested in expanding their business options should attend.
- *Black Enterprise/AXA Advisors Ski Challenge.* This event offers African American executives a forum for networking while enjoying leisure activities. Held during Presidents' Weekend, in Vail, Colorado, attendees can enjoy conquering world-class slopes, being pampered in the spa, or attending a financial seminar. No professional should miss this exciting winter event.

Networking is the foundation of a successful career search. The costs of hiring and training new employees is skyrocketing and, for that reason, many hiring managers want a personal recommendation from someone they know, or who already works for the company, to refer job candidates to them. Take the time to network with everyone you know and everyone they know. It will pay off.

4

HUNTING FOR THE
RIGHT JOB

Searching for a job is a job in itself. You must do research, plan wisely, focus, and not give up easily. Auto mechanics cannot get jobs unless they have their own tools, and most mechanics spend thousands of dollars on a good set. They know that when good tools are coupled with good training, they can always find good employment. That's also the case with any other job—you must invest in the tools that are going to advance your search and get you the job you want. It also helps to be totally prepared. Many employment professionals warn that it is not unusual to spend six months finding the job you want.

DO YOUR HOMEWORK FIRST

Researching a company is the most important—and often the most discounted—first step of a job search. There are several ways to find out what you need to know about a particular company. You can ask people who work in the organization or the industry; you can do online searches; or you can gather books, annual reports, or other relevant literature at a library or from companies themselves. It's interesting how some people determine the company for which they'd like to work. It could be the manufacturer of their favorite morning cereal. It may be the network that broadcasts their favorite music videos, or the ad agency that consistently produces first-rate television commercials. If your only link to a prospective company is its clever TV commercial, you have a lot more research ahead of you.

First, determine whether the company is in the industry you want to enter. Use journals, newspapers, and online resources to determine the industry's trends and future prospects; its challenges, especially in areas of growth and stagnation; and the key players or best companies in the industry. Next, really think about whether the industry is right for you. If you like the outdoors and travel, then maybe the airline, hotel, or resort industry is right up your alley and buying and selling photocopiers is not for you.

At your local library, peruse *The Encyclopedia of Associations* (Gale Research, Detroit, Michigan), which offers a comprehensive list of trade and industry organizations, names of contacts, and addresses and phone numbers of members and chapters. Almost every company has its own Web site. When you log on, you can find out everything: the company's history, the names of the top executives, the career opportunities, and the recent revenues (if it is a publicly traded company). Attend industry conventions. Many key issues, trends, and industry challenges are discussed at these gatherings. If you can't afford the registration fee, try to get on board as a volunteer. Reach out to experts. Investment bankers, sales professionals, economists, journalists, regulators, trainers, and graduate students can be wellsprings of information.

SEARCH THE WEB

The Internet has taken the job search to a whole new height. In the past, you had to resign yourself to sending out countless paper resumes and cover letters, which became costly if you were using the prescribed high-quality paper and stamps. Today, the job search has gotten easier with the help of the Internet. No longer at the mercy of the U.S. Postal Service, which can slow down the process, or of fax machines, which often gave poor reproductions, resumes can now be transmitted, with the help of a computer, a modem, and a phone line, almost anywhere on the globe in seconds. Hundreds of Internet job sites offer everything from career advice to free resume postings, seminars, and training. However, with so much to choose from, where do you start?

The Internet provides access to thousands of jobs, from entry level to CEO status, around the world. And, these positions are in a wide range of industries, not just the technology field. It's convenient for you to sit in your home and scan the electronic want ads, but not all employers will come to you. You might have to go to some of them. To do this, consider posting your resume online. Personnel managers and recruiters often scan resume databases for candidates by using a keyword search. Job seekers on the Net should include, at the bottom of their resume, a separate line of key words related to their occupation.

But before taking that step, do your homework. Read several industry magazines and books to determine which sites are reputable. If you're going to market your resume, you don't want it to fall into just anyone's hands. Ask for references, a list of participating employers, and how long the company has been in business. The company should also give a disclaimer that it will not sell your name and address.

Another issue you should weigh is the possibility that your current employer may see your resume on the Internet. Many sites will allow you to post your resume as "confidential," omitting key identifying elements such as your personal information and the name of your current employer. Evaluate sites based on their level of confidentiality. A private database should seek permission from the candidate before releasing a resume to an employer.

The Internet has experienced unbridled growth. Almost every company, big or small, has a presence on the Internet. However, the Internet is only one tool in your job search arsenal. You have to do more than just post your resume. You have to search job lists and e-mail a resume to every job that is even close to your skill set. The more resumes you e-mail, the better your chances are.

CLASSIFIED ADS

Classified ads generate hundreds of responses, often from unqualified applicants. With that in mind, human resources professionals spend seconds surveying a resume before they hit either the perennial "cylinder file" or their "in" box. That tells you how important it is to have your cover letter stand out. It should be a teaser of what's to come in the accompanying resume. Include a paragraph that zeros in on your particular skills. For example, mention that you developed a market plan, expanded your sales territory, or saved the company thousands of dollars with a new time-saving process.

Avoid some common mistakes that can cost you your current job and reflect badly on your ethics. Don't use your company's letterhead, fax, or postal system. Nothing is worse than a faxed resume that has your company's name and fax number printed at the top. It's fine to use formatted cover letters, but tailor them to the specifications of the job you're seeking.

No response from classified ads? It may be that you're only approaching companies that are advertising their openings. Often, those are the worst prospects because they get inundated with applications. Have you sought out some of your professors in the finance and marketing departments, and asked them for help? They often do consulting work and get phone calls from employers who need help in finding good candidates. Check out your local One-Stop Career Centers (Unemployment Office). Its database of jobs is open to the public.

Another suggestion: Call up some nearby companies, and ask to speak with someone who is working in one of those areas. Your goal is to buy that person lunch or a cup of coffee and listen as he or she tells you about the job and how it was landed. Do not ask for assistance in getting hired by the company; just try to gather information. Chances are good that he or she will recommend that you speak with a hiring manager within the company, or perhaps a hiring manager at another company that has similar needs. You may then be able to speak directly with the person who has the need and authority to hire you.

GENERAL CAREER WEB SITES

Here is a list of the most popular and comprehensive Web sites to date. Don't relegate yourself to contacting just one; post to several that you feel confident are potential job prospects.

- www.blackenterprise.com   The *Black Enterprise* career center offers tailored job search and resume postings, as well as a list of almost 100 minority executive recruiters who specialize in diversity recruitment for the nation's top companies. Find your job (search by location, salary, job type, and job title) and apply online. It's confidential, easy to use, and, of course, FREE!

Every day, your Personal Search Agent (PSA) will search B.E.'s job postings for positions that meet your search criteria. When it finds a match, it will send you an e-mail with an abstract and the Internet address of the job posting.

- www.careerbuilder.com   Formerly careerpath.com, this site allows job seekers to instantly search more than 75 of the Internet's best career sites, using just a couple of clicks. It also provides personalized career services and advice. The Career-Builder Network includes careerbuilder.com—the flagship career center—and the career centers of premier destination sites, including MSN, Bloomberg.com, USA TODAY.com, iVillage.com, latimes.com, Philly.com, chicagotribune.com, and BayArea.com.
- www.collegerecruiter.com   Students seeking part-time jobs and internships, and graduates seeking full-time employment, can post resumes and scan more than 25,000 job listings. There is also info on resume writing, scholarship applications, and student loans.
- www.cruelworld.com   This site's wealth of career management content makes it easy for mid- to senior-level professionals to evaluate their career progress, prepare for a job change, or negotiate salary, among many other resources. Areas covered are marketing, finance, sales, MBA, developer, database, and Java.
- www.gotajob.com   This site is for hourly and entry-level jobs in industries such as retail, restaurant, entertainment, office/ clerical, and service.
- www.hotjobs.com   This site boast hundreds of thousands of jobs and offers advanced privacy features and searching technology. Corporate hiring managers, as well as staffing firms and executive recruiters, post jobs here. Jobs not posted by corporate members are clearly marked.
- www.jobdirect.com   For students and recent college graduates, this comprehensive site lists internships, co-ops, seminars, and holiday jobs. Its parent company, Korn-Ferry, is one of the nation's largest executive recruiting firms. Resume posting is available.
- www.monster.com   The perennial source in online job search engines. Monster.com is a career network that job seekers can use to expand their careers. It provides continuous access to

the most progressive companies, as well as interactive, personalized tools to make the process effective and convenient. Features include resume management, a personal job search agent, a careers network, chatrooms and message boards, privacy options, expert advice on job seeking and career management, and free newsletters.

- www.vault.com   Vault offers extensive insider company information, advice, and career management services.
- www.wetfeet.com   This a good site for finding job descriptions that include expected salary levels, for all types of careers. For a fee, you can purchase career, company, and industry insider guides. Look for "day in the life of" descriptions of the lives of real people and their jobs.

CAREER-SPECIFIC WEB SITES

- www.allretailjobs.com   A listing of hundreds of jobs in the retail industry, from apparel to auto to specialty stores; catalog and health and beauty to toys and hobbies. From logistics, supply chain, and distribution to buyers, finance, and IT job listings. Free resume posting.
- www.geoweb.com   Jobs in technology and science, and a free technology salary survey.
- www.healthjobsite.com   Offers job seekers thousands of healthcare positions. In addition to clients' job listings, visitors may post their resumes. Once your resume is posted, you can easily submit it to any job listed in the job databank. Search more than 3,000 jobs in nursing, medicine, physician employment, and pharmaceuticals. Resume can be posted for available employment!
- www.hcareers.com   Search thousands of hotel jobs, restaurant jobs, casino jobs, resort jobs, chef jobs, cruise ship jobs, catering jobs, and all hospitality industry employment, and post your resume.
- www.prsa.org   Lists conferences, career resources, firms, services, and members of the Public Relations Society of America, 33 Irving Place, New York, NY 10003-2376; 212-995-2230.
- www.telecomcareers.net   Currently contracted by over 500 leading telecom firms. The site offers news, training, and career

tools, and is a complete online telecommunications employment center. Search thousands of telecommunication jobs and post a resume for free.

BOOKS

- *Rules for the Road: Surviving Your First Job Out of School* by Eve Luppert (Perigee). Everything you wanted to know about entry-level jobs but didn't know whom to ask.
- *The Five O'Clock Club Guide to Targeting the Job You Want* by Kate Wendleton (The Five O'Clock Club). The founder of one of the nation's top job-search strategy groups tells you where the jobs of the future are, where you fit in, and how to have job security during turbulent times.
- *How to Identify, Research and Penetrate an Industry* by Robert Davis (Robert Davis & Associates, Mira Loma, California; 909-681-0686).

NOT YOUR ALMA MATER? NO MATTER: CAREER PLACEMENT OFFICES CAN HELP

Some colleges and universities offer reciprocity services for free; others charge one set fee or a per-service price for use of their college placement offices. Services vary but may include access to job listings, use of computers and the Internet, resume preparation, and career development seminars. To get started, call the college that is of interest to you, and ask about its requirements for reciprocity. Perhaps you'll need only a letter of reciprocity from your alma mater, or proof of an affiliation with a state school or a consortium of schools, such as historically black colleges and universities.

TEMPING MIGHT BE YOUR BEST ROUTE TO SUCCESS

Too often, people discount temporary assignments and view them as just a way to make extra money. However, says Monica Mancebo,[1] CEO of Selective Staffing Inc. of New York and New Jersey, they should approach temporary assignments like a full-time position.

That means dressing professionally and conservatively from the start. In addition to making sure that individuals have the prerequisite skills for a particular company, temporary agencies have to consider how well they will fit into an organization's corporate culture. Once on assignment, keep an eye on the job postings and inform your agency representative of the ones that interest you. He or she may be able to speak to the client on your behalf.

It's also critical to exceed the expectations of the job and develop a good relationship with the supervisor. He or she will be the person who can speak in support of your performance if you interview for full-time employment, advises Mancebo. If there is a job posted that requires skills you lack, inform your agency. You may not get that job, but the agency can look for future assignments that will offer you that experience. To get your foot in the door of the company you desire, you must put the best one forward.

The entire temping industry has changed. Now, instead of only traditional clerical and blue-collar workers, a gamut of professionals is needed on a temporary basis—accountants, engineers, lawyers, middle and senior management. In rare instances, temps have even stood in for CEOs, says Bruce Steinberg[2] of the National Association of Temporary and Staffing Services (NATSS), in Alexandria, Virginia. The organization reports that there were more than 2.8 million temporary workers in 1998. Temp work, which can last from a few days to more than a year, now accounts for 2 percent of total U.S. employment. Include independent contractors and America's contingent workforce tops 20 percent.

If you're a student who is trying to reenter the workforce, or is between jobs or seeking diverse work environments, temping may be for you. The lack of real job security and the inability to build long-term relationships with coworkers may be drawbacks. But those who have tried it say temp work offers flexibility, independence, competitive salaries, and the chance to gain valuable skills. It may also be a bridge to permanent employment. A NATSS survey indicates that 66 percent of temp workers view their assignments as a way to gain new skills.

As more people find themselves between jobs, the stigma of temp work as a "dead end" has virtually disappeared, and temps are gaining more respect. With temp agencies' increasing competition for good candidates, some agencies are now offering benefits. Typical temporary benefits at the nation's largest personnel agencies, such as Manpower,

Kelly Services, and ADIA, can include medical insurance, paid holidays, vacations, and 401(k) plans. Some even provide dependent-care reimbursement accounts and tuition refunds. Temporary agencies are in a unique position to track the types of skills the local workforce must have in order to match companies' needs. The more highly skilled the temp, the higher the fee the agency receives. As a result, many temporary firms offer their workers tutorials and training in order to meet clients' demands and remain competitive.

There are, however, some drawbacks to temping. The big problem for contingent workers, says Helen Axel,[3] senior research fellow for the Conference Board and author of the report *HR Executive Review, Contingent Employment,* is that they don't have the underpinning, the security of a permanent job, unless they're highly placed, highly specialized, well-trained consultants who can write their own ticket. Axel says the huge disadvantage of temporary work is insecurity. Even though many of the temporary agencies provide benefits, they do it only after a certain amount of service.

The flip side of flexibility and independence is that coworkers may not accept temps or establish bonds with them because they're not "full members of the club." Temps are not looked down on anymore, but the positions they fill are usually transient, high-turnover slots. Permanent staffers may treat temps differently and not listen to their ideas as readily. Not all agencies have temporary workers' best interests in mind. An agency may send temps on jobs they have no interest in. Because it is insincere about the opportunities it can offer, it may not be able to place the temp. Be clear about your objectives. It's important to build a good relationship with your agency. "Out of sight, out of mind. It's like a parent–child relationship; they will look out for you if they know you," says Tony Johnson,[4] CEO and owner of ACJ & Associates Inc., in Atlanta. For some of his temps, Johnson has made special accommodations such as salary advances, or has provided transportation to an assignment.

If full-time employment is not on the horizon, don't rule out the benefits that come with "professional" or "career" temping. In today's job market, a series of temporary positions on a resume is no longer a stigma. Most employers actually view a number of temp assignments as full-time employment. Temping demonstrates to prospective employers that you have the initiative and skills required for permanent employment. At the least, temporary work provides an intriguing career alternative until you land the job you want.

FIVE TIPS FOR CHOOSING A TEMPORARY AGENCY

1. Find an agency that treats temps like individuals; avoid clearinghouses that simply process people. Some agencies go out of their way to develop real team spirit. They have employee-of-the-month awards, recognition for good attendance, and even company picnics.

2. Choose an agency based on recommendations from people whom you respect. Then, call for references. Try to speak with employees as well as company reps who outsource through the agency. Shop around.

3. Look for an agency that is offering benefits that fit your lifestyle. Many firms offer health and vacation benefits; inquire about the qualifications.

4. Locate an organization that shows concern about you as an employee. The firm should do troubleshooting for you and be an advocate or intermediary if you have any on-the-job problems.

5. If you have a choice of geographic locations, choose an area where there is a demand for your skills. Employers will probably pay more.

A SECTOR TO WATCH

All (Information) Systems Go

If you've ever watched daytime or late-night TV, you've probably seen the commercials for Apex, Chubb, and DeVry institutes. These technical schools promise to open the doors to lucrative information technology (IT) careers with just a few months of training. Years ago, these ads prompted laughter and snide remarks. Today, the schools and their graduates are laughing all the way to the bank.

A 1998 study conducted by Virginia Tech and the Information Technology Association of America (ITAA; www.itaa.org), in Arlington, Virginia, revealed a shortage of over 340,000 IT workers in the United States.[5] This deficit isn't expected to abate anytime soon.

With the need for workers so great, companies are looking to India, Eastern Europe, and South America for programmers, developers, and systems analysts. In 1999, talent-starved firms successfully lobbied Congress for an increase in foreign workers' visas from 65,000 to over 115,000 annually. Still, that's only a stopgap measure. Homegrown talent must be identified and trained in order to successfully fill the increasing void.

But what opportunities really exist? How do you get into an industry so complex that many fear to enter its labyrinths? You begin with education. There's a demand for IT people across all industries, says Bob Cohen,[6] vice president at the ITAA. And technical schools, vocational programs, and two-year colleges do a good job of preparing them. According to the Bureau of Labor Statistics,[7] technical careers make up almost half of the top 10 careers in the new millennium. They include everything from computer scientists to systems analysts to software testers. And everyone—from the novice to the technically adept, and from the recent college grad to the mid-career changer—can find a niche.

UP THE CAREER LADDER WITH A BULLET

Sometimes, a seemingly innocuous event can have a significant impact on our lives. For Cheryl White-Kelly,[8] the cover photo of a technology magazine she glanced at two years ago illuminated a new career path. Her childhood began in East New York, Brooklyn, one of New York City's toughest neighborhoods. She had the first of her four children while a senior in high school, and she weathered many unfulfilling jobs thereafter. Then, a picture of the earth, in which beams of light shooting from continent to continent depicted the Internet, compelled White-Kelly to pursue a career in technology. The fact that she was working in a high-tech environment (she was a billing assistant at a company that offered computer resale and support) was also a motivator.

Ironically, for years, she had been so close to a career in technology, yet so far. In 1990, as a student at New York City Technical College, White-Kelly majored not in computer science—the school's specialty—but in hotel and restaurant management. Three years later, she left school and worked at odd temp jobs so that she and her husband Donovan, her high school sweetheart, could raise their children. She tried landing a front-desk job in New York's selective hotel industry, but to no avail. Then, again, fate steered her toward technology. In 1996, while working as a billing clerk at a computer support firm, she found herself surrounded by computer software, hardware, and gigabytes. White-Kelly says she had always disliked computers because they were so complex; she would learn just enough of an application to get her job done. But eventually she felt challenged and hungry to learn.

On the advice of a friend, White-Kelly enrolled in the computer network engineering course at a local technical school. Three months and some $3,000 later, she went from computer novice to junior engineer. The design of LAN and WAN communication systems, and the ability to upgrade, install, configure, and provide support for these networks became her forte. In just weeks, White-Kelly had amassed enough knowledge to shut the mouths of coworkers who, months earlier, laughed when she asked what a file server was.

She advanced quickly by combining her lecture and lab work with diligent at-home study—a requirement for those serious about the profession. She also interned as a computer lab technician. By the end of the course, White-Kelly was building computer networks like those used by companies all over the world.

Like many alumni before her, White-Kelly found that success was virtually guaranteed. After graduation, she went to Paranet, a technology support firm. She waved bye-bye to her $19,000 billing clerk annual salary and said hello to $42,000 as a junior-level computer network engineer. After a year and a half, she took her technical expertise to Beth Israel Hospital in Manhattan for $55,000. With her network troubleshooting skills much in demand, she recently joined the network support team at media giant Viacom Inc. and landed a compensation package worth more than $73,000 a year.

With her long-range sights set on research and consulting, she offers this sound advice for others. "The industry is trendy, so don't become complacent and stuck in a position where technology might bypass you. Always keep your eyes on the next level."

BUSINESS AND THE VENERABLE MBA

If African Americans are going to participate in the higher echelons of business, an MBA is a must, says Daphne Atkinson,[9] director of MBA admissions at the Johnson Graduate School of Management at Cornell University. Thirty years ago, a college degree was a plus. Today, a graduate degree is how to distinguish yourself, and an MBA is important because it provides a functional specialty and a general management foundation. Today, individuals rework their career several times during their lifetime. An MBA adds to their flexibility.

With the great competition to get into some of the top business schools, schools have set the bar high. The ideal candidate should have three to five years of work experience, with a progressive track record. (On your job, volunteer for projects that place you in a leadership role and show tangible results.) Those with exemplary academic records and GMA total test scores above 600 can usually pick one of the top business schools. But that doesn't mean others can't get into reputable programs. Atkinson also suggests that minority students hone their quantitative skills while in college by taking core courses in economics and statistics. "You must be focused on your grades the first two years. If not, it will be difficult to excel the last two years," she adds.

Potential B-school students should also have significant internships and work experience under their belt. Schools look for a diverse population. A dual learning experience is going on, and students also learn from their classmates, notes Atkinson, who says that two years in an "analyst" position—for example, as a credit or market analyst— is a great feeder job into business schools. The more work experience and progress you show, the less weight is put on the undergraduate transcript. This is especially important for African Americans who may worry about their GMAT scores. No one is denied admission solely on a GMAT score, adds Atkinson. It was for some other weakness, not the GMAT alone.

PHARMACEUTICAL BREAKTHROUGHS

A Seller's Market

The economy has also boosted the market for sales professionals. Every industry, from consumer products to computers to healthcare, is providing lucrative career opportunities. Probably the most marked increase is in healthcare, pharmaceutical, and biotechnology companies, which are not only shoring up their sales forces but also revamping territories and creating specialties that never existed before. For example, two or more salespeople at a pharmaceutical company might cover the same territory, but one might be in cardiovascular drugs and the other in psychiatric, says David Marshall,[10] president of Target Pros, an executive recruitment firm in West Orange, New Jersey.

"There is always a new drug coming out with a different indication, thus opening up new, big markets and jobs, especially for African Americans. But you have to have what it takes." Marshall says companies want individuals who have perfected their sales pitch. Can you persuade? How are your leadership qualities? He adds, "You don't have to be a manager, but you must have the professional image, aptitude, and attitude to be a leader." Pharmaceutical companies desire an MBA or a master's degree in science or marketing. "If you are coming in with no sales experience but have the credentials, a company may put you into a training or marketing program."

A Day in the Life of a Pharmaceuticals Rep

It's 8:00 A.M., and Bonnie Mumford,[11] a sales rep for Pfizer Inc., is meeting with a hospital psychiatrist. Next, she makes a few cold calls and then has lunch with doctors in her Cape Cod, Massachusetts, and Providence, Rhode Island, territory. As friendly reminders of her visit, Mumford leaves behind pens and pads etched with the name of the sole drug she markets—Zoloft, the nation's most prescribed antidepressant. By 7 P.M., Mumford is at an educational symposium on depression, which she helped organize for an audience of psychiatrists. A hectic schedule indeed, but real life for a pharmaceutical sales representative.

A summer internship with Merck Inc., during her sophomore year at Florida A&M University School of Business and Industry, in Tallahassee, started her on this career path. She joined Pfizer after receiving an MBA in marketing from FAMU in 1993. Mumford saw pharmaceuticals as the most professional industry for a sales career, so she had worked with experts in the medical community and became an expert in her field.

Mumford had the foresight to adapt her skills to the needs of the pharmaceutical industry, which is projected to be one of the fastest growing businesses in the new century. She quickly proved that she could grow her market by courting managed health care facilities, teaching hospitals, and private-practice psychiatrists in her territory. And to the victor go the spoils: For two years running, Mumford exceeded her annual sales quota of $3 million by at least 25 to 30 percent, becoming Pfizer's No. 1 sales rep for Zoloft.

Despite the presence of Mumford and a few other path breakers in the industry, African Americans have not seized the career opportunities available in the booming pharmaceutical business. According to IMS America, a market research firm, the U.S. pharmaceutical industry generated $109 billion in sales from May 2000 to May 2001.

The goal of most companies is to keep new and better drugs in the pipeline and improve old ones, according to Louella Williams,[12] managing director of HR Strategies, an executive search firm located in Atlanta and specializing in pharmaceutical industry placements. When a company discovers a drug that will generate $100 million a year in sales, it's worth the price of all the failures. As a result, companies increase hiring in key areas such as human resources, finance, sales, and, especially, research.

For most sales reps, like Mumford, lofty expense accounts, company cars, base salaries between $45,000 and $75,000, and bonuses of up to $30,000 don't come without a price. Meeting stringent quotas in the evolving health care arena can get extremely competitive.

Managed health care has changed the dynamics of the marketplace. For reps, selling drugs has become even more challenging because there are so many restrictions. "Many times, a doctor may really like the drug I sell, but if that doctor is affiliated with a certain managed care group, my drug may not be on their list," notes Mumford.

Perks seduce some people to stay with the sales end, but other careers in the industry are just as lucrative. In the past few years, many companies have hired individuals with science-related backgrounds to work in the areas of drug discovery and research. These are areas where African Americans have typically been absent, says Williams. Technology is the basis of all new pharmaceutical jobs. Most of the downsizing and reengineering that companies did during the past decade, in fact, was done to make room for more technologically based jobs. African Americans with advanced degrees in science-related fields, says Williams, can command starting salaries of $50,000 to $75,000.

No one knows that better than Monique Carver-Clark.[13] Before graduating from California State University in Hayward with a degree in biology, she had considered becoming a doctor or physical therapist. But a junior-year science research project piqued her interest in biological research.

After graduating in 1982, she joined Genentech, a San Francisco-based biotechnology firm, as a research assistant. She quickly moved up to become a regional clinical research associate for the biotechnology firm. Having worked on developmental projects for years, Carver-Clark wanted more experience with patients and with the effects of drugs on the clinical end. Her job: to work with health care providers as they test new drugs on patients.

Spending at least 30 percent of her time traveling to various health care facilities throughout the United States, Carver-Clark acted as a liaison between the pharmaceutical company and physicians. The bulk of her present responsibilities includes ensuring that clinical drug trials are conducted according to drug company procedures and FDA regulations. Carver-Clark must make sure the data are accurately documented; that information is later assessed to determine whether the drug is safe for general release.

Carver-Clark says that the career is challenging, but part of her reward is knowing that her work has impacted someone's life. With few African Americans in research and drug discovery, companies are scrambling to hire blacks with research backgrounds. Carver-Clark says she receives about five calls a month from recruiters.

OTHER PHARMACEUTICAL CAREERS

Regulatory affairs specialist: Collects and compiles data from clinical trials for new drug applications that must be approved by the FDA. Salaries start at $50,000 with five years' experience in either clinical research or marketing.

Medical writer: Collects clinical data and writes proposals for FDA new-drug applications. A BS in biology or chemistry and a clinical research background are required. Salaries start at $35,000 to $40,000.

Project manager: Supervises the process from clinical drug trials to FDA approval. Individuals with an MD or PhD in chemistry or pharmacology and 10 to 15 years' experience can make $55,000 to $80,000. An MBA is a plus.

Drug information specialist: Handles drug inquiries from health care professionals and consumers. A PhD in pharmacology and 10 years' experience are required. Salaries start at $50,000.

Williams points out that health care professionals, such as nurses, physician assistants, and medical technicians, can easily cross over into clinical research. She encourages African Americans to pursue advanced degrees—specifically, doctorates in the biological sciences, organic chemistry, or pharmacology—in order to move into managerial positions, such as principal scientists in drug discovery, or directors of research. Many pharmaceutical companies sponsor doctoral programs with universities across the country, and offer scholarships and fellowships for minority students and employees.

Employers are really only looking for three things when they are hiring: Do you look the part? Can you be counted on? And can you do the job? You must keep this in mind and be prepared to convey your skills to employers. Simply being able to tell the employer what your skills are during an interview jumps you to the top 20 percent of job seekers! To make your job search a success, use all of the tools available to you and take the job search seriously.

5

PREPARING FOR AN INTERVIEW

Congratulations! You've been called in for an interview! Waiting for that call is sometimes the hardest part. However, no job-search activity creates more anxiety among candidates than the interview process. Having to impress strangers so that they will hire you is a daunting task. At some point in your search, you'll have to perform on cue in an interview. Gathering your thoughts and wits about you in order to smoothly maneuver through this task, which can sometimes be as short as 10 to 20 minutes, or may last a full day or more, takes work.

Many interviewees tend to cast themselves in the role of a beggar looking for a handout, but companies rarely hire individuals out of the goodness of their hearts. They're looking for people who can solve business problems. A candidate who understands what those problems are—and offers a method of solving them—will land the job.

Taking an active stance has lots of benefits too. It helps you manage your stress level and present your self in the best professional light. It also allows you to evaluate whether you really want to work for the interviewer's company. Just as there are imperfect interviewers, there are no perfect interviewees. This chapter will show you how to overcome some of your anxiety about the interview process by developing better skills and attitudes.

Don't rush to schedule the interview if you're not prepared. If you're asked to come in the next day, delay it; you need some time to prepare. If you can get an interview later in the screening process, the interviewer will have seen enough people to know what qualities to look for and will be more focused. If you are interviewed in the beginning of the process, be sure to follow up with the interviewer.

The first quality you will always want to project is optimism. Let it show through your attitude and the way you carry yourself. Imagine yourself to be playing the part of somebody else—a person who always gets what he or she is after. Try not to end your sentences with an upward inflection. It can make you sound nervous or timid. Keep good posture as well as good eye contact (not too much here; there is a fine line between a confident look and a stare).

You are essentially trying to sell your abilities to a potential employer. If the interviewer begins to get excited over a topic, you should too. If the interviewer leans forward and puts his or her arms on the desk, check that your own posture is relaxed, not rigid. Always be self-conscious of how you are acting. If you were to lean toward the desk while being interviewed by someone who is very calm and laid back, your move may be seen as an invasion of personal space, or a sign that you are too aggressive.

The key is: Know who you are and what you have to offer. Research the companies you're interested in and the ones that would be likely to hire you (Chapter 4). Learn those companies' needs and long-term goals, and, present yourself as someone who can really add value to those organizations. With this approach, your job search will be more effective and your self-esteem will grow.

Proper attire and grooming demonstrate respect and consideration for the interviewer and the company you are trying to enter. For example, if you are interviewing with an investment firm, you should dress as though you already work there. If this is your first job search, you may not own an interview outfit. You should make plans to buy at least two or three different suits so that you have one ready if another gets soiled or needs cleaning. You don't want to have to cancel an interview because your only suit is being dry cleaned. Also, if a company calls you back for a second interview, you would want to be wearing a different suit. Minimalism is key for a job interview.

The old adage, "First impressions count," couldn't ring truer than in a job interview. Your personal appearance is the first thing an interviewer evaluates, before he or she shakes your hand or asks you questions. Therefore, your overall grooming is critical. You can have the best credentials and experience, but if your appearance turns off your interviewer, you'll unwittingly be trying to overcome unspoken demerits. Here are some other things to be mindful of:

- *Maintain good posture.* Sit up straight and lean into the interview, to show enthusiasm. If your shoulders are slumped, you'll convey lack of confidence, laziness, and weakness.

- *Have a firm handshake.* Avoid a limp-fish handshake. Nothing is worse than a hand that is just dead weight in the interviewer's hand. It doesn't matter who extends a hand first; just make sure that the web between your thumb and index finger meets that of the interviewer. Apply a firm grip for three to five seconds. However, don't overcompensate and transform your hand into a vise-like grip. Men tend to do this with other men. Keep in mind that a handshake is not an arm-wrestling competition or a display of physical strength.

- *Display a calm exterior.* Do not fold your hands in front of you. It suggests that you have something to hide or are insecure. Granted, the inside of an office filled with photos, awards, and other desk accoutrements can cause your eyes to wander, but you must remain focused. When you enter the office, allow the interviewer to sit first or invite you to sit down. Don't just take a seat; you never know where the interview will be conducted. Not all interviews are conducted across a desk.

- *Stride confidently.* Keep your head up and your shoulders back. Approach the interviewer with eye contact and a smile. Your body language is being evaluated, and you want to exude your confidence that you are the right person for the job.

- *Display a positive attitude.* Energy and a bright personality count toward much of a person's total presence. Be confident, but not too aggressive, arrogant, or cocky.

- *Remove any gum or candy from your mouth before your interviewer calls you in.* Not only is it unprofessional to be seen chewing something, but you want to be able to speak and project your thoughts clearly. Also, don't come in carrying food or drinks, and avoid accepting anything that may spill on you or on the desk or chair of your interviewer.

OTHER THINGS THAT INTERVIEWERS EVALUATE

The Time You Arrive

Twenty minutes early is optimal. But arrive *at least* 15 minutes early. There may be forms to fill out before your interview. Or, you may have to park half a mile away, or find your way through unexpectedly long corridors. If the area is unfamiliar, you may get lost. Admittedly, some interviewers would love to have you arrive early because their day is running like a well-oiled machine and they are actually waiting for *you*. Arriving early shows your interest in the job and your respect for the interviewer's time.

It also keeps you out of the ugly "C.P. time" or "colored people time" zone. Oh yes, you know it well. Sadly, lateness is a common problem for many people of any persuasion; however, it has long been associated with African Americans. Late is late, whether it's five minutes or half an hour, and no matter what excuse you give, the interviewer will only remember that you were late. You'll have a red flag flying above you before you even open your mouth.

Just remember that even if you are early for appointments, for work, or for a class 99 percent of the time, that one late arrival will evoke in someone—perhaps the receptionist, or the interviewer's assistant—the thought that you are black and therefore lateness is to be expected. Wear a watch that day, even if you don't like to wear one. It tells the interviewer that you are conscientious about time and deadlines, and you take your job seriously.

How You're Dressed

It is always best to err on the side of conservatism; therefore, a suit is best. Blue or gray suits are considered "interviewing uniforms" and you can't go wrong with them. In the summer, khaki and taupe will also work, but try to stay with lightweight versions of the uniform. Brown suits are a no–no. They tend to make people look mousy and timid. Stay away from rainbow colors such as chartreuse, purple, and vibrant red. They immediately set a bad tone with the interviewer. No matter how toney or avant-garde the company is, the interviewer will spend the first 10 minutes trying to look beyond what you're wearing. Granted, information technology (IT) candidates at some firms can get away with a shirt, tie, and slacks when they saunter into a dot.com headquarters. But 97 percent of applicants must maintain the status quo and stick to the "uniform." Use this rule of thumb: Dress for the position that is one step up from the one you're seeking.

Unless you are a seasoned job hunter who has had experience in these areas, do a dry run the night before. Try on your clothes. If you don't wear suits every day, be sure that the suit you plan to wear is clean, pressed, free of lint, cat hair, and frayed threads, and has all its buttons and no torn spots. You're probably thinking, "This is a given. How would any self-respecting persons walk out of the house not looking their best?" You'd be surprised. It happens far more often than you would expect. Is the suit too tight, too big? If you have time to get it altered or can switch to an alternative, please, do it. Why do some people iron their clothes and others don't? I don't know. What I do know is that nothing is worse than a suit with a wrinkled shirt underneath, or slacks that bear a fold across the knee, letting everyone know that they just came off a hanger. If you can't iron a shirt like a naval cadet, send it to a laundry or dry cleaner.

Your Hands and Nails

Pay attention to your hands and nails. They speak volumes about your grooming habits and your personality. After your face and your attire, they are the next thing an interviewer will see as you hand him or her your resume or pass along copies of your work or career portfolio.

Women should wear a neutral color of polish, or no polish at all, on short, well-manicured nails. Ditch the Dragon Lady lengths adorned with airbrushing or decals. You don't want the interviewer staring at your hands because they look like they're headed for the Las Vegas strip.

For men, short, clean, groomed nails are best. Nothing is worse than showing up for an early morning interview where you're assumed to be showered and clean, but you have dirt under your fingernails. One Fortune 500 executive has said that the way a person's hands look helps her make her decision to hire. She relates a story of a very qualified job candidate who had impeccable credentials and gave an excellent interview. However, the position required someone with Zen-like patience in dealing with the public. One look at the candidate's bitten nails and chewed cuticles showed that she would not necessarily be graceful under fire. In fact, the hiring director thought that she might be a nervous wreck under pressure. Needless to say, the candidate was passed over for someone who had equally impressive qualifications but a much calmer demeanor and well-groomed hands. Was this just one hiring manager's pet peeve? Perhaps; but bear in mind that what may be acceptable to some interviewers may be red flags to others, so keep everything, from your attire to your accessories and grooming, simple and neat.

COVERING YOUR EXIT

You are not required to tell a potential employer that you have been fired. It is the responsibility of interviewers to ask what they want to know. But if you are asked directly, "Was your resignation voluntary?" or "Were you asked to resign?" never lie or blame others. Redirect the conversation to why you're the best candidate for *this* job. Being honest is key. Besides, depending on your particular industry and rank, the circumstances behind your exit may already be known.

If your termination was a result of poor judgment on your part—lateness or absenteeism—state that fact and explain what you've learned as a result and what you now do differently. For example, you now realize that you should have asked your previous employer for time off to care for a sick parent or child, instead of being absent and not explaining the circumstance.

Complaining too much about a former manager is taboo. It could signal that personality conflicts would develop if you're hired. Concentrate on your skills. Anticipate any difficult or challenging questions in advance, write the answers down if necessary, and find a way to end the interview on a positive note.

Accessories

Less is more, on this front. For women, wearing one ring on each hand and one earring in each ear is acceptable. Men should remove any earrings. Hands are the only areas where rings of any sort should appear. Ditch any eyebrow, lip, or nose rings until after work. Also, do not use this occasion to bejewel yourself in all your finery. For a man or a woman, a bevy of gold chains cascading down from your neck is too distracting and not appropriate for the workplace. Repeat: Don't forget to wear a watch—one that you can depend on.

Pantyhose are necessary for women going into a formal corporate setting, even if the interview is held in Florida or Arizona in the middle of August. If you're hired, you can evaluate the dress code and determine whether bare legs are acceptable in the workplace. For your interview, continue to err on the side of conservatism.

Also, scuffed toes and dull shoes say you lack attention to detail and to the value of how you're perceived. If you don't think you can bring your shoes to a high buff, then invest a few dollars in a professional shoeshine and be sure to fix any worn lifts and scratched heels. Think about it: If you are going for a job in sales, your appearance is half your technique. You may be able to talk a good game, but if you can't sell yourself to the interviewer or you don't represent the company in a good light, you won't be sent out to see clients who will base their impression of the company on how you, the salesperson, looks. Women should wear closed-toe shoes, although sling backs are becoming more acceptable.

Makeup should be subtle and appropriate for the daytime. No glitter eye shadow or blush, and no garish lipstick. I know it's liberating to want to express who you are, or to challenge the employer to accept you as you are, but why not wait until you get the job and feel out the tenor of the corporate culture.

Hair

This is a touchy issue; however, great strides have been made. Some cases taken through the courts have forced employers to be more accepting of the various hairstyles worn by African Americans. The greater acceptance of locks, braids, extensions, naturals, and color has given us myriad ways to express who we are. In the past, many companies were hit with discrimination suits for forcing African American employees to change their hairstyles. No more—or at least, not so often.

In most metropolitan cities, from the mailroom to the boardroom, individualism is accepted. However, as a newcomer to the job market, you might want to keep your appearance mainstream. The big bush or foot-long locks you sported around campus might not be embraced at all organizations. Clean, trim, and neat natural or relaxed styles are best. If you're hired, you can determine whether the corporate culture is open to anything more. If you're looking at anything to do in consulting, finance, insurance, banking, or a white-shoe law firm, you might have to rein in the tresses and adopt a more conservative natural look. Save the colored extensions and ornate hair accessories for after-work activities.

Resumes and Notepads

You may have faxed or e-mailed your resume beforehand. You might have even sent a crisp hard copy; nevertheless, bring at least two copies with you. You may be asked to see more than one person, or the interviewer might be reading an unformatted e-mailed version or a

NOT THE TIME TO LIGHT UP

Smoking has definitely become poor decorum in our society. If you're a smoker, be sure not to smoke before your interview, unless you're hoping for a job with a tobacco company. If your interviewer is averse to cigarette smoke, you'll never know that is the reason why you weren't hired, but why chance it. Walking into an interview with the smell of smoke on you send three negative messages: (1) you're possibly nervous, (2) you may falter when under pressure, and (3) more importantly, you will be sacrificing precious company time to satisfy your craving for nicotine. An unsympathetic interviewer realizes that if you're outside in front of the building, or in the smoking lounge four to six times a day, you may be losing up to an hour in productivity each workday.

CHECKLIST

ENSURING THAT YOU'LL BE PERCEIVED
IN A POSITIVE LIGHT

____ Arrive early or, at the least, be on time. DON'T BE LATE!

____ Be cordial to the receptionist.

____ Wear attire comparable to other employees at the firm.

____ Make sure your clothes are pressed, your shoes are shined, and your nails and hair are neat.

____ Bring extra resumes.

____ Make eye contact. Don't stare like a deer caught in the headlights, but have periodic eye contact when you are asked questions or are given information.

____ Address the interviewer by name.

____ Try not to ramble and *don't* try to be a comedian. Keep small talk to a minimum so you don't talk yourself out of a job.

____ Highlight your skills.

____ Don't discuss salary. If the interviewer mentions it, say that you are seeking an industry-competitive salary.

____ Ask questions about the company, the position, the qualifications being sought in a candidate, and when a decision will be made.

____ Don't discuss politics, religion, or sex.

____ Don't get too comfortable; you are being evaluated. No matter how easygoing the interviewer is, keep your hands off the desktop kitsch and photos, and don't ask personal questions.

____ Thank the interviewer for his or her time.

GET THE ANSWERS

Best Answers to the 201 Most Frequently Asked Interview Questions, by Matthew J. DeLuca (McGraw Hill), provides not only the most common Qs&As, but also tells how to answer awkward or illegal questions, personal questions, and trick questions, and still get the job.

curly-edged fax copy and will welcome a real one. Bring along a small briefcase or binder and a notepad. Take notes on things you want to research and remember after the interview. You should also document what your job responsibilities will be. Don't depend on your memory at such a tense moment. There might be follow-up information that you need to send, and writing each item down will ensure that you send the correct information to the right person.

BE A STAR

If this is your first foray into the job search arena, don't shelve or discount any of your scholastic achievements or examples of your work style during college or high school. Experience as a class president, a captain of a team, or a manager of a McDonald's points to leadership. If a company is interviewing for a job that is research-oriented, then talk about your research projects, math or science classes, computer skills, or Internet savvy. If the job is team-oriented, describe any of your earlier jobs that involved working groups or team sports. If the job requires public speaking and you were on a debating team or earned membership in Toastmasters (a national public speaking organization), let the interviewer know.

According to research, past behavior predicts future behavior, says Nancy Friedberg, a senior consultant with The Five O'Clock Club. Many hiring managers and personnel people are trained in behavioral interviewing. Their questions probe and unearth how candidates would handle job-related situations. Friedberg says that candidates can ace this type of questioning by employing The Five O'Clock Club strategy called the STAR method. Rather than listing their strengths, the candidates demonstrate how a strength has helped them achieve a goal. The acronym stands for a *Situation* or *Task* that *Achieves Results*.

In your head, or on a set of flashcards, select the *situation* that you will present when asked. List each action taken and end with a description of the results. For example, you can say that you already had a deadline to meet when a new project, due within the same time frame, was given to you. Then explain how your *action* prioritized the two projects by using strengths such as time management and delegation. Finally, explain the outcome or *results* of the situation, showing the success you had because of the methods you used.

"So when you're selling yourself during the interview, be sure to have a script in your head," says Friedberg. "If you practice and prepare, you will have a smooth delivery during the interview."

A STAR EXAMPLE OF GOOD CUSTOMER SERVICE

Situation or Task: "I worked in a store and was selling something to a very difficult client. The person became very irate because the product was not available."

Action: "Instead of letting this person be upset, I calmed her down and defused her anger. Despite not having the authority of my supervisor, I made a phone call to the distributor."

Result: "Within two days, we had the product delivered to the client. She was so pleased that she wrote a letter about me to the store manager."

An example like this will tell the interviewer that you understand the meaning of good customer service. Most people, particularly those in positions of little authority, would shrug their shoulders and say, "It's not my job." However, this candidate proved, through this scenario, an ability to take initiative. By practicing and charting out your script, you will also avoid candidates' common tendency to ramble. Interviewing is like show time; for any good show, there has to be some rehearsal. Don't wing an interview. You are going "on stage," so rehearse your lines. Think of yourself as an actor. Put your STAR examples on index cards and do a dress rehearsal out loud, as a preparation for your interview.

FILLING A QUOTA?

"There are companies that want diversity, but few companies are willing to compromise quality and performance to retain or hire a diverse candidate," says Willie S. Bright,[1] president of the Urban Placement Service in Houston.

During the initial stages of their careers, minority professionals may feel they are a "token," Bright says. However, most jobs offer a real place in the organizational structure of a company. "Disregard your suspicions because no job is officially a 'quota job,'" he explains. There are minority goals and objectives that companies try to reach, but if a position can't be filled with a minority person, someone else will be hired to fill it.

If a position offers you an opportunity to grow and advance, use it to get in the door. Your skills and potential will keep you with that company and allow you to progress.

THANK-YOU LETTERS AND FOLLOW UPS

A thank-you letter is one of the most commonly overlooked aspects of job hunting. Don't fall into the trap of thinking it isn't important. A handwritten note is best, but a thoughtful e-mail will suffice. Thank the interviewer for his or her time, and reiterate your skills and why you feel you're perfect for the job. Like your resume, your thank-you letter should be individualized. Don't copy a form or sample letter. What you write should reflect the mood and content of the interview.

At The Five O'Clock Club, members are not coached to write mere thank-you letters. Instead, they are told to write follow-up letters that imitate the form of the traditional thank-you letter but keep on delivering on their potential. If you really want a job that requires a particular software skill, go out and learn the software. Mention in your follow-up letter that you are learning it so that you will be up to speed when the hiring decision is made. Do a follow-up, but don't be a pest. Pace your follow-up and timing with where the hiring manager is in the process. If you call too much when interviewing is just beginning, you can screen yourself out. If you call only during the first few weeks and the decision is to be made in six weeks, you may have dropped from the interviewer's consciousness. A phone call a week is sufficient. It conveys your enthusiasm. Friedberg warns that it can take up to eight follow-up phone calls before you get a response!

TWO COMMON INTERVIEW QUESTIONS

Q: Tell me about yourself.
Generally, try to keep your response related to the job you're interviewing for. Talk about any relevant education, training, or experience. Even if the experience is not directly related, describe situations where the same skills are applied. Also talk about your expectations (your hope to get into management, etc.) if the company you are applying to offers you a job. The interviewer isn't looking for your life story, so just give a general summary of what you could bring to the table.

Q: What characteristics would you improve?
Find a point, like organizational skills or time management, and show how you rectified it. Don't offer something that you have no resolution for. For example, you might say, "I had too many post-its around and finally bought an electronic organizer." This shows the interviewer that you recognized your area of opportunity and then took steps to improve it. Ask yourself: "What area of my performance can be improved and what steps can I take to improve it?" What steps *will* you take to improve it?

   If you tell your interviewer your area of opportunity but you don't do anything to improve it, you are basically saying that you don't care to improve your performance. Pointing out your weakness will not do you any good in the interview if you don't have a plan to correct it.

HOW TO SELL YOURSELF DURING AN INTERVIEW WHEN YOU'RE NOT BEING ASKED THE RIGHT QUESTIONS

Despite the rapidly changing workplace, interviewers are still using many of the same criteria and questions that were used decades ago. Old favorites such as "Tell me about yourself" and "What would you describe as your strengths and weaknesses?" can be limiting—if you let them. Highlight the contributions you made at your last firm by turning the interview around. You must clearly articulate your achievements and be able to show how they affected productivity or the bottom line. Knowledge of how the company operated or of organizational operatives, and the ability to think critically by putting a fresh thought on an old issue are key.

When you feel you are up against a "bad" interviewer—one who seems ready to easily dismiss you, or is bored or preoccupied—be ready to volunteer information. Think about how your strengths— problem solving, attention to detail, or money management—can be used in the organization. Interviews should be dialogues. If the "right" questions aren't being asked, don't wait. Ask them yourself. It's perfectly acceptable to ask the interviewer what the company is looking for in a candidate. Remember, an interview is not one-sided. You are also evaluating the company. Putting your questions on the table may help you to better direct your answers and eventually land the job.

Questions to Handle with Kid Gloves

Q: What are the reasons why you left your last job?

A: I am looking for new opportunities and a way to continue my career growth.

Q: Have you received any other job offers? What other organizations are you considering?

A: Yes, I have received an offer or two, but am keeping my options open. (Answer truthfully. If you have offers on the table, do not provide too much information. Employers like to know that the candidate they have their eye on is also attractive to other companies. Try not to reveal too much about the competition.)

Q: What are your salary expectations?

A: I seek competitive industry compensation. (If you have done your research, you know the range the position pays and you can quote it.) However, you should wait until you are made an offer before discussing salary.

Q: Describe a situation where your work was criticized. What was your reaction?

A: Again, keep it positive. Describe a nonthreatening situation and show how you accepted the criticism and undertook measures to improve your performance. Use the STAR method here.

Q: Did you have a hard time finding the building/our office? Did your plane come in on time? What about this bad weather?

A: Keep your answer short and sweet, particularly if your experience wasn't pleasant. Avoid this type of conversational subject if at all possible. You don't want to reflect negatively on anyone or anything. Be succinct and polite. Do not complain.

PRACTICE INTERVIEWS

Set up interviews with companies you actually do not intend to work for. This will let you translate what you have read about interviewing into actual experience. There are many different interview formats (an interview by one person, by several people at once, or by several people in a row), and each person conducting the interview will add something new to the experience. Even if you walk in and forget everything you have read, be confident in yourself. If you don't appear confident, the person conducting the interview may be led to think that, if you were hired, you might have problems making decisions. The "practice" interviews can be invaluable when it comes time for the one you really want.

INFORMATIONAL INTERVIEWS

Okay, you might be very satisfied in your current job, but what about later? There is nothing wrong with testing the waters and seeing what's out there. You can do that with informational interviews. Many companies, if interested in your resume, will call you in even when no positions are available. They may be feeling you out for the future, and you can gain valuable information about the company and its networking connections. There will be less stress because you're not actually interviewing for a job, but you will still want to make a good impression.

Although many human resources managers are busy fielding stacks of resumes from candidates hoping to fill open positions, if you have some rapport with the HR manager or have a connection within the company, you can probably arrange an informational interview. If you are fortunate enough to speak with a manager in the department or business unit you're interested in, you can get even more insight into a potential career or job.

BEGINNING, MIDDLE, OR END? WHERE SHOULD YOU BE IN THE INTERVIEWING PROCESS?

Based on the pattern of memory our minds stick to, we tend to remember things in the beginning and end of a story or situation better than we can recall the middle (which is why experts advise students not to study for hours on end). It would be advantageous to be interviewed among the first or the last members of a group. You can get an idea of where you stand by asking when the company expects to fill the position. Just to make sure you get the most bang for your buck, send a thank-you letter and include a copy of your resume. This will be especially helpful if you were among a large group of people being interviewed.

REVERSE SELECTION: INTERVIEWING THE EMPLOYER

Savvy job seekers are screening potential employers as scrupulously as the employers are screening them. Many plum offers are getting thumbs down, and not just because of compensation. Candidates are also weighing corporate culture, benefits, and quality of life/work issues before signing on the dotted line.

After two years with a Chicago law firm, Deborah Telman[2] wanted to expand her legal skills. She interviewed with several big Chicago firms, stating her career goals and asking key questions that would help her assess whether that company was for her. "I asked if I would be working on corporate matters and if anyone would mentor me," says Telman. "I also wanted a firm where I would see successful people who looked like me." Her assertiveness paid off. After turning down several lucrative offers, Telman joined the law firm of Winston & Strawn.

For some employers, this turning of the tables has made wooing good employees that much more challenging. "These companies are looking at their turnover rates and trying to build more nurturing and diversified work environments," says Jean Maye,[3] president of VJM Associates, an organizational development consulting firm in Jersey City, New Jersey.

Before an interview, you should research the company and determine your questions, suggests Maye. The questions should uncover your job responsibilities, performance measurements, management style, organizational culture, and the resources that will be made available to you. "They shouldn't be a battery of detailed queries that might make the interviewer feel uneasy, badgered or drained," she adds. Act as a consultant and ask questions that unearth the employers' needs and pressing priorities. Don't oversell yourself. If you do too much talking and not enough listening, you won't know what they need. Push the right button, act like a consultant, and you'll sell them.

Asking some good questions can definitely make a good impression on your potential employer. Some good queries are:

- What happened to the last person who had this position? (fired, quit, promoted?)
- What plans does the company have for the position? (expanding? room for advancing?)
- What are the company's goals for the next several years? (Ask this only if you have researched the company and understand its full scope and the market share it competes for.)
- Who is my competition and how do I stack up? (You can't be timid here. You want to leave the interview knowing where you stand.)
- Are there any concerns about me or my background that might affect my getting the job? (People don't get callbacks and don't know why, but you'll leave knowing where you might be lacking.)
- Where does the hiring process stand and when will the company make the decision?

Some other questions to consider asking are:

- *What are the company's diversity initiatives?* The answer will give you some insight into the company culture and your career path options. If only the human resources person can discuss these initiatives, or there is apprehension in the interviewer's answer, perhaps diversity management is not embraced throughout the company.

- *How are new ideas and suggestions viewed?* If your question is met with "We never do this" or the process for implementation is bureaucratic, the company may not be very open to employees' input.
- *What are the company's short- and long-term business strategies?* Maybe they aren't in tune with your career goals. If the interviewer doesn't know what the company's strategies are, perhaps they haven't been made public. Do you want to enter into an environment where information isn't shared freely?

When Doris Mitchell Green,[4] associate director for geriatric services at Northwestern University Center on Aging, in Chicago, was offered a promotion, it looked like a coup. She would inherit two additional departments and would gain a 15 percent pay increase, lucrative benefits, and a flexible work schedule that would allow her to complete her master's degree in public health. "During the second

---

Q: I'm in sales. I know how to pitch products, but how do I properly sell myself during an interview?

A: Sales reps with at least two years of experience need more than just a resume. Sales ranking reports and letters of reference can make the difference, particularly for African Americans, says David Marshall, president of Target Pros Inc., an executive search and recruiting firm in Montclair, New Jersey. Sales ranking reports show how potential employees stood up against other reps. "If you say you were 130 percent of quota and can prove it, you help to close the decision-making process," says Marshall. "Employees easily overcome any objections when [companies] can see what type of sales rep they are getting."

If your company does not provide sales ranking reports or annual evaluations, some letters of reference from clients and/or customers can show a district or regional manager your people skills. Yet, despite the importance they place on these documents and on call reports, awards, and special projects, most potential employers won't ask for them, so you have to think ahead. Adds Marshall, "Companies want to see how you sell. If you can't sell yourself, then how can you sell the product?"

interview, I started inquiring about the kind of infrastructure support that I would have," says Mitchell Green, who would have lost five
years' seniority with the move. "The additional responsibilities
meant being on call 24 hours a day and losing out on sleep. Quality of
life was important to me, so I turned down the offer."

Turn an interview around to your advantage. The employer gets
to see your knowledge and initiative, and you get the essential information you need to make an educated career move.

WHAT SIGNS DOES AN INTERVIEWER GIVE THAT YOU *HAVEN'T* GOTTEN THE JOB?

There really aren't any definitive signals because personalities vary.
Often, the interviewer will not know (at the time of the interview)
whether you are "the one." Usually, interviewers need to go through a
large application pool, especially if the position was highly publicized.
Also, depending on the nature of the position, more than one person
may be involved in the final decision-making process. Many people
who have thought they interviewed poorly, have found out later that
they got the job. Unless the interviewer makes a job offer at the end of
the interview, there is no certain way of knowing. Just do your best.

DRESSING FOR AN INTERVIEW: WHEN EVERY DAY IS "DRESS DOWN," WHAT SHOULD YOU WEAR?

The general rule is: Dress at least as well as those who work at the company where you are being interviewed. However, these days, it's not
unusual to see professionals dressed in khakis and sport shirts rather
than in suits. As casual office wear continues to gain its popularity, the
requisite suit and tie still reigns.

Nevertheless, many companies, particularly those in the information technology, fashion, and entertainment industries, have virtually
abandoned the "corporate uniform." If you're interviewing with a company that has a business-casual dress code, ask what is appropriate.
Jeans and short-sleeved shirts at one company might translate to
khakis, dress shirts, and blazers at another. Before you meet, ask your
interviewer what attire is appropriate. The purpose of the interview is
to get to know you better. You and your accomplishments—not your
clothes—should leave the lasting impression. When in doubt, your best

---

DID YOU KNOW?

Linda Keene, Vice President of Market Development at American Express Financial Advisors, suggested a daring reorganization of a division while at Pillsbury. The recommendation could have cost her her job, but instead profits increased by more than 200 percent over three years.—*Black Enterprise*, August 1997

---

bet is to stick with a suit or appropriate business attire. Be well groomed. You should be polished and professional, even when your clothes are casual.

BE DISCREET

Q: When I'm conducting a job search without my employer's knowledge, what are some of the mistakes to avoid?

A: A notable risk is associated with job hunting while currently employed. Should you decide to conduct a job search without your employer's knowledge, be sure to have all bases covered. The job market is highly competitive. There is no reason to adversely impact your opportunity for success by making avoidable mistakes:

- Don't let fellow employees know you're job shopping. You don't know who is talking to whom.
- Avoid the use of company equipment, such as computers, printers, and copy and fax machines. Keep any resumes or cover letters out of public view at the office.
- Request that recruiters call you at home and leave a message if you're not there.
- Avoid speaking negatively of your current employer.
- If you normally don't dress for success, don't start now. Change before your interview or schedule interviews during your vacation.
- Don't overdo sick time. Too many single days off are cause for suspicion.

TELEPHONE INTERVIEWS

Telephone screening is one of the most difficult methods of interview. If you're not a telephone person, it can really beat you out of a job. Often, these are not just preliminary screenings; they are actually full-fledged interviews that last 30 minutes or more.

Companies are increasingly using this method, particularly before expending the time and money to, let's say, fly in a candidate. This method is not just relegated to long-distance candidates; it's used locally as well. A candidate who gets a face-to-face interview has often passed the first hurdle over the phone.

Prepare as you would for any interview. Learn as much as you can about the prospective company, the interviewer (is it the HR professional or your prospective manager?), and the position. One benefit of the telephone is that you can designate the time and place for the interview. Avoid having it at work or at a place where there will be interruptions or time restrictions.

During the interview, try to sound as natural as possible. Speak clearly and don't ramble. It's also important to ask questions. The interviewer will control the conversation. Before you hang up, inquire about the next step, if it hasn't already been mentioned. It will indicate your willingness to have an in-person interview. Allow the interviewer to close the conversation, and then end on a cordial note.

GROUP INTERVIEWS

Panel or group interviews are common for most managerial and higher-level jobs. They save the company time and money, and, more than likely, you won't have to return for repeated interviews. They also allow the hiring team to cover all their issues at once and to test your ability to handle multiple tasks with proper focus.

Before the interview, try to find out who are the members of the team that will be interviewing you, what their positions and roles are in the company, and who the final decision maker is likely to be. Panels reflect the corporate culture of an organization. The one you face will give you almost a panoramic view of the department or company where you may be working. Be aware that you will most likely be working with the interviewing team, and that they will be interested in your "team spirit."

This is an opportunity for you to shine. Make eye contact with everyone when you're answering questions. Keep your answers short. When appropriate, give examples of your accomplishments. Don't be afraid to ask for clarification, if necessary, or to have questions prepared. Bring additional resumes and maintain a sense of humor so you can relax.

WORKING THE CAREER FAIRS

How do you stand out in a room full of other candidates? This is a common question among those who attend job fairs. There you are, in a room sometimes the size of a football field. Several of the companies you're targeting, as well as many that you haven't considered, are there, and you want to make a good impression. If you have done your homework, you're holding a list of the attending companies, available earlier from the career fair organizers. With this in hand, you were able to log onto the prospective firms' Web sites and get some idea of the positions the companies are trying to fill. Once you've done this, you can chart your game plan.

Go early. Many recruiters see hundreds of people at these events, and their interests and enthusiasm may wane after lunch. Interviews with some candidates may be scheduled beforehand, and scant time may be left for random interviews.

You may have an urge to try and work the room and see as many companies as possible. Instead, visit the target companies that you researched. Afterward, you can consider your next choice of employers—those you may only know about through reputation or interest.

Take note of any literature that may be in the area of a booth. Some companies issue a listing of job openings, and it will give you some perspective on whether this company and you have something in common that is worth pursuing.

Introduce yourself to the recruiter. Tell him or her your current employment situation, and express your goals and interests. Don't walk up and ask, off the bat, "What are you hiring for?" You are likely to leave a bad taste in the mouth of the person on the other side of the booth. Typically, the interaction between a job applicant and a recruiter at a career fair lasts for about one minute, so make the most of it. You need to be assertive, but not aggressive. Be sure to have some type of evidence, such as a portfolio or letters of recommendation, that shows how you can be an asset to the company.

Get the interviewer's business card, and be sure to check on the progress of your resume within a week. Don't be afraid of possible rejection. Hundreds of resumes must be scanned and reviewed. Often, the person you meet at the booth is not the person who will be hiring you. Your resume may have been passed on to the respective department or hiring manager.

If nothing else, attending a career fair helps you make the right connections (see Chapter 3), and they can reap benefits in the future. With so many companies in attendance, you want to believe that you can land a job on the spot, but that might not always be possible. You might have to build a rapport with the interviewer—a strategy that can mean a job or referral to a job opportunity months later.

Career fairs aren't just for recent college graduates. Recruiters are there looking for candidates ranging from entry level to middle management. Fairs also allow you to test the job market and visit myriad companies in one fell swoop. It is also a way to brush up on your interview skills, which may open the door to a job later.

JOB SECURITY

The Working Woman's Legal Survival Guide: Know Your Workplace Rights Before It's Too Late by Steven Mitchell Sack (Prentice-Hall), can help tell you what to say when you're asked about your child care plans in an interview, or feel that you've been unjustly fired. The guide has many obvious and not-so-obvious illegal employment situations, followed by resolutions and helpful tips. It gives concise information to help you negotiate for better job security, as well as a list of things you should know if your job is in jeopardy. Although this guide is by no means a substitute for sound legal advice, the easy-to-understand, detailed information will certainly put you on the right track.

BACKGROUND CHECKS

Be aware that most employers conduct background checks on potential employees. Generally, employers verify education, previous employment, and references, and may examine criminal records. They may also conduct drug testing, inspect motor vehicle records, and investigate credit reports, current and previous residences, identity (Social Security number, etc.), workers' compensation, and civil records in each jurisdiction of residence.

In most instances, an employer needs your written consent to begin a background check. Submitting a resume does not give authorization.

Q: Why would a potential employer obtain my credit report? I'm not applying for credit; I want a job.

A: Integrity. Employers want to make sure job candidates are reliable. One way to determine this is to examine how they handle their financial obligations, says Kelvin Sims,[5] operations manager for Gleem Credit Services in St. Louis, Missouri. Frequently, if the job is one where the employee will be dealing with large sums of money, says Sims, an employer wants to ensure that outstanding debt, liens, or judgments won't tempt an otherwise honest employee to steal. A credit report also helps to verify information on the application, such as address and Social Security number.

You can obtain copies of your credit report for a nominal charge and in some cases for free. It's best to dispute any inaccuracies in writing. The credit agency has 30 days to contact the creditor and either clear your record or give you an explanation of why the negative reference will remain. If it can't be removed, you can attach a statement explaining the circumstances to your would-be employer. This statement will be included every time a copy of your credit report goes out.

Credit reports can be obtained, for a fee, from:

- **Equifax,** P.O. Box 740241, Atlanta, GA 30374-0241; (800) 685-1111; www.equifax.com.
- **Experian** (formerly TRW), P.O. Box 2002, Allen, TX 75013; (888) EXPERIAN (397-3742); www.experian.com.
- **TransUnion,** P.O. Box 1000, Chester, PA 19022; www.transunion.com.

"IS THAT LEGAL?" KNOW YOUR RIGHTS IN THE WORKPLACE

A potential employer says you have to take a "simple" polygraph test before being considered for the job. You agree, afraid you'll blow your chances if you decline. But is it legal? Michael Zigarelli[6] offers the answer to this and other workplace-related legal questions in his book, *Can They Do That?: A Guide to Your Rights on the Job* (Lexington Books).

Employees, managers, and many employers are not aware of the many facets of employment law. This easy-to-read guide sorts out many of the legal issues surrounding discrimination, interview questions, sexual harassment, drug testing, and more. Here are some sample items:

- Under the Employee Polygraph Protection Act (EPPA), it is illegal for most private-sector employers to require employees to submit to lie detector tests. There are a few exceptions: If your boss suspects you of a theft, or if you are responsible for money, classified information, or controlled substances.
- Candidates shouldn't be asked on an application if they rent or own their residence. This question singles out minorities, who tend to rent more than their white counterparts.
- You no longer have to suffer psychological damage or impaired work performance to prove sexual harassment. A 1993 Supreme Court ruling states that employees don't have to prove either of these factors in order to show that their work environment was abusive.

Today, a resume only functions as an entrance test to an interview. It's during the interview that a company decides if it wants to hire you. A job interview is the most important step in the job search process. But don't let that intimidate you. Take it as a chance to hop off the paper you've been confined to (your resume) and show the world what you're all about. So, arm yourself with a good resume, a respectable outfit, a reliable alarm clock, a solid knowledge of the company, well-thought-out answers to an array of questions, then practice and take a deep breath. Good luck!

6

GATHERING EXPERIENCE

SHOULD YOU CONSIDER GRADUATE SCHOOL?

Ask almost any college graduate, or anyone entrenched in a career, if he or she ever thought about grad school and you're bound to get a resounding "Yes!" People choose to go to grad school either to change careers or to advance in their current careers. Many recent college grads go because they have not found a job in their major, or their work is not fulfilling, and they think two more years in school will help them put their careers in perspective. Over the past four years, graduate school enrollment has decreased slightly. Chalk it up to a robust job market that lured many graduates (and some undergraduates) into jobs right out of college, particularly those in the computer science, engineering, business, and accounting fields, according to the Council of Graduate Schools.[1]

However, for people who are tired of their jobs or bored with the opportunities at their disposal, graduate school can offer new skills. A graduate degree can also reap a salary increase and/or promotion in a current job. For example, a high school teacher looking to move into school administration will probably benefit from a master's degree or a doctorate. You can't become a social worker or psychologist without certain credentials and licensing that are only obtained after a graduate education. It goes without saying that doctors and lawyers must earn special professional degrees. Many people with college degrees attend grad school just to expand their knowledge or to satisfy a personal goal.

Fortunately, those extra years of school often do pay off in terms of salary. Surveys show that people with a graduate degree earn 35 to 50 percent more than people with only a bachelor's degree. The Council of Graduate Schools reports that people with Ph.D. degrees earn 46 percent more than those with master's degrees.[2] But there are some exceptions. A Web site called Beyond College states that the average monthly earnings of someone with an advanced degree in liberal arts are actually less than those of an average bachelor's degree holder. Therefore, before you even pick up an application for grad school, it is important that you carefully weigh whether those extra years and tuition will pay off.

PICKING THE RIGHT SCHOOL

If you've determined that grad school is for you, there are some important things to consider: the school's reputation, size, location, and curriculum. Most schools have areas of concentration that are known to be exceptional. For example, Columbia University, in New York, has a strong journalism program, and Thunderbird American Graduate School of International Management is renown for its international MBA program. Research is important. Just as you examined various undergraduate programs while you were in high school, you must apply that same diligence to your graduate school search. There are myriad sources of information about graduate school—almost as many as there are U.S. graduate school programs (more than 1,800).

The information you gather can be at once confusing and enlightening. To cut to the chase, you must determine the best schools for your area of study, and rank them by their appeal and your chances of being accepted. Let's say that five schools peak your interest. Apply to two highly competitive schools, two moderately competitive schools, and one "safety" school. Keep in mind that size and location will play key roles. Ask yourself: Am I willing to relocate? Am I more comfortable

---

FREE MBA

In an effort to increase the number of African Americans in business schools, the University of Kentucky's Gatton College of Business and Economics is awarding full scholarships to qualified African Americans who wish to pursue an MBA degree. The African American Scholars Program was developed in response to the school's difficulty in recruiting African Americans to its MBA program.

The program offers scholarship winners full tuition, a $10,000 stipend, and a guaranteed summer internship with Kentucky-based company. There are no set minimum requirements; all scholarship applicants are evaluated on an individual basis. Degree concentrations are offered in banking, real estate, and finance; marketing and distribution; and information systems management.

For more information, contact Michael Tearney, associate dean/administrator, African American Scholars Program, the University of Kentucky Gatton College of Business and Economics, Lexington, KY 40506-0034; 859-257-3592; or e-mail TEARNEY@UKCC.UKY.edu.

---

on a small-town campus or at a large metropolitan university? It's also critical to evaluate the school's curriculum in the program of your choosing. Make sure that the school offers the classes that are going to deliver the best results *after* graduation.

GETTING IN

You might have the right grade point average (GPA) and a promising resume chock full of internships and jobs, but most schools require you to sit for a national exam before you're even considered. The most popular exam is the Graduate Record Examination (GRE), which is like an advanced SAT. Specialized programs may require a different exam, such as the LSAT for law school, GMAT for business school, and MCAT for medical school.

THE 411 ON THE MBA

For information on business schools and the MBA degree, go to www.gmac.com, the Web site of the Graduate Management Admission Council® (GMAC), composed of representatives of leading business schools worldwide. Get info on the Graduate Management Admission Test (GMAT). The site features a business school database that will allow users to search by program type (full-time, part-time, distance learning, etc.) for schools that most closely match their selected criteria with respect to geographic location, specializations/concentrations, entering-class size, percentages of female/U.S. minority/international students, program start date, application deadline, and so on. The Council's MBA Forums have hosted more than 275,000 potential applicants since their inception in 1975. During the 1999–2000 recruiting season, 264 business schools, four educational organizations, and almost 10,000 prospective MBAs participated in 14 forums (nine in North America, five in Asia).

The PhD Project (www.phdproject.org) actively recruits African American, Hispanic American, and Native American professionals who have an interest in pursuing a business doctorate. The PhD Project runs on the belief that by increasing the diversity of academic faculties, the end result will be an increase in minority workforce numbers.

If standardized tests are not your forte, consider investing in one of the myriad classes and study guides available. The most popular classes are offered by the Kaplan Educational Center. You may also want to consider the books listed later in this chapter.

COSTS

Keep in mind that advanced degrees don't come cheap. Perhaps you're already at an organization that offers partial or total tuition reimbursement if your advanced degree can be applied to the needs of the

---

LAUNCHING A SATELLITE CAREER

Satellite television and cable companies have served up a bevy of entertainment options for television viewers. All that programming has also resulted in a wealth of job opportunities. The T. Howard Foundation provides internships, scholarships, and career awareness programs for those interested in careers in the satellite industry. The foundation also partners with companies such as DIRECTV, HBO, and ESPN to recruit minorities and women into the ranks. For more information, write to the T. Howard Foundation, 225 Reinekers Lane, Suite 600, Alexandria, VA 22314; call 703-739-8346; or visit http://www.t-howard.com.

---

company. If so, then you've won half the battle. But if you're like most people, you're probably going to be looking for creative ways to finance your education. There are three basic ways to finance a graduate education, depending on the program in which you are interested. With a lot of footwork, you can unearth fellowships and traineeships, teaching and research assistantships, and loans. Even if you can afford to pay your way, don't rule out traineeships and teaching assistantships. They can provide valuable hands-on skills that will enhance your graduate school experience. Check with the school to find out what options it offers.

Help is available; you just need to know where to look. Most grad schools offer scholarships or fellowships. If you don't meet the qualifications, check out private scholarships or grants. You can also finance your education through assistantships, part-time employment, or more student loans. Before you dive into the pool of debt again, be sure to investigate all your options and find the ones that best suit your needs.

BOOKS ON GRADUATE SCHOOLS

The Index of Majors and Graduate Degrees by The College Board (College Board). This authoritative handbook lets students identify colleges, in preferred locations, that offer the majors that interest them. The *Index* includes over 600 recognized fields of study with a state-by-state listing of nearly 3,000 colleges, universities, and graduate schools that offer majors in these fields. Brief descriptions of every major are included. You can identify the right ones for you *and* find schools that offer these special academic programs.

The Best Distance Learning Graduate Schools: Earning Your Degree Without Leaving Home by Cindy Yager (Princeton Review Publishing Corporation). About 55 percent of colleges in the United States—and plenty abroad—offer some type of distance learning degree program. This book shows you how to find exactly the program you're looking for, and answers all the questions you may have along the way. Each entry includes everything you need to know about prerequisites, admissions, tuition, campus visit requirements, and delivery methods, plus all pertinent addresses (including e-mail).

Real Life Guide to Graduate and Professional School: How to Choose, Apply for, and Finance Your Advance Degree! by Cynthia L. Rold (Pipeline Press). This book takes on the graduate school admissions process, exposes many of its flaws, and offers readers a proven strategy for success. Topics covered extensively include the testing process, choosing a school, the application process, and what admissions professionals are really looking for.

African Americans and the Doctoral Experience: Implications for Policy by Charles V. Willie, Richard O. Hope, and Michael K. Grady (Teachers College Press). During the past decade, there has been a downward trend in the number of African American graduate students who successfully complete their studies. This book suggests how to reverse this trend by examining the relationship among financial assistance, social supports, campus experiences, family configurations, and degree-completion rates for a group of 65 highly motivated doctoral students.

Barron's Guide to Graduate Business Schools by Eugene Miller (Barron's Educational Series, Inc.). In addition to providing general guidelines for evaluating the various schools, the book includes factual and insider information about each business school. The business schools listed in this guide either are accredited by the Association to Advance Collegiate School of Business or have regional accreditation.

A CAPITAL CAREER VENTURE

For years, word-of-mouth recommendations and recruits from top business schools filled the ranks of venture capital firms. With unprecedented opportunity projected for the future, the industry must now develop a new generation of leaders. Through the Kauffman Fellows Program, exceptional young professionals can learn about start-up venture investing. The program partners fellows with seasoned mentors at venture capital firms for an 18-month apprenticeship.

Fellows must be U.S. citizens, preferably with a graduate degree in business, science, or technology and three years full-time professional experience. The annual stipend is $110,000, and some Fellows are eligible for travel and relocation expenses. Applications can only be submitted online at www.emkf.org. Fee is $45.00.

INTERNSHIPS

Internships and entry-level positions will give you experience, and if the right opening comes up you will be there to apply for it. Most companies would rather promote from within and fill the less costly entry positions from outside. Working, even at an entry level, will also give you experience to add to your resume. You can keep it out there and update it as you gain experience. People will begin to show interest, and a great job may come along. You must be persistent, as well as creative, in marketing yourself.

Pick at least three companies you would like to work for, and know which department, in each company, would offer you the best experience. Research is important here. Go online, or phone the company, and ask whom you should contact about internships. Be sure to get the name and address of the person who should receive your resume. You may receive a special recording that explains the requirements and gives you the necessary information. Remember to ask: When do internships begin and end? What is the deadline for resumes to be received? On what date will applicants for internships be notified? Include a cover letter along with your resume.

If you are truly interested in a particular career and you find a perfect match in a company, you must sell yourself to that company. Do not always set your sights on top companies. Smaller companies will usually give you more experience and may provide a springboard to "top" companies. You might then bypass the stage of getting coffee and making trillions of copies and sending them as faxes! Build your resume up first; then set your sights on the flagship companies. How do you get started toward a flagship? Pinpoint the industry you are most interested in, and get in touch with companies in that industry. Go onto the Internet. Go onto Monster.com, getajob.com, and similar sites. E-mail your cover letter and your resume to as many companies as you can each day. Does your school have a career center? If so, its resources can provide excellent help.

- Make an appointment with your career adviser.
- Talk to your teachers; they often know about internships.
- Networking is another way. Talk to your family and to parents of your friends. Let people know you are looking for an internship. Ask them to keep an eye open for you.
- There are lots of job sites out there, such as www.wetfeet.com and www.brassringcampus.com.

Talking to other students who have previously interned is also a good way to start; your school may help you contact them, and they can tell you a company's reputation. Ask them specific questions about what you will be asked to do. If you find former interns online, follow up with some form of personal contact. If one of these former interns still works there, ask whether he or she would pass along your resume within the company. That can be a great help, but you should still follow up. Researching the company will always help. What does it publish about itself? Does that match what other people say about it?

The first question you need to answer is: Do I need a paid internship, or can I manage with an unpaid internship? Unpaid internships are more available than paid ones. If time permits during this semester, or during your holiday break, line up a local internship or volunteer opportunity at a place that you can easily get to. Even if you are available for only five hours each week, this opportunity will give you a better sense of the direction that is most interesting to you.

SCIENTIFIC PURSUITS

Interested in a career in science? The Oak Ridge Institute for Science and Education (ORISE) administers more than 100 programs—from internships, to fellowships, to laboratory co-ops. As a partner to more than 60 federal laboratories, ORISE provides opportunities in physics, environmental management, nuclear engineering, worldwide emergency response and training, and other sciences. More than 3,000 individuals are chosen each year to work with some of the nation's top researchers in state-of-the-art laboratories. Research programs specifically for students at historically black colleges and universities are also available. For more information, access the ORISE Web site at www.orau.gov/orise.htm or request a research guide at ORISE, P.O. Box 117, MS 44, Oak Ridge, TN 37831-0117; 865-576-3146.

JUMP-START A NEW CAREER WITH AN INTERNSHIP

Get it out of your head that internships are only for students. The opportunity to gain valuable knowledge in another field is open to people in their 30s, 40s, and 50s.

"[Businesses] realize that people are not staying in companies from their 20s until retirement," says Sally Migliore, associate executive director for the National Society for Experiential Education, a Raleigh, North Carolina, association that promotes internships.

Whether they are available through a university, a job hotline, or a local branch of Forty Plus (a national organization that helps find jobs for people over 40), internship opportunities are flourishing. And in tough times, people of all ages and backgrounds use internships to break into new fields. Economics and downsizing, says Migliore, have left many companies with open positions. Filling an opening with an intern costs a business a fraction of the full-time employee price. Internship opportunities are open in everything from health care to television production. Some internships pay a salary; others offer college credit. And you have the option of interning for one month or several years. Best of all, many internships offer flex hours, which could allow you to keep your current job. Over the past five years, The National Directory of Internships has reported an 8 percent increase in the number of companies offering midcareer internships. To obtain information about internships, contact the National Society for Experiential Education (808-803-4170).

INTERNSHIP RESOURCES

Tap the following Web sites for information about internship opportunities. With thousands of unfilled internships available, you may be surprised to find hidden gems that suit you just fine.

www.CollegeRecruiter.com   Students seeking part-time jobs and internships, and graduates seeking full-time employment, can post resumes and scan more than 25,000 job listings. There is also info on resume writing, scholarships, and student loans.

www.everettinternships.org   Everett Public Service Internship Program provides a searchable database of internships at public service organizations.

www.interns.org   Part of the Washington Intern Foundation. Dedicated to helping individuals find internships on Capitol Hill and elsewhere in Washington, DC.

www.InternshipPrograms.com   A service of career Web site Wet Feet .com, which offers a database of opportunities organized by company or by region.

www.internships.com   A division of National Internships Online. A source for information on paid and unpaid preprofessional employment opportunities for college students and recent graduates.

www.internweb.com   Offers free searchable listings within a range of industries, plus job search links.

www.Jobdirect.com   For students and recent college graduates. Lists internships, co-ops, seminars, and holiday jobs. Its parent company, Korn-Ferry, is one of the nation's largest executive recruiting firms. Resume posting available.

www.usinterns.com   Provides students, employers, career service organizations, and business associations with alternative job-placement solutions.

BOOKS ON INTERNSHIPS AND FELLOWSHIPS

- *The Internship Bible* by Mark Oldman (Princeton Review Publishing Corporation): Lists hundreds of interns, internship coordinators, and career placement counselors across the country. The authors, founders of www.Vault.com, are the only nationally recognized experts on internships.

- *Jumpstarting Your Career: An Internship Guide for Criminal Justice* by Dorothy Taylor (Simon & Schuster Trade): Designed to assist students in obtaining valuable internships and making successful transitions to employment. Ideal for students of criminal justice, criminology, and other social sciences, who are beginning a criminal justice internship.

- *Breaking into Television: Proven Advice from Veterans and Interns* by Dan Weaver and Jason Siegel (Peterson's): Tune in and get, from seasoned TV veterans (all former interns!), insight and advice that will help you focus your job search and get you ready for your dream career. Find out what it's really like to work in television; learn from anecdotes provided by network execs and former interns; and explore internship opportunities.

- *The Backdoor Guide to Short-Term Job Adventures: Internships, Extraordinary Experiences, Seasonal Jobs, Volunteering, Work Abroad* by Michael Landes (Ten Speed Press): Check out this resource of over 1,000 easy-to-read listings for short-term, off-the-beaten-path work-and-learn adventures, and discover options you didn't know existed. There are 150 new listings for internships, seasonal work, volunteer opportunities, and overseas jobs.

- *Peterson's Internships* by Peterson's (Peterson's): This guide to more than 55,000 paid and unpaid positions worldwide can help students—and professionals interested in a career change—find the working experience they need. With information on more than 2,000 companies, ranging from Fortune 100 companies to national parks and art galleries, this is the largest resource available anywhere. Articles discuss a variety of issues crucial to understanding the internship experience, including the benefits of an internship, how to submit an application, and what sponsors are looking for in an intern.

- *The Kaplan/The Yale Daily News Guide to Fellowships and Grants* by Kaplan Educational Centers (Kaplan Books): This book

> ### DID YOU KNOW?
>
> John E. Jacob, executive vice president at Anheuser-Busch Companies, Inc., and former president and CEO of the National Urban League, was a U.S. Army Reserve captain and began his career as a social worker.—*Black Enterprise,* February 2000

features an abundance of helpful insights on everything students need to earn money for advanced study.

TEACH FOR AMERICA

Given the nation's need for good teachers, the Teach for America program was established in 1990. Teach for America is a national corps of recent college graduates, representing all academic majors, who commit two years to teaching in urban and rural public schools. Corps members earn a regular, full-time teacher's salary and benefits, paid by their school districts. The current range is from $21,000 to $36,000, depending on the region.

Corps members qualify for student loan deferral and payment of accrued interest during their two years of service, which means they need not make any payments on qualified loans during the two years. After completing each year of service, corps members receive an education award of $4,725 ($9,500 for the two years), which they can apply to their outstanding student loans or to their future education costs.

All applicants must have a cumulative undergraduate GPA of 2.50 at the time their applications are received *and* at the time of graduation. The fee is $25 for applications submitted electronically, or $35 for applications submitted through regular mail. Contact the Admissions Office at Teach for America, 315 West 36th Street, 6th Floor, New York, NY 10018, or call 800-832-1230, extension 225, and ask to have the application sent via mail. You can apply online at www.teachforamerica.org.

WORLD-CLASS LEARNING

Imagine jaunting past double-decker buses and looking right instead of left as you cross the streets of London on your way to class. Or taking in the baroque architecture of Brussels as you contemplate an upcoming exam on the intricacies of international commerce. These are not fantasy spring breaks; they are reality for individuals who have chosen to pursue degrees abroad.

Foreign study, whether for credit or a degree, is no longer just a perk of the intellectual or financial elite. Today, employers place a high value on candidates with a background in international business and culture. Thanks to an abundance of exchange programs, scholarships, and fellowships, record numbers of students are going abroad to study and soak up foreign culture firsthand. Most go for six weeks, a semester, or even a year. Others are enrolling for three or more years of undergraduate study or for completion of their postgraduate programs.

According to the Institute of International Education in New York, the number of Americans studying abroad increased nearly 14 percent in 1999–2000 to 129,770. Nonetheless, those numbers pale in comparison to the more than 500,000 foreign students who flocked to American institutions of higher learning during the same period. In fact, the number of Americans studying abroad represents less than 1 percent of total U.S. post-secondary-school enrollments.

Most of those pursuing degrees abroad major in the humanities or social sciences and go to Western Europe. In some countries, such as England, where only 20 percent of applicants are even admitted to college, admission standards are very high, says David C. Larsen,[3] vice president and director for the Center for Education Abroad, at Beaver College in Glenside, Pennsylvania. He adds that it's not an easy task to gain admission, but an international education allows you to get to know another culture. That can be a benefit to you and your resume.

However, costs can be a prevailing deterrent if the school you choose is not approved for U.S. financial aid. Even if tuition is cheaper than in the United States, the cost of living, depending on the country, might be much higher. You must also research a school's accreditation and what stature a foreign degree will have in the U.S. job market. Pursuing an education abroad will force you to push the envelope not only academically, but also culturally, as you adapt to a different environment.

A TRUE LEARNING EXPERIENCE

When Maya Kulycky[4] took off for London in 1996, it was to learn under a famed and respected professor. As a political science major at

Baltimore's Johns Hopkins University, she had become intrigued with the work of sociologist Paul Gilroy and his examination of African populations in the diaspora. With an unwavering interest in race relations, and having written her senior-year thesis on the history of race riots in the United States, she headed off for a year-long master's degree program in urban studies at Goldsmith College at the University of London, where Gilroy was head of the sociology department.

The Evanston, Illinois, native says she had always wanted to go to school abroad and had been planning for it even as an undergraduate. She could have found a university here, but she was interested in the black population in the United Kingdom, and thought the experience would give her a new perspective on racism in the United States. With the help of a $22,000 Rotary Ambassadorial Scholarship that covered her $10,000 tuition plus living expenses, Kulycky was on her way. (Ambassadorial scholarships can last from three months to three years.)

In addition to the challenge of the program, Kulycky found that the study was very independent. The eight hours or so spent in class each week was much less than she had expected of a graduate-level program. But with substantial reading assignments, and six papers and a thesis required, the work was also quite challenging. Goldsmith is located in New Cross, a low-income, integrated section of London inhabited mostly by African and Caribbean immigrants. Staying there allowed Kulycky to gain a better perspective of the black culture in London. Fresh from her experience abroad, Kulycky went on to Yale Law School and hopes to one day practice public service law.

A BUSINESS PROPOSITION

Living in a city that complemented his study was also the goal of Troy Flowers, Jr.[5] In 1996, Flowers took a leave of absence from his job as a flight attendant at American Airlines to earn a master's degree in administrative studies and multinational commerce at Boston University Brussels. "I was burned out," says Flowers, who flew European, South American, and Caribbean routes for five years while also earning his B.A. in comparative literature from New York University. "I was looking for another challenge, both professionally and academically." He chose Brussels, the European epicenter of business and politics, and the home of many multinational firms and the North Atlantic Treaty Organization (NATO). "I wanted to distinguish myself in the North American business job market, and this program is the best alternative to the MBA," says Flowers, a Winston-Salem, North Carolina, native. He graduated in 1998. His class of 100 boasted students from 25 different countries.

The program Flowers chose stresses hands-on training. He and many of his peers worked for major corporations in strategic planning posts. While interning as a market analyst for Dow Corning Europe, Flowers worked on a project aimed at determining new markets, in Europe and North America, for the chemical company's silicon technology. "I am making a valuable contribution to a company that might one day be a potential employer," said Flowers. Perhaps just as worthwhile was the fact that Dow covered his $5,200 tuition for a semester. The rent for his one-bedroom apartment was only $575. With food and other expenses moderately priced, Brussels is relatively cheap by European standards. After graduation, Flowers joined Cisco Systems in Brussels. His starting salary was $60,000, free of U.S. taxes.

CULTURAL TURBULENCE

An international education offers benefits, but they do not come without some caveats. While she was fulfilling her educational goals, Maya Kulycky had to contend with something else. In a class of students from all over the world, she was faced with the prevailing foreigners' view of African Americans. Their only perception had come from movies like *Pulp Fiction* and other American media that perpetuate black stereotypes. Kulycky roomed with six students, ages 23 to 35, from countries such as Saudi Arabia, Hong Kong, Taiwan, Sweden, and Norway.

This is not an uncommon occurrence, adds Margery Ganz,[6] director of study abroad at Spelman College in Atlanta, and history department chair. Ganz recalls the story of a Spelman exchange student who went to Japan and found that the Japanese were surprised that she wasn't a drug dealer, musician, or athlete. When the student informed them that she went to a black college, they were amazed. Her presence made them more aware of African Americans and black institutions. On the other hand, Ganz adds, African Americans shouldn't be discouraged if they're viewed first as Americans rather than as "returning brothers and sisters."

Perhaps more daunting than her efforts to counteract black and/or American stereotypes was the personal issue Kulycky faced—homesickness. Being very close to her family, it was hard for Kulycky, who traveled home for the holidays and found solace with a college friend living in Italy.

For Flowers, a small network of friends was essential to his speedy transition into Belgian life. "They helped me find a place to live and walked me through the bureaucratic circles you must maneuver through in order to get certain visas and work permits," he says. Informal gatherings with other African Americans working for international companies in Brussels also helped to ease the culture shock. For students who are entirely on their own, U.S. embassies or consulates can offer contacts or organizations that can provide a touch of home.

Besides researching a country's race relations history, you should familiarize yourself with local customs. Unlike their foreign counterparts, few American students speak a second language well enough to study in it. If you don't have a second language, make sure you target programs that are conducted primarily in English.

HOW DOES THE EXPERIENCE TRANSLATE?

Today's college students are taking advantage of study-abroad opportunities, not only to widen their horizons, but also to increase their hiring opportunities. Resumes that reflect overseas travel, study, and work experience stand out in a sea of job applications. But what is it really worth? Quite a bit, depending on your future goals. Those who have studied abroad present themselves with confidence because they have survived.

As the global economy becomes more competitive, American multinationals and international companies desire candidates with international experience. For example, graduates of Boston University Brussels with an MS degree in management have a 100 percent placement rate for jobs throughout the world. For American graduates who choose to work in Brussels, the rewards are high. However, it's difficult for Americans to get hired here. They can only get a work permit if they are placed in managerial positions at $100,000 a year or more, notes Joseph J. Heinlein Jr.,[7] director of Boston University Brussels.

Before you buy your plane ticket, research the university you've selected, and know what you want to get from the experience. Just because a country is intriguing doesn't mean that you'll get a five-star education that will transfer well to the United States. It's important to verify the accreditation of a school beforehand. Be very cautious of the school at which you choose to get a degree, warns Heinlein. Many schools have no solid accreditation, and a student may complete a degree in international policy and then learn that it's worthless. The U.S. Department of Education, the Council on International Educational Exchange, and the Institute of International Education provide information on studying abroad. You also can check *Peterson's Study Abroad* for information on the more than 1,600 programs in foreign countries. Check with the respective school for information about required board certifications and transfers of credits.

For learned individuals who return stateside, humility is a virtue. Travel tells an employer who you are and what you want out of life. But don't place too much emphasis on your international experience. It may be an asset, but it is only one among many that you must have.

WORLD-CLASS RESOURCES

Institute of International Education (IIE), 809 United Nations Plaza, New York, NY 10017-3580; 212-883-8200; www.iie.org. Publications include *Vacation Study Abroad; Academic Year Abroad; Financial Resources for International Study; Fulbright and Other Grants for Graduate Study Abroad* (free brochure); 800-445-0443; *Peterson's Study Abroad;* www.petersons.com

Scholarships and Fellowships

The Rotary Foundation of Rotary International, One Rotary Center, 1560 Sherman Avenue, Evanston, IL 60201; 847-866-3000; www .rotary.org

Robert Bailey Minority Scholarship Council on International Educational Exchange, 205 East 42nd Street, New York, NY 10017-5706; 212-822-2600; www.ciee.com

Graduate school and internships are a great way to learn a particular discipline or about an occupation and get work experience at the same time. It's important that you don't view them as layovers until you decide what you want to do in life. Research and examine the companies you want to intern for and the graduate program that will reap you the optimal career success. Chosen correctly, these experiences can only enhance your net worth to employers.

7

NEGOTIATING
YOUR SALARY

It's noble to believe that people get up every morning, endure arduous commutes and difficult superiors, and work on painstaking assignments—sometimes into the wee hours of the night—for *fulfillment*, but the true motivator for most of the world is *money*. Being able to enjoy a comfortable quality of living is an essential goal to which many working people aspire. But unless you are independently wealthy, win the lottery, or have a big fat trust fund, the route to that comfort is through work that pays fair wages and provides the benefits you need.

You have probably gone through various stages of interviews, or have submitted copies of your work or proof of your ideas to potential employers. Your presentation may have prompted one or more companies to make you an offer. Now comes the period dreaded by even the most seasoned professionals: talking salary. It can turn out to be a gratifying experience if the first offer put on the table is more than you imagined. Or it can turn into a poker-game standoff; you and the salary negotiator sit on opposite sides of the table and try to compromise on the best compensation package (salary, benefits, and perks).

If you are lucky and smart, you have avoided discussing this subject throughout your interviewing and evaluation process. You have managed to give the right answers and endear your future boss enough to create confidence in the skills you can bring to the company. You have smiled and chitchatted with everyone from the receptionist to the vice president of the department that has an opening. You may even know so much about the company by now that you're looking forward to the cafeteria's Thursday salad bar. However, one important fact has eluded you: if you take this job, how much will you be paid?

HOW ARE SALARIES DETERMINED?

Salaries are determined long before job seekers learn that the jobs exist. The first thing a company does, prior to making an offer, is analyze the available budget for that department, taking into account any raises that will become effective before the department's budget is adjusted for the following year. Next, the company will look at its industry's standard compensation for your position; how much you currently make (information gained from your previous employer or from you); and how much you're asking. The goal is "a reasonable offer," but company compensation specialists may have already determined a salary range for the position. Your next step is to get an idea of what that range is before the company makes you an offer. Don't go in blind; be prepared before you sit down to negotiate. Yes, I said *negotiate*. Don't think that just because you're not in the throes of your career yet, you don't have some negotiating leverage.

You can get useful salary information from trade and professional associations that survey their members on a regular basis. Often, these surveys are broken down by geographic region or by the size of companies (small, medium, and large). Believe it or not, your best bet for getting reliable advice quickly is: Ask people! Call recruiters or career counselors, and ask them to tell you the salary range for the position you're interested in. One of the benefits of working with an executive search firm or a recruiter is that the intermediary knows the job specs and salary range and can give you a ballpark figure of what the company is willing to pay (Chapter 9). When you combine their feedback with the salary information you already have, you'll have a better idea of how you want to approach the salary offer.

NEGOTIATING

Never box yourself in when you're asked what salary you want. Always say that you're interested in an industry-competitive wage, or that the amount is negotiable. Salary negotiations can vary. Never let an employer say that there is no wiggle room in an initial offer. (Only the various levels of government have fixed salary scales.) If you have a comfortable rapport with someone who works for the company, ask him or her what the position might pay. If you are asked to quote a dollar amount during an interview, explain that the amount would depend on all of the duties and responsibilities associated with the job. Employers try to get the best for the least amount of money. Savvy negotiators successfully showcase their skills while highlighting the contributions they can make to the organization. Keep in mind these points as you negotiate:

- Go in with a positive attitude.
- Check annual reports and the Internet to determine the company's financial standing and your potential future with the company.
- Don't bite the first offer. Even if you've been searching for a job for months, don't give in now. You've got to strike the best deal. Beyond salary, this is the time to get the most in terms of health coverage, vacation time, and other benefits.
- Ask for what you really want; it's more difficult to get more after you're hired. If you sense that an offer is on the horizon, see what dollar amount is put on the table. If the offer that is made is less than you expected, take a minute and relax. A pregnant pause is not bad at this point; it may cause the employer to rationalize the amount, and it will give you more time to think. The dealer may think your hesitation is a *no* and decide to increase the amount.
- Never make your decision on the spot; always give yourself at least 24 hours to think about it, even if the money is more than enough. If you believe you can bring something unique to the organization, then counter with: "I was really looking for more. I'll have to get back to you."
- Be realistic. If you know a position is paying $45,000 to $50,000, don't ask for $65,000. You must take into account the market and the company.

- Think about the big picture. If the employer can't meet your base salary needs because of the company's salary policy or "pool," ask for other perks. A signing bonus is usually given only at a managerial level and above, but additional vacation days, frequent performance reviews and their associated raises, a flexible work schedule, or performance bonuses may stand up as substitute perks.

FIND OUT WHAT YOU'RE WORTH

There are two excellent online sources for salary surveys: (1) Wage Web (www.wageweb.com) and (2) the Economic Research Institute (www.erieri.com). However, both cost money. *American Salaries and Wages Survey,* published semiannually, is usually available for free at local libraries. These are among the few sources that break down information by professions and location. Some other online resources and books:

- www.jobsmart.org   This *Wall Street Journal* job search site offers over 3,000 salary surveys culled from general periodicals, local newspapers, trade and professional journals, and recruitment and employment agencies. Learn about stock options and other benefits, as well as how to negotiate.
- www.salary.com   Users can obtain free salary surveys and compensation reports for dozens of industries. A job database and a salary-advice guide are featured.
- www.abbott-langer.com   Compare current salary survey statistics for more than 450 jobs in information technology, marketing and sales, accounting, human resources, consulting, manufacturing, nonprofit, legal, and other fields, from over 7,000 organizations.
- www.careerjournal.com   Provides salaries by industry. The database, maintained by the *Wall Street Journal,* reports average paychecks of employees in various industries. Locates advice and articles.
- www.nalp.org/jobseekers (National Association for Law Placement)   Job hunters seeking to join the legal workforce may want to check out the salary survey.

Are You Paid What You're Worth? by Michael O'Malley (Broadway). This book will arm you with the strategies and information needed to determine your market value and negotiate the compensation you deserve.

The American Almanac of Jobs and Salaries, by John W. Wright (William Morrow & Co.). This book provides hard information on job descriptions, salary ranges, and career opportunities for thousands of jobs and professions.

Q: I've received a new job offer and my current employer has made an impressive counteroffer. Should I take it and stay where I am?

A: There are critical things to consider before you decide to take your company's counteroffer or "buyback," advises Anita Ervin,[1] president of Aces Consulting, an executive recruitment firm in Linden, New Jersey. First, you must question why you weren't given this raise prior to your opportunity to leave. Perhaps you were denied a promotion or a raise in the past, and now, suddenly, it's feasible to honor it. The reason may *not* be that your company finds you invaluable. More than likely, the buyback was made to avoid a long and costly lapse in productivity while the company looks for your replacement.

With the job market so populated, warns Ervin, no one is so good that he or she can't be replaced. Companies like to have the upper hand; they don't like having their back up against a wall. She adds: "When a company has to negotiate from an inferior position, it leaves a bad taste in their mouth."

STOCK OPTIONS: TO TAKE OR NOT TO TAKE

Companies may use stock options or certificates as a means of balancing out their offer. Depending on the company's line of business and its competition, this perk could be extremely profitable for you. Start-ups have a great deal of potential, whether by making a name for themselves, or being bought by a larger, well-known company. But in the aftermath of the dot-com fallout, many applicants who join start-ups are saying "Nay" to options in lieu of cash.

Threatening to leave brings your loyalty into question. Don't be surprised, later, if you see a blind ad in the newspaper describing a job that sounds like your own. Your company cannot fire you, but it certainly can make things so difficult that you decide to leave voluntarily, says Ervin.

Q: I would like a raise, but my manager says he can't afford it. What should I ask for instead?

A: An employee must reap benefits from other budgets besides the salary pool, says Robert L. Livingston[2] of R. L. Livingston Recruiting and Staffing Consultants, in Atlanta, Georgia. Livingston says that many companies have adopted lump-sum bonuses in lieu of raises, and managers are willing to give an employee $2,000 in cash rather than upset the established salary scale by awarding a raise—especially if a salary is already at market rate. If you accept this form of compensation, negotiate for annual payments until the company is in a position to increase your salary.

Take advantage of perks such as educational money. An MBA could be worth more than a raise, not to mention giving your career a major plus. You can also opt for company stock or parlay your achievements into "performance awards." An entire department can share in a salary increase through variable payments. For instance, all employees in a department can agree not to call in sick for a year. This would save the company money in sick time benefits that trickles down to the department in the form of a raise, notes Livingston. There is no such thing as a company having "no money." You just need to know where to find it.

SEPARATION PAY

If you find yourself in a situation where the company is laying off employees or asking them to take early buyouts, you'll come face-to-face with severance pay. A severance package is usually offered to an employee who is laid off or terminated. Depending on the company and the employee, it can consist of two weeks' to one month's pay for every year spent with the company. It might also include six to 12 months of outplacement service.

"The problem is that it can take 18 months or more for some professionals to find a job they want," notes Wayne A. Newell,[3] managing director at Management Alliance Group, an executive recruitment firm in Summit, New Jersey. Like salaries, severance

WHAT IS EXECUTIVE COMPENSATION?

Executive compensation is an umbrella term that includes an executive's salary, bonuses and stock options, benefits, perquisites, and other (financial) contract provisions. Long-term compensation, such as performance awards, equity awards, and stock options, may also be included. Lucrative retirement programs such as SERPs (Supplemental Employee Retirement Programs), and perks such as company cars and health club memberships are also common at senior levels.

What many African Americans fail to realize is that employees get nothing unless they ask for it. Instead of a bare-minimum package, early retirement provisions, spousal travel and relocation awards, housing, financial and tax counseling, and other minor privileges may be yours for the asking.

If you're moving into an executive position, consider seeking the advice of a tax professional or financial consultant who can sort out the tax and financial implications of your new post.

packages are negotiable. Therefore, advises Newell, "If you're not satisfied, sign nothing until you're sure it's the best package possible."

Other benefits that may be negotiable are health and group life insurance, extended outplacement services, and continuing education reimbursement. If you have been relocated within the past six months, you may also request return moving expenses. Adds Newell, "The length of time it takes to find a job varies. That means you must know the market, and your worth, in order to get the best package."

The final step in preparing to negotiate salary and benefit packages is practice. Ask a family member or friend to interview you. Have them, at different times, throw in the question about how much money you want. Be ready to deflect the question until you have a solid offer. Practice asking for the salary you deserve. Practice telling them you are good at what you do and listing the benefits you will bring to the company. Do not be timid about negotiating for the salary and benefits you deserve! The company will not withdraw an offer because you have asked for more. So, do your research, develop a pitch that matches the company's needs, and practice, practice, practice.

8

MINING THE WORKPLACE

THE REALITY OF THE AFRICAN AMERICAN EXPERIENCE AT WORK

How should you plan for a senior path when the odds may be against you? The road to the upper echelons of business, government or the non-profit sector seem years away as you start on your career path, there are many who have paved the way for many African Americans with advice to offer.

Although the rewards were great, so were the challenges. For the few who have made it, their greatest obstacle to overcome, they say, has been making their organizations acknowledge the value of their skills and contributions. The pioneering African Americans who integrated corporate America during the '70s did so by working hard and not wearing their race on their sleeve. Nonetheless, for many of them the turned cheek was met with slaps to their intelligence and authority, underscored by a struggle for pay parity with their white counterparts.

For the next generation of black executives to succeed in the midst of this anti-affirmative action zeitgeist, they must understand that justifying their worth will be the norm. And a steady flow of black talent into the corporate pipeline will be the exception, unless businesses and those black executives already there embrace a "lift-as-we-climb" attitude.

DE-SKILLED, BUT NOT DEFEATED

Don't be stopped by career disenchantment. Many professionals never make it past the proverbial glass ceiling. A lack of challenges and feelings of isolation demoralize these executives before they even seek senior-level positions, says David A. Thomas[1] of the Harvard Graduate School of Business Administration. Thomas, professor of organizational behavior and co-author of *Breaking Through: The Making of Minority Executives in Corporate America,* has conducted over 10 years of filed study with more than 500 African American managers, who have great potential, enter competitive organizations only to become disenchanted after achieving some level of managerial responsibility.

For example, some managers may find that their suggestions on a project are being ignored. Others may have been promoted and be asked to continue doing the same work they were doing before their promotions. The manager then starts to look at the "equity equation" says Thomas. When someone is not getting back what he or she has put into a company they may start to under perform. In time, low expectations become a self-fulfilling prophecy; creating a phenomenon that Thomas calls "deskilling." To avoid getting stuck in this trap, Thomas advises managers to:

- Find diverse groups of people within the organization whom your comfortable talking to about culture and work style.
- Take part in multiracial organizations and events.
- Engage in regular, proactive career planning and self-assessment.

WORKING FOR AN AFRICAN AMERICAN-OWNED FIRM

There were more than 800,000 African American companies in the United States in 1997, according to the U.S. Census Bureau.[2] They employed over 700,000 people and generated $71.2 million in revenues.

DIVERSITYINC.COM TOP 50 COMPANIES FOR DIVERSITY

1. SBC Communications
2. Nordstrom
3. United Parcel Service
4. Bank of America
5. American Express
6. General Motors
7. Fannie Mae
8. Freddie Mac
9. Ford Motor Company
10. The Chubb Corporation
11. PepsiCo
12. Eastman Kodak
13. Xerox
14. Marriott International
15. Quaker Oats
16. Qwest Communications International
17. IBM
18. Hilton Hotels
19. JP Morgan Chase
20. JC Penney
21. Lucent Technologies
22. Darden Restaurants
23. AT&T
24. Verizon
25. Merrill Lynch
26. Johnson & Johnson
27. Prudential Financial
28. The Allstate Corporation

DiversityInc.Com Top 50
Companies for Diversity *(continued)*

29. Wal-Mart
30. Dole Food
31. Colgate-Palmolive
32. Pitney Bowes
33. Avon Products
34. Charles Schwab
35. McDonald's
36. Wells Fargo
37. Sears Roebuck
38. Philip Morris
39. FleetBoston
40. Aetna
41. Goldman Sachs
42. Pfizer
43. MasterCard
44. Ernst & Young International
45. Kmart
46. Motorola
47. DaimlerChrysler
48. Coca-Cola
49. Target
50. State Farm Insurance

Source: DiversityInc.com: An online magazine that provides news, resources and commentary on the role of diversity in strengthening business © 2001 DiversityInc.com, June 25, 2001

CRACKING THE CORPORATE CODE: FROM SURVIVAL TO MASTERY

Real Stories of African American Success, by Price Cobbs and Judith Turnock (Executive Leadership Council, Washington, DC). Published by the Executive Leadership Council (ELC), the book chronicles the experiences of 32 African American senior executives with successful careers in corporate America. Their stories are an inspiration to corporate veterans, rising managers, and those making their first foray into corporate America. The organization also offers the following programs for individuals at various stages of career development:

- *Shadow Mentoring Program.* ELC members welcome some of the nation's most promising graduate business students into their offices as part of Shadow Mentoring Week. Along with a firsthand look inside some of the nation's Fortune 500 companies, students benefit from one-on-one time with ELC members for career counseling and insight into corporate culture.

- *Mid-Level Managers' Symposium.* The symposium takes the young manager-attendees beyond business school education and technical competence. They learn to master the unwritten rules of the corporate world. Council members share their views on how choices are made, especially for organizational leaders, and how to handle the specific challenges every African American manager faces.

- *The Executive Leadership Council and Foundation.* Provides African American executives with a network and leadership forum focusing on business, economic, and public policies affecting African American professionals and students.

Regardless of the race of its owner and/or its employee population, a black-owned firm must be measured in the same way as any other company. Size, industry, career advancement opportunities, rewards—all these must be thoroughly investigated when looking for a job, especially a first job. Rather than trying to find the best black-owned company, your focus should be on locating the best company for you. However, given their rich experience, camaraderie, and career opportunities black firms are worth considering as options. (See the *Black Enterprise* BE100 list for a complete roster of the nation's top black-owned firms.)

LIFE ATOP THE CRYSTAL STAIR: WHAT PRICE SUCCESS?

Some say the route to the upper climes of corporate America is along a crystal stair—a path filled with bountiful salaries, chauffeured cars, and other lavish appointments. But missing from this fairy tale are the jagged edges beneath the beautiful, multifaceted facade. And for all its inviting color, reflection, and abundance of light, there is very little heat. For African Americans, there is often no wizard, or prince charming, or fairy godmother to help ease the way. It can be a lonely, cold ascent for African American executives, who inevitably may by stopped at the glass ceiling.

TALLYING THE GAINS

As first-generation black corporate executives reach the 20-year pinnacle of their careers, a mounting body of evidence has surfaced to prove that while some strides have been made, black executives have essentially been limited by their race. In 1996, the Federal Glass Ceiling Commission[3] found that African Americans held fewer than 5 percent of executive, administrative, and managerial jobs in all private-sector industries, and only 0.6 percent of senior executive slots.

    Black executives who have moved steadily up the ladder within America's largest corporations have gained increased compensation, influence, and status, and have pushed the "glass ceiling" ever higher. Many of the positions bestowed on them were disproportionately in affirmative action, personnel, and public, urban, and community affairs. Only a select few broke through to gain positions in finance, sales, and marketing. Yet, although ultimate power is still wielded by the "old boy network," senior black managers—through their performance and their sheer presence—continue to help redefine the paradigms of corporate culture.

Probably no executive has done more to change corporate thinking than Darwin N. Davis Sr.[4] During his 32 years at The Equitable Life Assurance Society, in New York, Davis was a stalwart who brought the virtues of African American clients and employees to the corporate fore. Davis has never hesitated to bring the black perspective to the table. His company expected that from him, says Davis, a former senior vice president now retired. He adds that he didn't start out intending to do that, but, as a black executive, he was thrust into a role that wasn't always comfortable but was necessary.

Executives who have the courage to take risks and carve out a place on the corporate mantel say that having their voices heard and valued is one of their greatest rewards. "I can pick up the phone and call the chairman. My counsel is often sought, and my responses have been incorporated into the bigger picture," says Paula Banks,[5] vice president of global social investment at BP Amoco Corporation. Banks, who joined Amoco in 1996 spent 24 years with Sears, Roebuck & Company prior. Banks says she was invited into the fold because she is a black woman who has done her homework and can offer a different perspective. Her challenge is to never get confused about who is in charge. She adds that it's not about you and your perceived power; it's about the company. As soon as a person gets confused, trouble begins.

SURVIVAL TRAINING

In a recent study of 111 black top corporate executives, conducted by the Kimbro Institute in Decatur, Georgia,[6] success for these individuals was defined as "having obtained the ability to affect change and the capacity to enjoy their work." Those profiled reflect career moves that have been propelled by a desire for increased responsibility and challenge. Undaunted, they took the risks that eventually led to high visibility or promotions. They work between 55 and 62 hours a week. Their average age is 46, and most of their careers have been spent in sales or marketing.

The most important factors cited for their success were hard work and alignment with the right people. Racial discrimination, company mergers, and reorganizations were perceived as the principal threats.

Sadly, many believe that, with the political climate the way it is, their successor will be neither black nor female.

For some, racial bias is a reality. Davis remembers a superior whom he unabashedly refers to as a "bigot." It was clear that, under him, Davis would never be promoted. Davis realized that he couldn't fight every day; he had to get around the bigot. He went to the CEO of the company and told him of his plight—a move he does not suggest for all. The result: a veiled threat from the accused manager that Davis had better watch his back. Months later, the manager was dismissed for other reasons. Davis, meanwhile, had learned that he had to dot all the i's and cross all the t's. To avoid being unfairly judged, he would become a better manager, correct the glitches in his personality, and make himself infallible.

As black executives scale the higher echelons of corporate America, the air gets thin and they struggle to play down the "only" and "first" factors. "When I first entered the organization, I was viewed as a novelty and drew a lot of attention without even trying," says Ursula Burns,[7] president of Xerox Worldwide Business Services. Burns joined the company as an intern in 1980. She had earned a degree in mechanical engineering, but the native New Yorker quickly learned that the general consensus at Xerox was that African Americans—especially African American women—are viewed as being less competent than whites. People translated her achievements into either "She is super brilliant" or "She must have floated through." She couldn't just be a regular employee, "and that is an insult," notes Burns. At various times in her career, Burns has served as assistant to the chairman, was on international assignment in London for two years, and oversaw a $3-billion unit—Xerox's largest.

Burns was elected to the elite group of Xerox corporate vice presidents in 1997, a coveted level of policy decision making that was held by only 40 other individuals. Burns says that she can't control being a black woman, but she did have control in being the youngest person to pass through all the gates. The fact that she did it faster than others has nothing to do with her race and gender, she states. It was her performance. Despite the fact that the coveted title was also bestowed on three white men, she still hears the whispers of detractors who say she "took" the position.

Unfortunately, there are those who find it too difficult to walk the executive tightrope. Sylvester Green,[8] executive vice president at Chubb & Son Inc., in White Plains, New York, says that one of the gravest mistakes black managers make is to blame others when things go wrong, rather than recognizing how they could have done things differently. "People should not take themselves too seriously. They end up leaving the company without asking questions and finding out where the real problems are," says Green, who has seen many African American managers come and go during his more than 30 years with the firm. He warns that black managers must choose their battles carefully. "When you do," he says, and when you stand behind your belief with evidence to support it, "you gain tremendous credibility."

A DOLLAR SHORT

Some highly qualified executives have found few roadblocks along their career path, but, for most employees, promotions are few and far between. Sometimes, obstacles present themselves in subtle ways: a lackluster assignment, a marked depreciation in workload, or "new" positions created above, which others are brought in to fill. "This company has never considered me for the position of chief insurance officer, and I have dealt with that. I always know that the glass ceiling is there because racism catches up with your successes," says Darwin Davis, who had been one of Equitable's top performers and is a recipient of every management award given by the company. (Only one other headquarters officer, the chief of insurance operations, shared that niche.)

Even when opportunities are seized and promotions come frequently, disparity is often found in compensation and severance packages. Executive pay can include lucrative six- or seven-digit salaries, stock options, access to corporate jets, and membership in exclusive clubs. Those perks might sound glamorous, but the Federal Glass Ceiling Commission reports that black men at the top of management earn 79 percent of the amount white men earn, and black women in those roles earn only 60 percent of the amounts awarded to their white male counterparts.

Davis, who says that even as a senior vice president he suspected that he made less than his colleagues, echoes this sentiment. "You don't get what you deserve, you get what you negotiate," he says.

STAYING AHEAD OF THE PAST

Sharon Collins,[9] an associate professor of sociology at the University of Illinois in Chicago, says that, in order to remain competitive, the next generation of executives must meld the lessons learned yesterday with the corporate strategies of today.

The first step is to learn how to "read" a company. "Find out who gets ahead and how; then try to replicate the process," Collins advises. "Learn what is rewarded and desired by the company, and give it to them." African Americans are inherently "outsiders." The ability to appeal across race and gender lines and transcend those barriers—given the race-conscious nature of the American society—is difficult but critical.

Part of the success of trailblazers came from their ability to maneuver through the labyrinths of their organizations. Black executives should avoid or move out of support areas. Performance standards in support jobs are tied to subjective rather than quantified measures, such as profit, sales, or production figures. Playing a soft role in a hard and increasingly competitive environment is not how to put "points on the board."

Do not get comfortable, however, warns Collins, who spent nearly a decade studying the black corporate elite in Fortune 500 companies and authored the book *Black Corporate Executive: The Making and Breaking of a Black Middle Class* (Temple University Press). "Black executives should be prepared to move up on the open market rather than stick around and make a lifelong commitment to a company."

Similarly, they should be proactive and entrepreneurial rather than conforming to the old models of "team player" and "company person." Their performance must stand out, she adds, and they must learn how to aggressively promote themselves in order to accumulate career opportunities both inside and outside the company.

But in the end, it all boils down to the following question: Do black executives lack support from each other, the most basic of foundations? Many would argue that the summons to "lift as we climb" falls on a tone-deaf flock. "In the 1960s, pressure from black constituencies on corporations created new opportunities that we exploited. Times have changed," says Collins. "Since blacks are vastly underrepresented in the executive ranks, the concept of 'similar treatment' has vastly different group consequences today that are not always fair. Solidarity between blacks, both inside and outside the corporate walls, will at least ensure some level of equity."

Yes, over the years, African Americans have been viewed more favorably in the workplace. Verbal slights, insults, and overt prejudice were more the norm of a generation ago. But where there were once these crimes of commission, there are more crimes of omission. In other words, affirmative action at least forced corporate America to recognize the abilities and contributions of blacks. But as the "A" in affirmative action grows more scarlet, African Americans must find more astute ways to get in the door and move up. More importantly, if companies truly live up to their diversity mission statements, African Americans might find the glass at the top of the crystal stair a little easier to break.

9

USING A RECRUITER

As a potential candidate, you should know the rules for dealing with executive recruiting firms. If you know the differences among various types of firms, you'll operate with more realistic expectations and gain more control over the hiring process. Two alternatives of executive search exist to this day. Retained and contingent firms both have the same objective—hire someone—but they go about it differently. Because these firms vary, both in approach and in payment, you'll need to know how to approach each one to get the best results from your efforts, or how to know whether you should even pursue a relationship with either one.

THE RETAINED FIRM

- Works for the employer, not for the candidate.
- Receives a fee from the employer, whether a placement is made or not.
- Usually signs exclusively with the client for the assignment.
- Executes searches for salaries in a range of $50K+.
- Offers a limited and tailored number of opportunities to the candidate.

- May present a candidate to only one client.
- Confidentiality is generally assumed.

THE CONTINGENCY FIRM

- Fee is paid when a candidate is placed on a job.
- Probably does not have an exclusive contract with the employer.
- Looks for candidates in the $20K to $100K+ salary range.
- Wants to get candidates hired so that its fee can get paid.
- Provides exposure to many opportunities because of its large clientele.
- Confidentiality could be at risk.
- Sends numerous candidates to the same employer.
- Freely circulates resumes.
- Potential conflicts can occur between rival firms or between a firm and its clients.

SEARCH FIRM RESOURCES

Blanketing search firms with your resume is neither effective nor endearing. To identify proven recruiters that have a track record of successful placement in your industry, try these resources:

- *Black Enterprise Guide to Executive Recruiters* (www.blackenterprise .com). Online listing of the nation's top black-owned recruitment firms committed to serving the diversity management needs of U.S. corporations and organizations.
- *Secrets from the Search Firm Files: What it Really Takes to Get Ahead in the Corporate Jungle* by John Rau (McGraw-Hill). This book provides proven strategies and guidelines for advancing your career, plus tips and cautions from executive recruiters, such as how they target candidates, interviewing mistakes, and ways to make employers come back even though you've said no.
- *The Directory of Executive Recruiters* (Kennedy Publications). With over 1,000 pages, the directory lists more than 10,000 recruiters at more than 5,000 offices across the country. They are segmented by specialty, industry, geography, and whether they are retained or hired on a contingency basis. The directory also

offers valuable tips for how to deal with executive search professionals.

- *Job Seekers' Guide to Executive Recruiters* by Christopher W. Hunt and Scott A. Scanlon (John Wiley & Sons). Lists hundreds of recruiters and gives advice on how to effectively approach them. Includes tips on interviewing.

EXECUTIVE ROUTES

Q: I've sent my resume to a number of executive recruiters. Why have I not received a response?

A: Executive search firms work for *companies,* not job candidates. Their focus is to find a match for a company's specific employment needs. Time is money. With commissions averaging 20 to 30 percent, or even as much as half of a candidate's annual salary, recruiters, unfortunately, don't give much time to corresponding with individuals who lack the skills the recruiters seek. Some firms acknowledge the receipt of unsolicited resumes, but most do not.

Generally, when a resume is received, information such as industry, education, special qualifications, salary requirements, and geographical preferences is entered into a database. Some firms keep the data on file for up to a year; others toss it if the candidate doesn't qualify for any of their positions. Some tips: Use a functional resume, which emphasizes your skills, if you want to go out of your field—say, from sales to accounting. Otherwise, use a chronological resume, which emphasizes your work experience.

DOS AND DON'TS OF WORKING WITH EXECUTIVE RECRUITMENT FIRMS

Dos

- If a counteroffer appeals to you, tell the recruiter that you may consider staying if your present employer makes the offer.
- Build relationships by referring colleagues or friends who meet the qualifications a recruiter is looking for. As recruiters become familiar with you and your work, you will be exposed to opportunities yourself.
- Don't deal with a recruitment firm that requests that you pay a fee.

- Be selective about the firms you work with. Check their references, and ask if you may contact someone who has been placed by them.

Don'ts

- Don't contact a client company directly. Go through the recruiter until you are given the green light.
- Don't lie about your current salary, job title, or education. (These things are easily and routinely checked.)
- Be professional. Don't get too familiar or informal. As a representative of the hiring firm, the recruiter will not refer you, despite your qualifications, if he or she is not comfortable with you. Treat your relationship like any other professional encounter.
- Just because recruiters call, don't think you're hired. The recruiter is calling for candidates. You may only get as far as an interview. Companies scrutinize all qualified candidates on the same basis, whether they are referred by a recruiter or walk in off the street.
- Don't jump at the first attractive offer. If a position is not in line with your career goals, you won't be making a good career move.

Keep these tips in mind to establish the best working relationship with an executive recruiter:

- Make sure they have an updated resume.
- Be honest. Don't fudge the facts or play coy when ask how much you earn. It all comes out in the background checks done by the employer and you risk damaging not only your credibility, but also that of the recruiter.
- Do your homework when an interview is arranged. Find out everything you can about the company that might hire you.
- Return phone calls immediately. Although that courtesy may not always be reciprocated, recruiters need to know if you are serious about pursuing a position.

There are no guarantees that a recruiter can land you your dream job, but they certainly can be an important part of your job search arsenal.

10

MAKING A
CAREER SWITCH

There comes a time in everyone's career when change is necessary. When a job becomes less challenging or yields fewer rewards, you may feel compelled to change employers—or maybe even industries. How do you make the switch, particularly if you have logged many years at a single company or in one industry or sector?

Youthful bravado has a way of helping career dreams flourish, but somewhere along the way the implementation process gets stalled. The reason could be marriage, relocation, the birth of a child, getting too comfortable in a current job, a change in education plans, or simply a change of mind.

If you are midcareer, it's not too late to consider another type of industry and job function. However, you must do a reality check and look at the various opportunities that are available—the job outlook. Regardless of where you are in your career, it's important to do informational interviews with people in the field or company you want to enter. Also, expand your research to libraries and the Internet. Then set your goals and devise a job search strategy. Don't forget: Networking is still an important key to getting the job you want.

BE PREPARED FOR CLOVERLEAF PATHS

One thing to remember: Career planning provides a guide for your career track, but your plans may not always be absolute. Every career plan is subject to change, again and again. Jay Curtis Hutchins found that out, early in his career.[1]

Determined to make his desire to hold public office a reality someday, Hutchins, 32, earned a BA in political science and public administration from Winston-Salem State University, in Winston-Salem, North Carolina. In 1992, he worked on Capitol Hill for New York Democratic Congressman Edolphus Townes for a year before earning a JD from Howard University School of Law. After graduating in 1996, Hutchins worked on the Clinton/Gore reelection campaign in Essex County, New Jersey, in the area of antivoter intimidation and voter fraud. What seemed like a surefire track to public office took a slight detour. "A career plan has to be subject to amendment," says Hutchins. "A person has to be open to change and evolution." And change he did.

After the presidential inaugural, Hutchins entertained thoughts of corporate law. In a leap of faith, he went to work for Prudential Insurance Company in Newark, New Jersey. "It was a learning experience, but what it really did was validate the path that I was already on." He adds, "I quickly realized, in my heart of hearts, that I didn't want to pursue that line of work." In 1998, Hutchins was back in Washington as a senior research associate and was assigned to a new post that he helped create: director of African American Affairs at the Democratic Senatorial Campaign Committee. He was also on the short list for a presidential appointment. He landed in the Peace Corps in the office of congressional relations, where he worked to recruit Peace Corps volunteers.

By February 2000, the newly married Hutchins and his wife Renee, also an attorney, moved back to East Orange, New Jersey. Still driven by his passion to help people, Hutchins became corporate program manager for Jersey Cares, a nonprofit organization in Morristown, New Jersey that provides volunteer opportunities for individuals and corporations. Today, Hutchins has so squarely positioned himself, both professionally and in the community, that he has been tapped to run for mayor of East Orange. "I am extremely excited that my dream of public service is becoming a reality," says Hutchins. His growing sphere of influence, his desire to serve the public, and the encouragement he has garnered from the community make him a prime candidate.

The biggest mistake of career planning is having no plan at all or a poorly developed one. Far too often, people find themselves in a career rut. They think that too much time has passed and it is too late to do their dream job. There is nothing wrong with doing the job you really want on the weekends or part-time. You can hold down the job that pays the bills and pursue your entrepreneurial or artistic goal during your off-time, until you determine how to do it full-time.

Career planning is an ongoing effort that never really ends. Your goals should not be only in the present; you should picture them when you look ahead. Ask yourself: "Where do I want to be in the next two to three years?" It's very important that you don't stop your career planning once you get a job, even if it seems to be the ideal job today. All in all, it is essential to do what you do best; to enjoy your work, the working environment, and the people with whom you work; and to meet your financial goals. You spend most of your waking hours working. For an investment that large, you have to have a plan.

LIVE YOUR IDEAL CAREER ON THE SIDE

Years ago, Shirley Hailstock[2] wanted to follow one career path: the U.S. space program. Instead, she had four careers: accountant, sales manager, college professor, and author.

While a chemistry major at Howard University, she joined the ROTC, hoping that would help to open the doors to NASA. But when she graduated in 1971, no jobs in the space program were to be had. A national wage freeze had dried up government jobs, and not even chemical companies were recruiting. On the strength of an associate degree in accounting, Hailstock resident crunched numbers at an insurance brokerage. In 1975, she joined the pharmaceutical company, Johnson & Johnson, in New Brunswick, New Jersey.

While there, Hailstock really got to work. Within five years, she had earned an MBA in chemical marketing from Fairleigh Dickinson University in Teaneck, New Jersey, was teaching accounting at Rutgers University in the evenings, and had switched to a job at Squibb (which later merged with Bristol Myers). She stayed in accounting until the 1980s, all the while continuing to broaden her skills. She

TURN A LIFE EXPERIENCE INTO A CAREER OPPORTUNITY

Whoever said "You need to have a job in order to get another one" didn't realize the value of life experience. With today's heavy concentration on credentials and paid work experience, some people feel left in the lurch. But even if you don't have a sterling resume, you can still highlight your assets and return to the workplace as a valuable employee. The key is to identify the life experience skills that will transfer to today's workplace, according to Fern Lebo,[3] president of Lebo Communications, a communications and training firm in Markham, Ontario. Lebo counters that homemakers must not downplay that they work at home. Instead, they should "highlight the time-management, problem-solving, interpersonal, and organizational skills required daily," adds Lebo, author of *Your Outplacement Handbook: Redesigning Your Career* (CRC Press).

If you were a fund raiser or a coordinator for a volunteer organization, or treasurer of your neighborhood block association, your resume should reflect the leadership, motivational, diplomatic, public-speaking, and financial skills you gained. "If you were the one writing the checks, research how your experience might translate into that of a budget manager or bookkeeper," suggests Lebo. "Everything you've accomplished before today is preparation for a job you may have tomorrow."

To unearth your hidden skills, ask yourself the following questions. Use your answers as the foundation of your resume and as responses to the most commonly asked interview questions.

- What activities do I do for work (paid or unpaid)?
- What activities do I do for leisure (focus on those with responsibility and teamwork requirements)?
- What skills have I gained from my life experience?

learned financial systems and absorbed as much as she could about computer programs, eventually becoming less reliant on others to write COBOL (a new system at that time). When her company wanted people with knowledge of both systems *and* accounting experience for a new financial project, they tapped Hailstock.

By 1991, she'd given birth to her two children and had weathered a divorce. Her division was sold and she became the senior sales systems manager in charge of consolidating and developing sales systems.

Yet, through these transitions, the creativity of a romance writer lurked deep beneath the analytic skills required for her day job. In her spare time, she wrote, took writing classes, and joined organizations such as the International Women's Writers Guild, Women Writers of Color, and Romance Writers of America.

Part-time or voluntary experience allows you to explore your dreams and still have a safety net. Let's say, for example, that you dream of working at a bed-and-breakfast. If you don't have the time to work at one during the summers or on weekends, then do informational interviews to find out more about the field.

Harlequin Books, the largest publisher of romance novels, rejected Hailstock's first manuscript but gave her valuable writing advice. Her 1994 debut novel, *Whispers of Love,* and, later, *Clara's Promise,* were greeted with critical acclaim and awards. Hailstock, who serves on the board of the Romance Writers of America, has seven novels and three novellas to her name—all published by Pinnacle Books. "For me, professional fulfillment has been the freedom to do what I've wanted and not be boxed in. I also never set unattainable goals," says Hailstock who hopes to be able to write full-time some day.

To ensure that you too can make the transitions, organize your work around satisfaction, serenity, and self-esteem. You don't have to be at the mercy of technology, economic decisions made five time zones away, or someone else's "manifest destiny."

HOW DID A FORMER ASSISTANT DISTRICT ATTORNEY MAKE IT TO STARDOM?

Star Jones's twinkle has worked like a beacon, launching the New York attorney from the courtroom to the small screen. Jones,[4] a former NBC News legal correspondent, currently co-hosts ABC's *The View.* Her relaxed style and keen jurisprudence helped Jones land the half-hour series *Jones & Jury* some years ago, and served her well when she was a Brooklyn assistant district attorney.

Jones says that, early in her law career, she chose prosecution over defense and any other aspect of the law because "it's the only avenue of the law where you can do the right thing," she says. "The law shouldn't be influenced by politics or the next job you're trying to get, but because it's the right thing."

Starlet Marie Jones spent the first six years of her life with her grandparents in Badin, North Carolina, and later moved to Trenton, New Jersey, with her mother and stepfather. Her grandmother's loyalty to TV's daily soap operas helped influence her future career choice. "My grandmother used to watch *Another World*, and, for one character in particular, she would always say, 'That child needs a lawyer.'"

Jones put herself through American University by taking clerical jobs and racking up student loans. In 1986, after receiving her law degree from the University of Houston Law Center, she joined the Kings County (Brooklyn, New York) District Attorney's office. She served in the General Trial and Homicide bureaus after being promoted, in 1991, to senior assistant district attorney.

The transition from practicing law to analyzing it came easy for Jones. When an associate at the district attorney's office turned down an offer to do legal commentary for cable television's *Court TV*, she recommended Jones. That windfall was a direct result of contacts made through networking, Jones now says.

Jones's *Court TV* commentary on the William Kennedy Smith trial led to a career shift. "I was sitting in my office in Brooklyn, trying to convince a teenage witness to testify, when the phone rang," she recalled. The call was from an *NBC Today* show booker. "I thought it was a prank call and hung up," she adds.

That afternoon, Jones got the teenager to testify. The defendant was sentenced to 25 years to life, and Jones landed a job as an NBC legal correspondent.

Her quick wit and infectious humor haven't compromised her stellar legal record as a veteran of high-profile, highly sensitive New York City felony cases. One of those was the 1991 Crown Heights controversy in which a Hasidic man was accused of driving the car that injured one black child and killed another. In addition, she won a 66-year prison term for a serial sex abuser who had escaped conviction in four previous trials.

PRESTO CHANGE-O!: WHEN YOUR PLAN CHANGES

Even though you may have a plan that works and seems crafted for success, there are some instances when a career needs a change. Some people expect to make an early decision about a career and then to stick with it for their entire work life. True, some people have clear goals and pursue them throughout their lives. But others go from experience to experience, not always sure what is coming next, but trusting that there is a next step. People who crave change but are afraid of leaving behind the familiar may feel more boxed in by life each day. Change may be scary, but just putting in time or being bored in your career is deadly to the soul.

Many working people seem to agree. A 1998 American Management Association survey of more than 4,500 executives found that 71 percent had held two or more positions in the 1990s.[5] Of those, 39 percent had held three or more positions. Managers age 35 years and under showed the most mobility: 90 percent of them had worked at more than one job (the average number was three jobs).

To be successful as a career changer, you must be information-oriented and self-responsible, and must have good people skills. The important factors are: your willingness to accept change, the support system you've developed, and your focus on making your dream a reality. In the end, your determination and sacrifices will lead to new levels of satisfaction in this crazy thing called *work*.

PREPARE FOR CHANGE

Through derring-do, pluck, or accident, Stephen James learned these things early.[6] "I became a 'roads scholar'—a black guy who grew up in the South Bronx, went to Harvard, and got a PhD," he says of the winding road that led him to a professorship at Lehman College, a unit of the City University of New York. "People think that's a big transition. For me, it was a transformation."

As a child, James found more comfort in the cello, gymnastics, and his mother's collection of mail-order books than in the rigors of the classroom. In 1969, when he was 17, he dropped out of high school and became one with the sociopolitical movement of the day. He sold the Black Panther newspaper along Bronx streets. As a community worker for the nationalist organization, he often landed on local college campuses. Lehman College, one of the many colleges that make up the City University of New York, would later play a pivotal role in James's life.

In 1971, he traded his Black Panther combat boots for the hard hat of a carpenter's trainee. "Construction was the best hiding place for a radical," says James, who had just married. "I had been politically active and had no plans of going back to school." Yet, as much as he tried to hide, "school" found him. Construction sites became his classrooms. "When you work with your hands, you get to use your mind," says James. "There is a lot of opportunity to think and talk." He also became a student of tai chi, the ancient Chinese discipline of meditative movement. It helped him to relax, especially during the times to come.

By 1978, the construction jobs had diminished and his marriage had ended in divorce. He was a driver for a commuter bus line, working three-hour stints during the morning and evening rush hours. On his second day at work, he drove to his familiar haunt, Lehman College, and registered for classes right on the spot. "I was driven to finish what I didn't when I was younger," says James, who attended classes in between his bus runs.

The first part of preparing for change is figuring out what burns inside of you and pursuing that goal. Although James had shunned his early schooling, he now had a passion for education.

Nine years later, James earned his degree in English and applied to graduate school. He checked the box on the GRE exam that permits having scores sent to universities, but he never imagined that Harvard would respond. Harvard and Columbia accepted him. In 1987, with a stipend in hand, James was off to Cambridge, Massachusetts, to study English and American literature. A Dexter Fellowship from Harvard sent him to England in 1989. He also traveled throughout Switzerland, France, and Spain. The overseas experience prompted the knowledge-hungry academic to take a four-year break in his formal studies to hang out in Europe and immerse himself in African American literature and language. A visiting professorship at Columbia University and his daughter Joy's high school graduation finally lured him back to the States in 1992. Four years later, after completing his dissertation, he was hired by Lehman College.

James's strategy was different: he had none. "All my career decisions were arbitrary," says the assistant professor of English and black studies. "I wouldn't tell someone to necessarily do what I've done. I had interests in certain things and pursued them. I don't know if I'm finished yet. This profession suits me now, but at some point, I may decide to do something else."

Whatever happened in your first life, you can plan for a successful second life. Do your planning now. The future is going to happen whether you're ready or not.

STRIKE A BALANCE BETWEEN WORK AND YOUR PERSONAL LIFE

Do you frequently have lunch on the run, or at your desk? Are you "dropping by" the office for a few hours on the weekend? Do family and friends complain that they never see you?

Many workers forsake their personal life and then shift into overdrive at the office, says Val Arnold,[7] senior vice president of Personnel Decisions, a human resources consulting firm in Minneapolis. Ask yourself the following questions to see if you "have a life." If you don't, then try to reclaim it.

- *Are you focused?* Does your task contribute to a major organizational or personal goal? If you can't answer these questions, then you're not clear on what projects are important and worth your effort. Take a break and get back on course.

- *Does time escape you?* You look up at the clock and find that you're late for dinner or your child's school play—again! Your workload is making decisions about your life. Instead, you should be setting the boundaries for your work. Establish clear limits on the amount of time you'll devote to a project, and stay within those limits.

- *Do you talk about work 24/7?* If your off-hour conversations revolve around the office, you've lost your perspective. There is more to life than work.

- *Do responsibilities overwhelm you?* You may be at the wrong company or, even worse, in the wrong job.

- *Are your relationships fulfilling?* Heed the cries of your friends and family when they say they never see you anymore. These are sacrifices you shouldn't have to make.

- *Why am I here?* Humans are inherently spiritual creatures, yet many of us are so consumed by our jobs that spirituality takes a back seat. Stop, look, and find the soul inside you again.

HOLDING OUT FOR THE RIGHT JOB: CONFESSIONS OF AN MBA GRADUATE

Often, no matter how you set the stage for success—secure top-notch credentials, gain coveted skills, craft a killer resume, or hone communication skills—your career path might not track as planned. Darryl Scott had undergraduate and graduate degrees in computer science from the nation's leading universities, several years experience working in the IT departments of telecommunication and major banking companies. He even had an MBA in strategic planning from an Ivy League business school.

Ordinarily, professionals like 31-year-old Scott have lucrative job offers before they even begin their last year of business school. However, Scott had his sights set on an entrepreneurial venture seeking to make a transition out of IT and into business development. He rebuffed the many job offers that came his way, but after nine months, his business had faltered. A year after graduation, Scott was still unemployed. He refused to accept a "safety" job that would limit him to IT functions. Instead he held out for a position that would allow him to expand his business skills in a medical and technological environment. Today, Scott is senior manager of business technology at a major pharmaceutical firm and doing a job he loves. But his decision to wait came at a high price. Here is his story.

Q: As a child, what did you want to be when you grew up?

A: I wanted to be a doctor in 3rd grade, a programmer in 8th grade, and a scientist in college. Toward the end of college, I became very interested in combining medicine with technology.

Q: What were your career plans?

A: In college, I saw areas where the integration of technology and medicine could be improved. There was a new frontier opening up that would lead to enhancements in how doctors treated patients and how patients could take on a greater role in deciding on the medical care they received. Granted, companies had been integrating technology into the medical field on the business side, such as in billing, but were still in the infancy stage of applying technology to the way patients are treated.

I planned to get advance degrees in computer science, biomedical engineering, and my MBA. The plan was to develop my skills in information technology, business, and healthcare within 10 years so I could run my own business that focused on medical-diagnostic consumer products.

Q: After business school, you delayed your efforts to seek employment, why?

A: I was set on starting a business and developed a business plan while in business school. I also thought that if the business didn't take off that the start-up experience would be attractive to potential employers. However, when the business faltered and I began looking for a full-time job, recruiters pushed me toward technology-related jobs (development, etc.) because of my background. I wasn't satisfied with that and held out until I found something that was right for me.

Q: Cite one or two career obstacles you have faced?

A: Unexpectedly, after you get one master's degree, people seem to be less supportive when you try to get another. Also, employers met my desire to transition immediately from business school to business development with skepticism. The response was that they sought people with previous consulting and marketing experience—mine was very limited.

Q: You transitioned to a new career. What do you think contributed to your success?

A: In my previous jobs, I had gained experience developing IT systems. In business school I gain business strategy experience. I believe that these skills, combined with my interest in the healthcare field helped me make the transition into business development at a pharmaceutical company.

Q: Many friends and family members disapproved of your decision to wait for the right job to come along. What was the fallout of your decision and how did you handle it?

A: Many people from business school thought that I just didn't want to work. This theory fit in well with the comments of me being a "professional student" because of my multiple degrees. This was compounded by the fact that I was trying to start a business—something that was counter to what people had come to expect of me. (Professionally some started to question why I wasn't working and thought that I just couldn't get a job.) Financially, I was set back pretty hard. I exhausted my savings, got into a lot of debt—my credit took a hit. At one point, I even took temporary jobs to make ends meet as an administrative assistant making photocopies all day. Socially, I distanced myself from naysayers, instead seeking out a circle of people who were supportive and/or in the same situation. There were many people who understood what I wanted to do and offered financial and emotional support.

Q: Have you achieved your goals? What are the next steps in your career track?

A: In my current role, I am able to gain experience and an understanding for how consumers use and want to use medical information/technology, the role the government plays, and how physicians are willing to use technology in medicine. In hindsight, trying to start my own company gave me a broad strategic perspective into how business works: what it takes to develop it, the various logistical factors, and how to put things into action. This experience was invaluable and was noticed during the interview process by my potential employers. Within six months of accepting the offer, I was out of financial straits and had made significant steps to repair my credit.

I am currently taking classes in medical digital imaging and I plan to take courses in biomedical engineering. The convergence of medicine and technology will be a huge market for pharmaceutical and biotechnology firms, for surgeons in the use of remote surgery and telemedicine, and for patients who want to take charge of and monitor their own health.

Q: What's your advice for others who are waiting for their dream job to come along?

A: Don't wait. Make it happen. Acknowledge what your strengths are and what it is that you want to do. If you have long-term goals, shoot for that job first. If you are not currently qualified or ready for that job, then take a job that plays to your strengths and will help you gain the skills for the long term. Also, pick a company that provides an environment where you can move within the company to the next stage of your career development.

HOW ACCOUNTABLE ARE YOU FOR YOUR SUCCESS?

The key to career and personal empowerment is: Take responsibility for yourself and others.

An African American female manager is promoted to head a business unit at a large corporation. Over the past three years, she has proven herself to be an excellent candidate, possessing all the technical qualifications necessary for the post. But her employees resent the appointment. They feel that the job should have gone to a white male, long rumored to be next in line for the position.

The employees begin to sabotage her efforts. A small faction of managers in her unit spreads rumors that her appointment was a classic case of reverse discrimination. Department productivity and morale take a plunge.

Not surprising, the manager is called in by her superiors and told she has three months to reverse the situation. It doesn't happen. The company vice president then informs her that "things aren't working out" and offers her a lateral move—a position with less prestige and responsibility. Instead of accepting a job she views as a demotion, the manager resigns.

This woman was faced with what, for some, would be insurmountable odds. She suffered unfair treatment and discrimination. But could she have prevented her failure? It's easy to place blame elsewhere, but how different would things have been if she had been more accountable for her own success?

WHOSE FAULT IS IT, ANYWAY?

It is no secret that racism and sexism exist in the workplace. Despite the fact that many organizations are now addressing diversity, company initiatives are not strong enough salves for the wounds caused by decades of social inequality in the workplace. But you can't expect your company to do everything. You have to hold yourself accountable for your future.

"Personal accountability is the willingness to claim 100 percent ownership for the results produced as a consequence of your involvement, both individually and collectively, with others in your workplace," says William A. Guillory,[8] CEO and founder of Innovation International Inc., a management consulting firm in Salt Lake City, Utah. "The lack of empowerment for African Americans is partly discrimination, but the other part is preparing ourselves," he adds. "Ask yourself, 'If discrimination disappears tomorrow, am I still prepared?'"

Although the manager was capable of handling the position from a technical standpoint, she had limited skills and experience in managing people—as do most women and minorities who are moving up the corporate ladder.

The company said it would "treat her equally"—and that's where the problem began, Guillory explains. Under the rules of diversity management, people shouldn't be treated alike, but as individuals. The manager was not equipped to handle her new role without proper skills and support. The company should have recognized the manager's unique circumstances and put the proper systems in place, and she should have asked about the support she would receive during her transition. ("How will things be set up to ensure the highest probability of my success?")

Her objective should have been to produce the result required, even though her subordinates didn't want her to. One way to do this would have been to go to her superiors and inform them of the difficulties she was having with her staff. She also should have developed a support network of people to whom she could go for advice, and built alliances with her superiors.

If she had done all that and had still felt that the level of support offered was not adequate, she could have chosen not to take a job in which she would inevitably fail. If, by resigning, she walked away feeling as though she was set up for failure, then she learned nothing. Her experience was a self-fulfilling prophecy. On the other hand, if she learned to assess her strengths and weaknesses, to continuously upgrade her skills and request the tools needed to work efficiently, then her experience was a success.

MEASURE YOUR ACCOUNTABILITY: A QUIZ

Being more accountable involves giving up some behaviors, beliefs, and attitudes, rather than concentrating on behaving a different way. One of the most common defense mechanisms used to avoid accountability or responsibility is to become upset. Obviously, if you're upset, you can't handle the matter.

Going "unconscious," is another, says Guillory. "This is done by simply tuning someone out, or by having your own mental conversation while someone is attempting to point out how you could have assumed greater responsibility."

Playing the role of a victim is another way to escape accountability, adds Guillory. Expressions common to the victim are "I can't" and "I'm unable." These statements are really saying, "I am unwilling." To see how accountable you are, take this test and then rate yourself on this scale:

SA—Strongly Agree

A—Agree

N—Neutral

D—Disagree

SD—Strongly Disagree

I am totally responsible for my success at work. _____

I am exceptionally productive, irrespective of the work
    environment. _____

I am accountable for the results I produce, even if a situation
    is unfair. _____

I take training to upgrade my skills and competencies on a regular
    basis, without having to be told. _____

I am exceptionally skilled at the work I do, as demonstrated by my
    performance. _____

I trust coworkers (or employees) without interference when I delegate
    tasks vital to my own success. _____

I have demonstrated exceptional interpersonal skills where mentor-
    ship or coaching is concerned. _____

I hold coworkers to their commitments, even when that policy pro-
    vokes confrontation. _____

I hold others proactively accountable for their commitments, regard-
    less of how that policy may affect our personal relationship. ____

I am willing to work through in-depth personal issues in order to
    achieve team success. _____

SA response _____ × 4.0 = _____
A responses _____ × 3.0 = _____
N responses _____ × 2.0 = _____
D responses _____ × 1.0 = _____
SD responses _____ × 0.0 = _____
Total   _____

Multiply the total by 2.5 to obtain your total percentage of personal empowerment, based on a scale of 100 percent.

Total _____ × 2.5 = _____ percent

[Average score is 77 percent.]

91–100
Extremely empowered. Your success is ensured. You accept unfairness as something you have to deal with, and you ask, "How do I get beyond this?"

81–90
Very empowered and successful most of the time, except if you are put in an extremely unfair situation.

71–80
Somewhat empowered and probably experiencing success 50 percent of the time if you are in a fair system.

70 or below
Marginally empowered, and your success rate is low. You're aligned with people who have long conversations about how racist society is, and how, if it weren't racist, they would be successful.

HOW TO IMPROVE YOUR ACCOUNTABILITY QUOTIENT

- Change your attitude about colleagues and work. Take 100 percent responsibility for events in your life. Ask yourself, "Am I avoiding responsibility?"
- Learn self-management skills. Managers may be disappearing, but managing is not. Plan, prioritize, execute, and focus on your own work.

- Assess your competency level. Your skills should be consistent with the market. Make sure you're not easily replaceable.
- Accept continuous learning as a way of life. Take advantage of the training programs at your organization. Tapes, books, classes, seminars, and, most of all, a personal and professional mentor, should be mainstays. White males take five times more, and white women take three times more training classes than African Americans.
- Consult resources such as: *Empowerment for High-Performing Organizations,* by William Guillory and Linda Galindo, and *Realizations,* by William Guillory. Both books are published by Innovations International. To order, call 800-487-3354.

Knowledge is the only key to security. It also gives you the ability to integrate information and create new systems. Learn all you can, process what you've learned, and then apply it.

Make a Quick Career Comeback

No matter who you are or what you do, losing a job is a dramatic event. It's an unexpected upheaval that can change your life. That's why it's crucial to respond with an appropriate action that can get you and your career quickly back on track. Before you make any major decisions, take time to deal with your feelings. Get mad, cry, scream, bend a friend's ear—do whatever you must to allow yourself to grieve and eventually move on. Next, focus on your goals. For obvious reasons, the closer you stay to your previous job profile and industry, the less time and effort it will take to land your next job. But you must decide what's more important: quickly finding a job, or landing a fulfilling occupation? Often, finances drive the need to find a job fast, but if you have the benefit of a severance package or ample savings, take some time to reflect on where you've been. It will help you decide where to go. Ask yourself these important questions:

- What impact did you have in your job?
- Were you pleased with your position?
- What things were you especially good at?
- Did your position put your best skills to use?
- What did you like most about your last job?

- Were there areas of your performance that needed improvement?
- What areas of your job did you most dislike?
- Do you want to continue doing the kind of work you were doing?

Searching for these answers will help you determine whether you're interested in—and suited for—the kind of work you have been doing. No one wants to be out of work, but loss of a job provides an opportunity to stop and evaluate some options and perhaps select a new path. You may also be compelled to start your own business. Whether you start your own outfit or land a nine-to-five, you should lean on your contacts to help you make the transition. Chances are that the "who-you-know rule" will open the door to your next gig. Let old colleagues and clients know that you've left your job and you're in the market. Even if you're still feeling angry, try to be upbeat with those who might provide you with contacts. No one wants to refer a sourpuss.

Above all, keep an open mind. Be flexible as you evaluate the kinds of positions you're willing to accept. If you find yourself facing a job loss, it will hurt a while. But, all is not lost. If you plan carefully, losing your job may actually be a blessing.

Q: What are the signs that there is no promotion in sight and I should leave my job?

A: "It is critical to know what you're worth to your organization, yet people fail to find this out," says Mallory Sanford,[9] president of Execu-Search Inc., an executive recruitment firm in Philadelphia. Your performance appraisals will clue you on how the company values your contributions. A red flag should go up when someone who joined the company after you did, and has the same work assignment, is promoted to a higher level than yours. Frequent changes in management are also sure signs that you should test the job market.

Before taking a job, ask about the route of mobility. Speak to individuals who have moved up the track. If you don't get the right answers, focus on getting maximum experience and then leaving.

Periodically, test the job market by building a relationship with an executive recruiter. Companies call recruiters to find out whether their salaries are competitive, so why shouldn't you? If you don't ask, you could end up on a treadmill instead of the fast track. If people at

TURNING A PENCHANT FOR
MOVIES INTO A CAREER

When you think "behind the scenes" in Hollywood, think Gregory Jones.[10] Before a camera can roll or a director can yell "action," Jones, and entertainment insurance brokers like him, write the insurance deals of their producer clients.

Jones, an executive with a major entertainment insurance company, analyzes a film's script and budget to determine how much it will cost to insure production. He then shops the film around to insurance companies to get the best deal. But marrying his passion for entertainment with the pragmatism of the insurance industry, Jones has proven that some hobbies can make for quite intriguing careers. Before first grade, Jones was memorizing film credits, jingles, and sports statistics. "My mother would say, 'Tell your uncle who does the music for *The Lucy Show*,' and I would answer, 'Wilbur Hatch,'" recalls Jones. Soon thereafter, Jones was reeling off the names of producers, directors, and writers. By the age of 12, the gifted student with a photographic memory was auditioning for drama roles in New York City theaters.

But as a boy growing up in Harlem, Jones says his acting wasn't popular with his sportsminded peers, and he abandoned it. Nonetheless, his strong interest in the arts motivated him to earn a degree in English literature. After college, Jones flirted with the idea of teaching, but opted for business instead. He took a job as an underwriter trainee with American International Group, a New York insurance company, and later moved to Chubb Insurance where he was a commercial property insurance manager. About a year later, Jones was bored.

"I was unhappy and feeling unfulfilled," he recalls. But one day, after overhearing an entertainment broker and a producer talk about scripts, actors, and the use of animals in a film, things changed. Jones drilled colleagues on the ins and outs of entertainment brokering and within a year obtained his broker's license. Later, an associate's degree in risk management helped Jones better understand how movie studios purchase insurance.

TURNING A PENCHANT FOR
MOVIES INTO A CAREER *(continued)*

Jones soon moved to Los Angeles, worked for several prominent insurance companies, and has negotiated more than $3 billion in production insurance placement for more than 200 films, television shows, and commercials. He must take into account everything from general liability to props to actors falling ill to determine the cost of a film's insurance. It could cost up to $800,000 to insure a $40 million film from script to distribution, and most brokerage firms walk away with 10 percent to 15 percent in commission. Brokers get a percentage of the fee and easily rake in $100,000 to $200,000 a year. Those salaries are sure to keep pace with film production costs that continue to jump 20 percent annually.

Despite the aura, the industry is not as glamorous as people think, notes Jones, who occasionally gives lectures on producing insurance. He can count on one hand the number of actors he has met. "Producers call me all times of the day or night with questions," says Jones. "Success in this business is measured by your accessibility." Adds Jones, "Insurance is not just a guy with a briefcase knocking on you door. There is a niche for any interest."

---

your current job aren't talking about you, asking for your input, or assigning you to special projects, it may mean that you won't be missed if you leave.

Q: I've been in marketing for the past three years and want to prepare myself for career growth. What should I do at this stage, in order to advance?

A: "While marketing is a great area of business, those who have made it to the executive suite have also cut their teeth in finance or operations—areas that provide a broader view of the company and make you more marketable," says Jeffrey Greene,[11] of Goodrich and Sherwood International, an executive search firm in New York. "Even marketing-driven organizations seek product developers who can balance a profit and loss sheet." Yet, notes Greene, opportunities are lost because many

African Americans are less willing to take risks. "For example, a manager's spouse gets a promotion that will force them to relocate, but the manager is reluctant to move, so the opportunity that might have meant career advancement tomorrow is lost today," says Greene.

You have to be a risk taker, and that may mean doing rotations in various cities or even in other countries. While racing can most certainly have a negative impact on your career, you want to alleviate all other barriers or potential shortcomings. "Volunteer for projects that show you're willing to do the grunt work, and take on less popular jobs," adds Greene. "Your flexibility will also lessen the likelihood of being pigeonholed." True career success means positioning yourself to win the advancement you want.

Q: How do I go about showcasing my skills when I lack traditional credentials?

A: When employers challenge your lack of a college degree, they are saying they don't think you have the intelligence or the potential to do the job, says Terry Simmons, president of Simmons Associates Inc., a human resources consulting firm in New Hope, Pennsylvania. What many companies fail to recognize is that they really don't need the credentials—they need the skills. You can highlight yours by changing the direction of the interview.

If the position you want requires good leadership skills, ask the interviewer if community leadership is valuable and then market your community or social activities. If you're looking for a promotion, ask your manager, "What skills would a person with a degree have that I don't have?"

Once the skills you lack are identified, get to work acquiring them. If an advanced degree is necessary, take the first few courses of the program. Bringing back good grades will answer the question about whether you're competent. Don't be intimidated by what you don't have. Spotlighting what you do have is a way to stand toe-to-toe with the competition.

Returning to Your Old Job

Some things in life are cyclic, and that includes careers. Now that the downsizing dust of the past decade is beginning to clear, many workers have been invited back to their former companies. Good news? Perhaps.

Whether they are contractors, temps, or full-fledged regular employees, those asked to return shouldn't do so in haste. "Control your involvement," advises Joan Moore,[12] president of the Arbor Consulting Group, in Plymouth, Michigan. "Consider your long-term needs, establish goals, and ask yourself, 'How will this move help me to manage my career?'" Whether you're offered a short-term assignment or permanent employment, when negotiating your return you must factor in the elements that will give you future leverage and not make you a pawn in the industry.

In 1992, after 10 years with IBM, Timothy McCanelley[13] opted to take the buyout package offered to employees when the company began streamlining its operations. Since then, he has returned to Big Blue in Research Triangle Park, North Carolina, as a contract employee on two separate occasions. He was well aware, both times, that a permanent position was not guaranteed, but McCanelley looked at his return as a strategic career move.

"During my career, I observed this industry carefully. I was aware of where the jobs would be, and returned each time for skills, not money," says the Alabama A&M University computer science graduate. Going back on a contract basis allowed him to take only the jobs he wanted. The first time, he moved into a position as test coordinator in a client/server platform. He returned in 1996 for a tour of nearly two years in a networking hardware division. "I took jobs that offered transferable skills," says McCanelley now a system integration verification testing director at a Dallas telecommunications firm.

If you're offered a permanent position, come to terms, during your comeback, with the fact that things will be different. People, jobs, even the decor may not be what you remember. There might also be resentment from coworkers who feel that you got a better deal. "Often, you may be returning with more money or at a higher position. Old colleagues may think you're getting special treatment and not trust you," says Margaret Munzel,[14] senior consultant at the Arbor Consulting Group. Consider these other points before you go back:

- *Any bennies?* Inquire about health benefits, seniority, and becoming revested in the company pension plan, advises Moore. Find out if your employer will bridge your benefits. Other benefits such as stock options, vacation time, and use of a car can be especially important, particularly if you return with a cut in pay, says Liv Wright,[15] an outplacement counselor at Lee Hecht Harrison in New York.

- *"Toto, this isn't Kansas."* Because things will be different, ask whether you will be handling the same type of projects that you did before your departure, and whether procedures have changed. Get the new terms and job description in writing, so that your return doesn't seem capricious, advises Wright. It's also important to know whether mentoring or growth opportunities will be available, and whether layoffs are projected for the future. "You don't want to be on a dead-end track," states Moore.

- *Just say no.* If you left with a bad taste in your mouth, do you really want to go back? It's easy to get lulled into the security and safety of your old job instead of taking the risk of doing a job search. The assignment may be better for the company than it is for you.

Above all, set goals and determine what you want to get out of this reconstituted relationship. Whether you return or move on, stay actively involved in changing and reinventing yourself every day.

How to Make the Transition from Peer to Boss

Promotions are great, but they can be difficult when you're faced with managing individuals who are friends. There are ways to make the transition easier. Val Arnold, senior vice president of executive consulting services for Personnel Decisions International, a Minneapolis-based human resources consulting firm, offers some tips for when you go from coworker to supervisor.

Realize that authority impacts relationships. Face it; your relationships with your peers will change. Now that you're in charge, be prepared for different expectations and behavior from them. Come to terms with the fact that things will be different.

- *Define the new relationship.* Ask yourself: What kind of boss do you want to be? How will you treat employees and, in turn, how do you want them to treat you? If this relationship is clear, achieving your goals will be easier.

- *Don't take things personally.* Everything from envy, anger, and mistrust to overfriendliness may cloud your relationship with your former peers. These reactions have less to do with you than with your new status. Stay focused and continue to maintain harmonious relationships.

- *Pull back on the reins.* Don't turn into the boss overnight. Discuss with your coworkers the roles they see themselves playing. Listen to what they have to say about their expectations. Doing this will help you spot potential problems early.

- *Learn by example.* Remember the boss you liked the best? Try to mirror that relationship. Apply those same skills in asserting your authority positively and effectively.

- *Seek advice, but do what's best for you.* Other managers will tell you everything from "Stay friends" to "Let them know who's boss." Find a management style that works best for your goals, needs, and personality.

Quell Job-Hopping Fears with the Right Approach

You've had five jobs in as many years, and now fear that your kangaroo act has caught up with you. Don't worry; you're not alone. Whether corporate trends, such as downsizing, or career growth opportunities kept you hopping, jumping no longer carries the stigma it once did. Companies are aware that the volatile job market has displaced many people and that workers have found more creative forms of employment. "Contract employment is becoming more prevalent, and the rise of mergers and acquisitions and downsizing has actually made job jumping commonplace," says Julia Hartman,[16] author of *Strategic Job Jumping: Fifty Very Smart Tactics for Building Your Career* (Prima Publishing). Nonetheless, some employers are on the defensive. Here's how to counter their skepticism:

- *Bring up references.* Offer references who can vouch for your performance in spite of your short tenure. If you were a productive, results-oriented employee, they'll be able to give tangible examples of your work.

- *Show your portfolio.* Seeing is believing. Compile awards, sales performance records, and other pertinent documents in a professional-looking binder, and present them during your interview.
- *Prove your worth.* "If you were hired by all those companies, then you must have had the skills to do the job," says Hartman. In addition, you bring with you a broader industry perspective and numerous contacts that can benefit the organization.

"The companies most accepting of this are those that embrace change and are not very traditional," says Hartman. "If the firm frowns on this type of strategy, you might not be happy there in the first place."

Go for It!

Sometimes, the dream that you want can't be fulfilled in the confines of an office or the award of a lofty title. For some, the thought of pursuing their dream career, no matter what, is a compelling force. Bailing out from the workday world can be exhilarating—and hair-raising. Throwing caution to the winds and venturing out on one's own can be the start of a fulfilling adventure—and a satisfying new way of life—even in today's volatile economy. Many individuals don't have the time, money, or guts to walk this economic tightrope.

For most, starting a business, spending time with family, teaching, or just taking some time off to regroup would be enough. The problem is that these aspirations often amount to nothing more than dreams deferred: they happen either too late or not at all. But these days, more individuals are taking the risk and rewriting the script so that they can be in charge of the show.

Despite the strong work ethic embraced by many baby boomers, a recent study reflects a definite change in this group's attitude toward work. According to the study presented at the Academy of Management's national meeting, held in 1997, nearly 40 percent of the 874 middle-income managers surveyed said they would quit their jobs if they had enough money to live comfortably.[17] A similar study, done in the 1980s, found that only 23 percent would quit; and back in the 1950s, only 14 percent said they would opt out.

Today's respondents said that if they could change jobs, they would work for smaller companies or become entrepreneurs, notes Frieda Reitman,[18] a professor emeritus at Pace University in New York, who coauthored the study with Professor Joy Schneer of Rider University in Lawrenceville, New Jersey. "Only a small percentage focused on living a life of leisure. It was much more a desire for self-employment and more involvement with the family and community."

STOP THE WORLD, I WANT TO GET OFF

Longer hours, increased responsibility, and little free time have created a legion of stressed-out workers who have no real outlet. Others have found that the grind of a nine-to-five job no longer offers them all they thought it would.

"It's part of the natural evolution of human beings to want to feel that their work is valuable and that they are making a contribution," says James C. Gonyea,[19] founder and host of the America Online Career Center in New Port Richey, Florida. "As people move higher up in an organization, they become distanced from the people they were intended to serve. They begin to feel unfulfilled."

Another reason some individuals want to change their line of work is their realization that they were in the wrong field to begin with. Many people are not fully aware of their interests, abilities, values, and needs—the elements that make up their personality type. "It is very difficult to identify occupations that are right for you if you're unsure about who you are," states Gonyea. "Unfortunately, the realization that you're in the wrong job doesn't usually come until after you've been there for a while, which, in time, leads some to make a change."

Still others have grown tired of the threat to financial and career security that decades of downsizing have brought. Many have sought refuge in entrepreneurship or family matters. Meanwhile, technology has created new possibilities and careers that were only imagined five years ago, and has opened a door to new vocational possibilities, says Gonyea.

Stress, a major reason for discontent in the workplace, costs employers an estimated $150-to-$200 billion annually, according to the Society for Human Resource Management, located in Alexandria, Virginia. In response, more companies are recognizing that employees are more productive if they are given a chance to periodically take time off to focus on personal priorities.

As a result, sabbaticals are becoming popular. They allow employees time to reflect on their careers and the overall operation of the business, away from the daily pressures of the office. With a three-, six-, or 12-month leave, employees get a break from job stress, and employers get workers who return refreshed and ready to go.

SPOT THE SIGNS

How do you know when it's time to make a change? Gonyea offers 10 common road signs for your feelings or ongoing situation:

1. Bored and unchallenged.
2. Demeaned and dehumanized.
3. Given assignments well beyond your capabilities.
4. An outcast with no bridge to coworkers.
5. Burned out from emotionally exhausting work.
6. Seriously and consistently underpaid.
7. Extensively overqualified.
8. Unrecognized or unrewarded for your labor.
9. Expectations, from your boss, that are unrealistic or overly demanding.
10. Little room for personal or professional growth.

If most of these points apply to you, a change may be in order.

DEVISE A GAME PLAN

The good news is: Making a change is possible. The bad news is: It isn't easy. There is clearly some risk; few people can shift career gears on a whim and be successful. Therefore, you must develop a strategy. Whatever you choose to do, part of your game plan must involve getting your finances in order. That may mean paying off all debt, building a nest egg to last you six months to a year, and curtailing expenses. If you're worrying about paying the rent, it's hard to focus on your dreams. Your survival needs cannot dominate your long-term goals.

Look inside yourself to be sure of what you want. Preparing the groundwork entails headwork, legwork, and paperwork. You must decide on the specifics of your leave and do some in-depth research into its costs, benefits, and personal and professional feasibility. All in all, consider these goals when negotiating with yourself:

- Determine how much time you want off.
- Establish a budget and pay off any outstanding bills.
- Discuss your decision with family and friends who may be apprehensive of your motives.
- Set down objectives by asking yourself what you want to accomplish. Just because you are not in the office doesn't mean you're not working. You still need to have goals.

Profiled here are three individuals who made a conscious decision to leave their jobs and engage in more fulfilling pursuits. They pursued wildly divergent paths, but all the subjects agree that making the switch was one of their best decisions ever.

The Drive to Teach

Terry Caliste[20] walked into the math department at Southern University in 1980 with every intention of dropping out of school. Two years in the Air Force and four years as general manager of several fast food restaurants should have prepared him for many of life's challenges, but after being scorched by a failed algebra test, the 23-year-old wanted out. "You're not dropping out!" shot back Dr. Myrtle Smith, the department chairperson. "It was the symbolic kick in the butt I needed," recalls Caliste whose necktie of choice is peppered with algebraic problems. "She taught me how to acquire knowledge, and built my confidence in a subject that was intimidating." In a dramatic turn of events, Caliste fell in love with math and ended up tutoring others. In three years, he graduated—with honors—with a major in mathematics and a minor in computer science.

Two successful college internships at AT&T Bell Laboratories (which later included Bell Communications Research and NYNEX) in

Holmdel, New Jersey, opened the doors to a job in quality assurance in 1983. Caliste, who is extremely analytical, was quickly targeted for the management fast track. AT&T sent him to Iowa State University, where he earned a master's degree in statistics. By 1986, Caliste was troubleshooting problems in technology projects and conducting quality audits and inspections for clients such as MCI and Simi Valley high-tech companies.

Nonetheless, Caliste, a high-spirited man with a contagious smile, missed seeing the familiar light that went on the moment a student grasped a difficult math concept. He longed to pursue his dream of teaching. "I thought that if I didn't leave now, I would be stuck. I was taking risks for these people every day. I wanted to take a risk for me and my family." So, in 1992, after nine years as a technical statistician, he "retired" with a $30,000 buyout, nine months' severance pay, and modest savings. For his family it meant a lot of belt tightening. "I was humble enough to take some great steps back, financially—we ate a lot of beans," jokes Caliste, who loves the Creole cooking of New Orleans, his hometown.

However, his mother was horrified, and friends thought Caliste was crazy to leave the security of a $60,000 job and put his family in jeopardy to work as an adjunct math teacher. His combined salary from two local colleges and private tutoring classes totaled $25,000 a year at best.

He was happy teaching, but the classroom allowed Caliste to reach only 20 or 30 students at a time. He wanted a larger audience. In 1993, with just a blackboard, some chalk, and loads of enthusiasm, Caliste launched his company, Knowledge Base, in Red Bank, New Jersey. He conducted math seminars and workshops in schools across the country, and soon launched the show "Knowledge Base" on New Jersey public access television.

His income slowly increased, yet Caliste began to feel as though he had run his course. "I had reached the curve that made me a man in this business. I cried some nights about the sacrifice I had made, and reached a point where most people bail out." His only inspiration was the 60 to 70 phone calls and hundreds of letters he received each week from thankful parents. They made him press on.

Knowledge Base won a Cable Television Network Award in 1995 and was recognized as the number-one public-access show in New Jersey. Called the "Pied Piper of Math," Caliste developed in 1995, a four-part video series, *Mind Over Math,* which provides problem-solving strategies and techniques to help increase standardized test scores.

"To the kids, I'm entertainment, but when I say 'SAT scores,' Mom and Dad listen because then I'm talking about their child's future," states Caliste, adding that the SAT scores of hundreds of his "students" have increased by more than 75 points. "Math is a universal subject that transcends all races and people. By making it uncomplicated, I knew I could offer something to everyone."

Stay-at-Home Mom

"Take a piece of candy for you and one for your brother," says Janice Glenn Kershaw[21] to her son, Matthew. To a five-year-old, the number one is relative. Clack! Clack! Onto the floor go the brightly wrapped hard candies that won't fit in Matthew's tiny hand. Mom gently coaxes her son to surrender half of his bounty. Content with four, Matthew scurries off to share them with his three-year-old brother, Philip.

Kershaw knew such negotiation skills would be par for the course when she left her job at a major Washington, DC, university in 1991. Matthew was four months old when she returned to work. The former associate director of Affirmative Action asked her boss for a flexible work schedule so she could have more time at home. Her job, which entailed investigating complaints and developing training programs, "didn't require me to be in the office every day. I wanted to arrange to work at home two or three days a week," recalls the Upper Marlboro, Maryland, resident. Her request was denied.

She had a long discussion with her husband, John an Air Force pilot at the time and now a Lieutenant Colonel and military aide to the Assistant Secretary of Defense at the Pentagon. Before Matthew's birth, they had considered all possible child care options, including a nanny, but at more than $1,000 a month, hiring one was unrealistic. Kershaw was uncomfortable with home-care providers, afraid that they wouldn't be able to give individualized attention because they are allowed to care for up to six children at a time in the state of Maryland, and day care centers could not give the Kershaws the attention and environment they wanted for their son. The decision was easy: the best person to care for their young son was his mother. Her aunt baby-sat for seven weeks before Kershaw walked away from a job that paid in the mid-$40,000 range. The family income was severed almost in half.

"We quickly realized that life as we knew it was over," says Kershaw. "We were prepared to downsize." With solid long- and short-term investments, low debt, and some money in the bank, the Kershaws hunkered down for the long haul: limited dinners out, less travel, cloth diaper service, breast-feeding, and homemade baby food. Her sisters, both teachers, contributed generously to the over-300 children's books the boys have. A box full of outfits would arrive "every so often" from Kershaw's mother.

Kershaw dispels the myth that working in the home means not working at all. Since her husband's transfer from Albuquerque, New Mexico, to Andrews Air Force Base in Maryland, in 1989, Kershaw has been quite busy. Today, her days are spent keeping her sons occupied with educational activities and art projects, and getting Matthew ready for preschool before embarking on her daily errands. It's not uncommon for Kershaw and the boys to visit her husband at work for lunch or dinner.

Her home is regularly filled with preschoolers. No stickler about territory, Kershaw says her entire home is for her children. Any doubts? One need only to take notice of the drawing pad and easel that hold permanent residence in the breakfast nook, next to the miniature kitchen set. On special occasions, such as birthday parties, "weed and mud soup," made by Philip, can sometimes be found in the backyard.

To maintain her skills and stay in the loop, Kershaw stays in touch with old colleagues. "I keep up with trends and let them know how I've been keeping my resume 'warm.'" One way that she has been keeping it warm is by consulting various organizations on human resources issues. For her, one of the biggest challenges is that "people don't feel they have to pay you what you're worth because you are not in the workforce," notes this graduate of Winthrop University in Rock Hill, South Carolina, who has a master's degree in public administration from New York University. Eventually, when her sons are in school full-time, Kershaw would like to either work in an organization that supports the family or start her own business.

"Some women say they wish they could afford to make the decision to stay home. Others never tire of asking me when am I going back to work," says Kershaw. But affordability is relative for this mother who takes seriously the raising of two African American males in this society. "We can never afford it all," she says, "but I can afford the value of my time and the impact it will have on the lives of my children."

A Sports Dream

When Charles Howard,[22] fresh out of Southern Methodist University Law School, took a job with Sun Oil in 1978, he planned to stay two years—max. Afterward, he planned to pursue his real interest: criminal law. But two years turned into five, and eight years later, Howard was still drafting agreements and exploration leases.

In 1986, the former track star dislocated his kneecap while playing basketball and was sidelined for a month. It gave him a lot of time to think about his life. "If I was going to make a move, I had to do it then," recalls Howard. "I wasn't sure what I wanted to do, but I knew my job wasn't giving me what I needed." Soon after returning to work, Howard paid off some bills and cashed in his company stock options. With six months' salary in the bank, he said good-bye to his $49,000-a-year job.

He "enjoyed life" for the next six months. When he wasn't going to the gym or riding his bike, he was traveling throughout the United States, Mexico, or the Caribbean. However, his physical and spiritual retreat was periodically interrupted by a Greek chorus of friends and family. "They would say, 'Don't you think it's time to go back to work?' They were afraid I would start to drift," says the Dallas native. But even Howard had to admit he was becoming bored. "The experience was great, but I soon realized that what we do in our jobs helps to define who we are. I felt as though I was losing my identity," he recalls. Even socializing was met with trepidation as he tried to avoid the most commonly asked icebreaker, "What do you *do?*"

Soon after, he began working part-time as a court-appointed attorney, living out his dream of practicing criminal law—or so he thought. It paid the bills, but the personal fulfillment he yearned for was absent. Reluctantly, he decided to go back to corporate America. By January 1987, the oil industry had taken a plunge. The arena he thought he could always return to had dried up and offered few opportunities. His anxiety began to mount as his job hunt dragged on longer than he had expected. Howard wondered if he had done the right thing in leaving. A year after breaking with Sun Oil, he joined Hexter-Fair, a now-defunct

Dallas real estate firm, as a staff attorney. Two years later, Howard was disillusioned with corporate America—once again.

A magazine ad for a sports management program at Kent State turned his life around. In May 1990, Howard packed up and headed to Ohio for the one-year master's program. He had finally found his calling. On a full scholarship, Howard lived off of savings and the $500-a-month stipend he received as a graduate assistant. He interned with the National Collegiate Athletic Association (NCAA) in Kansas for a year. A professor suggested he consider college athletics and, in 1991, he took a job with his alma mater as assistant athletic director in charge of compliance. "I love it!" says Howard, who combines his love of sports with law by ensuring that the university, its athletes, and coaches comply with NCAA rules.

"I could have made more money in the legal arena, but personal happiness is more important," says Howard of his $52,000-a-year job. "I'm willing to sacrifice some income for peace of mind. But you never know unless you take a chance."

THE INTRIGUE OF INTERNATIONAL ASSIGNMENTS

If you're prepared, career advancement, leadership opportunity, and a diversified experience can be yours. In 1994, when Belinda Miller[23] embarked on a two-year assignment as director of human resources for Swissotel Beijing, she envisioned an alluring experience awaiting her in a country rich with history and culture. For the most part, that proved to be true, but her international sojourn was not without a few bumps.

Miller, a Norfolk, Virginia, native, was shocked one day by the re-action of a Chinese employee to a piece of innocent advice that she had given. "I calmly explained to her how she could have handled a partic-ular situation better. She became extremely upset and started crying," recalls Miller, whom hotel employees respectfully call *loaban*, or boss.

Although Miller had spoken to the woman as she would to any American employee, she quickly learned to use a subtle, more Socratic approach. "I had to phrase things differently, such as 'Have you thought about what is the most effective way to perform this task?'" It was a les-son she would not soon forget.

Being sensitive to cultural differences and nuances is just one as-pect of an overseas assignment. Today, recognition of those differences is crucial, now that more and more companies target fast-growing foreign markets while requiring their managers and executives to have international experience.

Many of those who work abroad, like Miller, see an international assignment as an exciting, rewarding, sometimes even glamorous career move. Still, gaining those newfound business and management skills may come as a culture shock for the uninitiated. It can also mean a loss for any company that doesn't utilize the skills of these wayfaring employees upon their return.

PREPARING FOR THE JOURNEY

Three factors are necessary for a successful assignment overseas, says Martin F. Bennett,[24] senior partner at Bennett Associates, a cross-cultural and global management training firm in Chicago:

1. Evaluate whether an international assignment is right for you.
2. Get cross-cultural training.
3. Utilize and apply those skills after your return.

The employee and the company must be clear on the reasons why the assignment is being undertaken, and what is expected. It's also important to determine how an international experience fits into your lifestyle and career plans, emphasizes Bennett. The successful expatriate is an open-minded, flexible individual—someone willing to take risks. More than just professional and technical skills are needed to thrive. An ability to adapt to different cultures is essential.

That's where cross-cultural training is important. Yet, despite an increase in the number of their overseas assignments, many U.S. firms don't provide employees with cultural and language education. A recent study conducted by Runzheimer International, a Rochester, Wisconsin, management consulting firm, found that only 42 percent of the 54 multinational companies polled had any formal training program for acculturating expatriates with their host country.

Even employees who are independent and well traveled should get some form of cultural or language training before departing, according to Bennett. For example, some expatriates may expect America's strong work ethic to cross all borders. As a result, they may misinterpret a more relaxed attitude toward work—seen, for example, in many European countries—as laziness. "The key to global competency is to develop the skills to cope, and that means integrating into the dominant culture and realizing how to properly interpret and analyze behavior," says Bennett.

Reading the Signs

Belinda Miller certainly had her job cut out for her in China, the leading destination for international assignments among emerging countries. The Wharton School of Business graduate landed the job of recruiting, training, and managing employees—a job traditionally held by ethnic Chinese—quite by accident.

In 1991, Miller was wooed away from her job (director of travelers' cheques marketing at American Express) by the Swiss hotel firm. Working as a marketing adviser at Swissotel locations throughout the United States, Europe, and Asia, she was assigned to China for a six-month stint in 1994. Her mission: to develop strategies to increase hotel revenues and make the five-star Swissotel Beijing attractive to international travelers. Her ideas were so impressive that, after five months, she was asked to stay and implement them. With a $1.5 million annual budget, one of Miller's main areas of focus was to train the property's more than 1,000 employees, most of whom were Chinese, in the art of first-class customer service.

Despite having worked in Turkey, Amsterdam, Zurich, Düsseldorf, and Seoul, Miller was surprised by the cultural differences in China. In a country where people are fed information, memorize it without question, and don't take well to criticism, "I had to learn not to be too direct with my employees," she recalls. Miller, who didn't start taking formal language classes until she was nine months into her assignment, says that learning the semantics of the language gave her important clues about the culture. "The Mandarin word for 'question' is the same word for 'problem.' Knowing that helped me better understand that people who ask too many questions, or are too challenging, are viewed negatively."

In retrospect, Miller says that while she could have benefited from some form of cross-cultural training, she has no regrets. Her naïveté led her to attend certain social events and to personally recruit from the area's vocational schools—functions normally attended only by native Chinese. These forays—however accidental—gained her a high degree of popularity among her colleagues and showed her respect for the culture.

LEAVING FAMILY BEHIND

International assignments hold tremendous appeal for the young and single, but they can be quite daunting for those who are married and have children. Still, an offer, from New Orleans-based Doley Securities, to become a market maker on the Johannesburg Stock Exchange proved irresistible for Ralph Wright.[25] Consequently, Wright is now the only African American trader on the floor.

Nonetheless, taking the job was a hard decision for the Marlboro, New Jersey, resident and his close-knit family. With an 18-year-old son in college and another son, 24, in the workforce, the separation proved to be a painful, albeit educational experience for all. "Initially, my sons thought life would be great with their parents away, but they eventually missed having us to come to for advice." Wright and his wife Sallie, a homemaker, telephone their sons at least twice a week, and a bevy of aunts, uncles, and neighbors check on them periodically.

Family obligations are the number-one reason that many overseas assignments are refused. Taking into consideration the toll on loved ones is crucial, particularly when young children must be relocated or spend long periods of time away from one or both parents.

MAKING ENDS MORE THAN MEET

An international assignment doesn't always involve an increase in salary, but it may still mean reaching a higher rung on the economic ladder, depending on where you live. After allowing for taxes, Belinda Miller's salary is comparable to the $90,000 she earned while working with Swissotel in New York. Her expenses, including meals, laundry, and living accommodations, are covered by her employer.

Most firms give cost-of-living stipends, along with lucrative leaves and vacations. Miller, who works six days a week, gets about two weeks off a year, plus an 18-day vacation. Her company foots the bill for her trips home once a year.

ON THE REBOUND

Many companies claim to be committed to globalization, but most don't take advantage of—or can't quantify—their returning employees' newly acquired skills, especially their flexibility, diversity management, and interpersonal growth. As a result, many expatriates remain on the international circuit for much of their careers, or they start their own businesses. In fact, 20 to 48 percent of expatriates leave their companies within the first year after they return from an international assignment, says Martin Bennett.

In a *Business Horizons*[26] survey of 135 repatriated employees, only 39 percent felt their firm was using their newly acquired skills; a meager 29 percent claimed that the assignments helped their careers. Bennett says such post-repatriation dissent occurs because goals were not discussed before commencing the assignment, and most employers fail to properly reacclimatize their world travelers.

On the flip side, many employees who have been on overseas assignments assume that they are special or "chosen ones," and expect to be treated as such when they return, warns Bennett. "Instead, they come back and move right back where they were." With international assignments becoming more commonplace, few companies are suggesting that any career advancement is granted for taking one. Still, the rewards can be significant.

Many African Americans say that international assignments have gained them the promotion they otherwise would not have had. For others, it's a way to escape the sometimes blatant, often subtle, racism and sexism they experience here at home. Bennett recalls how one black senior executive, on assignment in China, remarked that "for the first time in his life he felt that his success was based 100 percent on his efforts and not on EEO."

Many white employees get their first taste of racism when they go overseas. Particularly if they are sent to countries where they are the minority, says Bennett, they realize what minorities have been going through for years. Frequently, they then become active in the diversity efforts of their operators.

For those, like Miller, returning home can be tinged with melancholy. "In China, I was a big fish in a small pond, looked at as an expert in my field, but when I returned, I lost that 'star' status," Miller laments. Yet, she adds, the knowledge she imparted will reap immeasurable benefits for her Chinese employees. Those benefits also await African Americans willing to join the fray. Many agree that overseas experience can neither be matched nor outdone at home. And once undertaken, the rewards tend to far outweigh the losses—especially now that the once impenetrable borders surrounding the burgeoning global marketplace are slowly dissolving.

FIVE WAYS TO GET ON THE INTERNATIONAL CAREER TRACK NOW

1. Attend courses or conferences that focus on the international aspects of your field. Join professional operators that have international arms, such as the National Black MBA's Association or the Society of Human Resource Management.
2. Ask a colleague who has returned from abroad, or one currently on international assignment, to mentor you.
3. Rework your resume to reflect your cultural experience. List the languages you speak and any international travel you have done. Volunteer for projects or assignments that will give you international insight or exposure.
4. Take courses in the language of the country you wish to venture to. If you're not sure of the country you'll be heading to, learn a language that piques your interest.
5. Consider pursuing a master's degree in international affairs, business, or management. Your firm might even finance your tuition. Some schools offering international curriculums are:
   American Graduate School of International Management (Thunderbird), Glendale, AZ.
   Cornell University, Ithaca, NY.
   Georgetown University, Washington, DC.
   Monterey Institute of International Studies, Monterey, CA.
   University of Southern California, Los Angeles, CA.
   Florida State University, Tallahassee, FL.

REFERENCES

International Jobs: Where They Are and How to Get Them (Fourth Edition) by Eric Kocher (Addison-Wesley).

Competitive Frontiers: Women Managers in a Global Economy by Nancy J. Adler and Dafna N. Izraeli (Eds.) (Blackwell Publishers).

Kiss, Bow, or Shake Hands: How to Do Business in Sixty Countries by Terri Morrison, Wayne A. Conaway, and George A. Borden, Ph.D. (Adams).

Global Assignments: Successfully Expatriating and Repatriating International Managers by J. Stewart Black, Hall B. Gregersen, and Mark E. Mendenhall (Jossey-Bass).

GET THE MOST OUT OF TEAMWORK AND TEAM-BASED PAY

As companies seek to empower employees, work teams have fast become the latest management trend. This has given rise to variable pay systems such as "team-based pay," which awards raises, bonuses, and incentives based on team performance.

"It's certainly an idea whose time has come," says Robert L. Heneman,[27] director of the Consortium for Alternative Reward Strategies at the Fisher College of Business at Ohio State University in Columbus. "But it hasn't gotten off the ground yet," he adds, "because some employees 'ride along' with a team, letting the more talented and motivated people do the work."

What happens next is that the "stars" suffer because team performance is undermined, and, as a result, everyone's paycheck is jeopardized. "Society," Heneman adds, "is conditioned to be rewarded for individual accomplishment; therefore the concept of pay being linked to group performance is hard for many individuals to grasp." Heneman offers these tips for increasing team members' accountability and ensuring the best compensation for all:

- *Be informed.* Ask your boss how he or she defines a good team player and what factors go into determining team compensation.
- *Peer pressure.* Confront those team members who are "social loafers." Describe their faults in concrete, behavioral terms. For

example, "You're always coming to meetings late and you're never prepared. You need to start pulling your weight."

- *Be observant.* From the synchronization of an orchestra to the synergy of an emergency room medical team, examples of teamwork abound. Watch other teams, read management books, and help your team members model their finer points.

Q: My boss constantly asks me to complete assignments in unrealistic time frames. I'm afraid that if I complain, I would jeopardize my performance rating and future growth. What can I do?

A: Your boss may not have the same perspective as you do regarding the deadlines she sets. "If you believe the deadline is unreasonable, prepare to negotiate," says Robert Davis,[28] author of *Implement Now, Perfect Later* (Robert Davis Associates). Successful negotiation on deadlines begins when all parties involved take a realistic look at the amount of time available and required to complete an assignment. Davis suggests developing a list of the steps you must take to complete an assignment, and making a fair estimate of the time required to complete each step. Prepare a flow chart to compare available time to the time required, and share the chart with your boss.

Be prepared to present alternative ideas that involve either adding resources to complete the work faster, or eliminating steps to cut down on the time required. Presenting the flow chart to your boss will ensure that the two of you have a common understanding of the work required to get the job done.

"But don't offer all your strategies up front. Save at least one. If your boss is not receptive, be prepared with some other choice," says Davis. "The key to negotiations is not taking 'no' for an answer and being persistent."

In uncertain economic times, when layoffs become the norm, staying informed without overwhelming yourself with the fear of what might happen is important. So is empowering yourself with the skills necessary and a good solid awareness of where you are on your career path and where you would like to go next. Remember that you cannot completely control whether you will land the dream job or if the job you have today will still be yours tomorrow. You can keep your ear to the ground, your skills at the ready, and reestablish faith in yourself and your abilities, which is the best possible insurance.

11

SUCCEEDING AT WORK

BUILDING YOUR CORPORATE FOUNDATION: WHAT YOU SHOULD KNOW TO CREATE YOUR CORPORATE IMAGE

You've landed a promotion or broken a sales record, but who knows about it? Interoffice memos and informal company announcements may inform colleagues within your organization, but getting your name out among your peers and in the forefront of your industry creates a vital career tool.

"Visibility is a very valued existence," says Randolph W. Cameron,[1] president of Cameron Enterprises, a New York-based management consulting firm. "You must strategically create your own corporate image if you're looking to advance in your career," he advises.

"Overlay an image of responsibility with an image of reliability and knowledge," suggests Cameron, whose book, *The Minority Executives' Handbook* (Amistad Press), has been revised and is available in paperback. "Take steps to build on those blocks," he adds. "It may mean doing grunt work, but in order to lay the proper foundation, you need to market this image." But what if your corporate image is tarnished? You don't have to live behind that cloak forever. If people have lost trust in you, you can do things to change your image. "All executives will have some failures," says Cameron. A failure should be taken as a learning experience.

"You must be offensive, not defensive," Cameron explains. Seek out and volunteer for projects that will put you in a better light. "Your intent is to wipe out the past stigmas," he says. "Make sure you do it in arenas where your critics and people who matter will notice." Your corporate image matters, both inside and outside your organization. One of the first steps that public relations firms advise for executives is: Get involved with trade associations. When you find an association that reflects the kind of image you want to be identified with, take advantage of opportunities to hold a position of leadership in that organization.

"We tell executives to try to be a speaker on a trade association panel, and to write articles for their company newsletters and trade publications," says Judith H. Sussman,[2] executive vice president and general manager of Pezzano+Company. But Cameron cautions against joining too many groups. "Don't become a corporate social responsibility butterfly." Moving from one volunteer organization to another gives the appearance that you are everywhere but in the office conducting company business.

When you are "overexposed" in the corporate world, adds Cameron, your business associates tend not to take you very seriously. If you're always out of the office, how serious is your commitment to your profession?

SHOW WHAT YOU'RE WORTH: DEMONSTRATE HOW YOU AFFECT THE BOTTOM LINE

To succeed in today's workplace, you must often lead a double life: being a team player and still standing out from your coworkers. The only way to really set yourself apart is to show proven results. Now, more than ever, you must act like an "internal consultant" for the company. Professionals who can adapt their functions to the changing role of an internal consultant are proving their contributions to their companies' operation and bottom line. To become an internal consultant, you must:

- *Know your company's goals.* Be familiar with what your company does and how it does it. Build a network of leads, both inside and outside your firm, so you can better understand how it competes in the marketplace.

- *Think strategically.* Tie your expertise to corporate strategy and the needs of your clients. Find out what keeps line managers— those with bottom-line responsibility—awake at night, and offer solutions.

- *Be flexible.* Enhance your listening skills and create partnerships with other employees. If you're an information systems professional, for example, avoid creating even more sophisticated software applications when users are having trouble with the present system. Instead, offer hands-on training to help users become more effective with what they have.

- *Demonstrate a bottom-line impact.* Link your recommendations to your company's strategies and initiatives. Learn the financial reporting system, and get involved in the budgeting process. Once you can talk about finances, emphasize how you can add value to the company rather than focusing only on cost.

SUCCESSION PLANNING: THE KEY TO A SMOOTH TRANSITION

James D. Brown's[3] promotion at the Guardian Life Insurance Company of America, in New York, was a picture-perfect transition. A senior financial executive had left, enabling Brown, then manager of tax accounting, to become director of financial analysis—a natural chain of events in the company's employee succession plan.

In some organizations, an employee's departure creates havoc until a replacement is found. But, at Guardian Life, "Six people were promoted as various managerial and executive slots were filled," says Brown, president of the Northeast Region, and Director of the National Association of Black Accountants. Even more impressive, those who were promoted trained their respective successors for the next four months while still carrying out their new roles. Had Guardian not had a succession plan in place, things might not have been so smooth.

When companies restructure for downsizing, a formal employee succession plan is critical. Companies must identify and develop existing talented employees who can take over when key employees leave, are promoted, or take extended leaves of absence. Used effectively, a formal succession plan or program maintains productivity and ensures that your customers continue to receive quality sales and services.

The majority of firms have formal succession plans, but most small and midsize companies don't. If your company has no succession plan, you can still ensure that your department will continue to operate smoothly after you're gone. First, assess your staff to determine who would be the best person for the job. "Managers should also evaluate their own biases to ensure they are assessing *all* qualified people in their department," says Joan Burnett,[4] principal of Path Ways International, an executive recruitment firm in Windsor, Connecticut. "If you are not thoroughly acquainted with your staff, a fair assessment is difficult and you might overlook some high-potential employees." Other factors to consider as you choose your successor are:

- Target individuals who have the technical, leadership, and administrative skills/competencies required for the job. Don't look only at those whom you like or know well.

- Ask yourself: How does this person interact with coworkers? The candidate should possess good interpersonal skills and be able to effectively lead and motivate people. "The higher you go up the corporate ladder, the more influential you have to be," adds Burnett.

- Talk to the potential successor. Let him or her know about your recommendation for the job. More importantly, find out if he or she is interested in the position.

- Give your chosen successor increased responsibilities. This will keep him or her from competing with you or possibly looking for advancement elsewhere.

- Set up a career development plan. Send your hand-picked successor to executive education or management training classes. He or she should be ready to fill your shoes quickly and with minimal guidance.

- Discuss with your successor your department's long-range plans and seek his or her feedback. Sharing decision making early will make the eventual transition easier.

- Don't set someone up for failure. Coach your chosen successor along the way, and provide the necessary support. "That person may never get another opportunity if they fail," says Burnett, "Not only do they lose, but so do you."

- Keep in mind that you may be judged by how your department functions without you. If your heir apparent fails, it may be assumed that he or she inherited a problem you created.

Q: I left my old company last year for a job at another firm. Now they've asked me to come back. What do I do?

A: Downsizing and restructuring have left some companies talent-starved. A growing number of executives are being asked back by former employers, sometimes as consultants, says Joseph Dickerson,[5] principal of Penn Associates, an executive search and recruitment firm in Philadelphia.

"Firms often do extensive searches for candidates who meet the skill levels, but with whom they are not comfortable," explains Dickerson. They may then consider a former employee. "The advantage is that you know the environment and the company knows you," he says.

If you get such an offer, assess thoughtfully the reasons why you left in the first place. Will your contributions be valued? "The job should offer a better work environment, growth, and security," he notes. "You and your employer should lay out a very clear career path."

Realize that you can never truly "go back." Things will be different. If you've been away 10 to 12 months, there may be new faces, and you, too, will bring new skills and experiences.

If the problems that coaxed you out the door the first time still exist, warns Dickerson, chances are you'll leave again.

Q: I feel under attack at work and have lost the full support of my staff. I think my job might be on the line. How do I avert a disaster?

A: What you must do is regain the rhythm and flow of work within your department. "Nothing should happen in and around your territory that you're not aware of," says Randolph W. Cameron. To get back that control, Cameron advises managers to:

- Check and recheck important assignments to reduce the margin of error.
- Network vertically and horizontally.

- When delegating work assignments, use reliable subordinates who can get the job done right.
- Spend time with the operational people, or people in the field who impact your bottom line.
- Be sure to have all paperwork in order. Reports, budgets, and forecasts should be done well and on time.
- Read everything that comes across your desk.
- Most importantly, he says, "Find ways to help motivate your people without stressful tactics, and don't forget to reward those who support you in times of trouble."

"IT'S NOT MY JOB."

"It's not my job."
"I'm so busy, I forgot."
"I just work here; I'm not paid to make decisions."

These are just a few of the excuses that cloud the workplace and drain companies of valuable time and profit.

If left unmanaged, excuses can grow into an iceberg—a visible tip of a host of larger problems below the surface. These problems can include pessimism, procrastination, and feelings of victimization that may later spill over into staff conflicts, communication gaps, and excessive absenteeism.

Excuse making is natural and common. "Most excuses exist in the workplace because companies tend to operate out of a personality of fear. Employees are afraid to admit that they are wrong, for fear of being viewed as failures."

To avoid negative consequences, employees try to rationalize their behavior. Companies can rid themselves of excuses if failing is viewed as a positive learning experience. Some suggestions:

- Discuss with your boss or colleagues all the things that can go wrong with a project before it's undertaken. Determine what should be done if these problems arise.
- Level the playing field on employees' appraisals. Try 360-degree evaluations, which judge employees by the opinions of colleagues as well as superiors. Set a target date for your organization to be excuse-free.

- Ask job candidates questions that measure their accountability. This will clue you in as to whether they are responsible and results-oriented, or are excuse makers.

BE FRANK, BUT CONSTRUCTIVE, ON 360-DEGREE APPRAISALS

The tables have finally turned. You've been asked to rate your boss's performance in a 360-degree evaluation, and you raise your pen, poised for retaliation. But before delivering that *coup de grâce*, consider this: Being constructive, not destructive, may create a whole new boss for the liking.

Over the past decade, more companies have embraced 360-degree evaluations, which allow employees to evaluate their own performance while receiving feedback from direct managers, peers, subordinates, and those in other departments. "These evaluations are designed to help the employee develop and advance professionally," says Jean Maye, president of VJM Associates, an organizational development consulting firm in Jersey City, New Jersey. "But they're also confrontational and force the persons being evaluated to take a hard look at how their behavior is perceived." To ensure that your feedback is constructive, Maye offers these tips:

- *It's not personal.* Make your evaluation concise, professional, and directly linked to your superior's work performance. Also, stick to the time frame in question. Don't rehash incidents of days gone by.
- *Word it right. Say it nicely.* "Ed needs to be more of a team player on projects" is better than "Ed just doesn't get along with anybody." Or, "Ellen can benefit from enhancing her interpersonal style" rather than "Ellen always has an attitude."
- *Shh!* These evaluations are anonymous and confidential, so avoid referring to specific incidents that will link you to your responses. This isn't a "water cooler" discussion, and sharing your answers will relinquish your anonymity.
- *What should you do if confronted?* Simply remind your boss that the evaluation is confidential, and suggest that he or she focus on the total feedback and not individual responses. "This isn't a gripe session," adds Maye. "Being an evaluator should make

you assess your own behavior. Who knows? One day, you too might be on the receiving end."

FLEX SCHEDULES, JOB-SHARING, TELECOMMUTING: WHAT'S IT ALL ABOUT?

Welcome to the twenty-first-century workplace. *Workplace* is actually a misnomer because now it's not one place; it's anywhere there's a telephone and a modem. If you're fortunate enough to work for a company that offers flexible work arrangements, you know that may mean job-sharing, telecommuting one to five days a week, a compressed workweek, or flexible hours in the course of a day. No matter what your company calls it, this new approach allows you to spend less time in the office while, hopefully, getting the same, or more, work done. The lack of, or limited, commuting; fewer hours or days spent in a chaotic or demanding office; shared job responsibilities— these are perceived to allow individuals to have a better quality of work life, less stress, and an environment that allows them to be equally, if not more, productive.

If you're job-sharing, you have found a colleague with whom you can share a five-day workweek. More than likely, you both work in the same department and have similar duties, but you split the week or the day in half—one of you works in the morning, and the other works in the evening. With a compressed workweek, you may be at the office as long as 10 or 12 hours for three to four days, and be off the rest of the week. If you already work 12 hours a day, minus the free day, perhaps telecommuting one or two days a week, without the interruptions so characteristic of office environments, will allow you to be more productive. As a telecommuter, you sign in from a home computer that has been configured to handle programs used at the office, and you rely heavily on e-mail and the telephone to get your work done. Flexible work hours might allow you to change the hours you work each day. Instead of working from 9:00 A.M. to 5:00 P.M., you might work from 7:00 A.M. to 3:00 P.M., or from 10:00 A.M. to 6:00 P.M., depending on your duties. All in all, these options can improve your quality of work and even your personal life.

Your company might offer flexible work schedule seminars monthly, posters in the cafeteria and other common areas, and repeated interoffice e-mails that coax and invite employees to take advantage of a flexible schedule. So why is no one beating down the human resources manager's door? Despite how sophisticated and open some traditional organizations say they are, not being in the office every day is viewed as a career derailer.

Flexible schedules were once scoffed at by bosses who thought their employees were goofing off. Some coworkers felt a sting of favoritism. Employees dreamed of a flex schedule but were afraid to ask for one, for fear of being viewed as a slacker or missing out on promotion opportunities because of their diminished visibility.

Most of the first pioneers in flexible work schedules were working mothers. When the boom in dot-coms arrived, everyone—from company presidents to 22-year-old computer engineers—had some form of flexible work arrangements. Some companies are even encouraging flexible work arrangements, not only to retain employees by offering schedule alternatives, but also to meet some important business factors. For example, in metropolitan areas like New York, office space is at a premium. It costs hundreds of dollars per square foot for midtown office space. If more people work at home, less office space is needed, and expenses are lower. Companies also want to be seen as good corporate citizens who offer a place people are clamoring to work at because of its accommodating work arrangements.

Conversely, some bosses, particularly those being pulled kicking and screaming out of the industrial age and into the information age, may have difficulty with flexible work arrangements or be against them totally. There is a tendency for your counterparts who trek into the office each day to think that you're on vacation two days a week. Natural responses when someone is granted a telecommuting or flex schedule may be: "When did that happen?" "How did they get that?" "Why do they get to work from home?" Some companies keep flex arrangements quiet, to avoid a stampede of potential telecommuters into the human resources office. When someone is granted a flexible work schedule, that announcement is made discreetly—and, usually, just as that person's computer is being hauled off to his or her home.

When you're conducting conference calls from the comfort of your living room, or you're out with your children two days a week scot-free, what happens to your career? Is it out of sight/out of mind when it comes time for a promotion? If you do the right thing, the answer is *no*.

Telecommuting requires trust. Your boss has to trust that you're working, and you have to trust that the company hasn't forgotten about you when it comes time for promotions and new assignments.

Unfortunately, that old "face time" routine, where people have to be at work every day at the requisite time so that their boss can "see" them working, is alive and kicking. Therefore, be sensitive to your coveted, often envied position and don't let yourself fade into oblivion. Don't let this be a typical conversation at the water cooler:

"Hey, did you hear that Susan had a baby girl?"

"Who's Susan?"

You must stay in the loop. Keep your boss and coworkers well informed and update them regularly through e-mail and telephone calls.

- *Keep in touch.* This is not your opportunity to sneak into oblivion. With pagers, cell phones, e-mail, and two-ways around any corner, you cannot just disappear. You should be accessible within a short, usually fixed, period of time during your flex days. In fact, before most flex schedules are granted, there is usually a lengthy proposal that must involve you, your boss, and a human resources representative. You will be required to show how you can get your work done away from the office and how your absence will not have a negative impact on the business operations. It would also help to periodically review your career development plan with your superior, to ensure that you are still on track.

- *Keep up.* Return phone calls right away, and be available at the time someone says he or she will call. For every phone call that is not picked up or returned in a timely manner, someone is thinking you're out on your sun deck or at the gym, instead of working.

- *Have the right stuff.* Make sure you have the communication and work essentials. Your company can probably provide you with access to your company e-mail; it may also reimburse or support a computer, fax machine, printer, or Internet access. You need reliable equipment. Nothing is worse than having an important fax rejected, or a phone call missed, because of your

---

DID YOU KNOW?

Ray M. Robinson, President, Southern Region, AT&T, was relocated 11 times over the course of his 32 years with the company.—*Black Enterprise*, February 2000

CAREER AT A GLANCE—A MAJOR PRODUCTION

Occupation: TV news producer

Duties: Finds, preinterviews, and coordinates sources. Develops story ideas and ensures that shows run smoothly. Must be able to juggle multiple tasks under close deadlines. Frequent travel.

Salary range: $25,000 to $90,000

Training: College degree in journalism, communications, or media studies preferred. Entry-level experience usually as a news clerk, production assistant, and assistant producer. Internships at media outlets are a must.

For more information about a career as a news producer, contact: Producers Guild of America, 400 South Beverly Drive, Suite 211, Beverly Hills, CA 90212; 310-557-0807; or the National Association of Black Journalists, University of Maryland, 3100 Talafero Hall, College Park, MD 20742-7717; 301-405-8500; or e-mail: NABJ@jmail.umd.edu.

---

hardware. If it happens too frequently, it might lead your boss to reassess your telecommuting arrangement.

- *Don't move out totally.* If you have a five-day-a-week telecommuting or flex schedule, try to arrange some "face time." Arrange lunch dates with colleagues, or project reviews with key managers or executives; or come in for a meeting in lieu of a conference call.

RATHER FIGHT THAN SWITCH

Q: My new boss seems to be trying to push me out, but I don't want to leave. What should I do?

A: First, you must determine whether your boss is intentionally trying to derail your career or is merely implementing a new strategic process. If you are excluded from meetings you were once a part of, or your bottom-line responsibility has been usurped, it may be that new organizational changes are being put in place. Don't take the changes personally, but do defend your career.

CAREER AT A GLANCE—
SELLING MILLION-DOLLAR TURF

Occupation: Real estate broker

Job description: Helps clients buy or sell real estate. Manages price negotiations and devises marketing strategies. Must be sensitive to clients' needs and adapt to a fluctuating real estate market. Brokers, unlike agents, can own their own firms.

Salary range: $15,000 to over $100,000. Most work is done on commission, which ranges from 3 to 6 percent of a property's selling price.

Training: Hours of formal classroom training vary from state to state. Brokers must also undergo a series of examinations and log some experience before receiving their license.

"Tell your boss, in a nonthreatening way, that you're concerned about some of the new practices that are being instituted, and you feel that your position may be in question," advises Johnson. "Express that you want to be part of the process, and show where you can add value." If he or she is aloof and offers no logical reason for your exclusion, then perhaps your job is in jeopardy.

The next step is to go to a higher authority and discuss your future with the company. Follow up with a letter stating that you look forward to a prosperous relationship with the organization. In the event that you are terminated and you feel the discharge was wrongful, this letter will serve as legal documentation that you tried to salvage your job.

PERFORMANCE APPRAISAL ANXIETY

Despite their bad reputation, performance appraisals are important to everyone involved. After all, they allow you and your boss to assess the needs of your department and your contributions to it. Usually conducted annually, an effective appraisal will focus on your accomplishments, based on goals you and your boss agreed upon during a previous appraisal. It also includes a plan for your future development.

Whether you expect good or bad news, you have to be professional and flexible. Normally, a boss doesn't have it out with an employee or be vindictive. Concern centers on the productivity of the department and ensuring that your contribution meets the company's business objectives. Nonetheless, appraisals can be especially tough to endure. Even the most confident individuals shun criticism, even if it is constructive.

Keep in mind that you and your boss have certain responsibilities to each other. A manager must create an open environment and provide ongoing feedback and review. You should not be surprised by the outcome of your appraisal meeting. In turn, you need to be open-minded and receptive to the suggestions and advice offered for your career development. Determine your role in the company and the required duties of your job. Think of ways in which you can improve your performance, and ask for the tools that you'll need to do a better job. Make sure that you and your manager are on the same page. You may see your job one way, whereas he or she may see it differently.

HOW TO HANDLE RACIST REMARKS IN THE WORKPLACE

You'd like to believe that an air of equality and respect runs through the civilized corridors of the average work environment, but that is sometimes not the case. Racist behavior does rear its ugly head. But before you lash out unprofessionally or begin to harbor negative feelings about the person, your job, or even yourself, analyze the action. The person's seemingly racist behavior may very well be that individual's personality or style. Perhaps the person is sarcastic by nature—it may be how he or she acts around everyone. Maybe the person is overly assertive and dismissive of the ideas of others.

Do an internal audit and assess your strengths and weaknesses as well as those of your coworkers. Develop clear communication skills by listening and speaking clearly. Be aware of the corporate culture and how situations like this are handled. Not every culture is open to quelling these situations. A company may be conflict-averse and try to dismiss it or pretend it's not there.

This may be difficult, but discuss the situation with the offending employee. Most people deny that they harbor racist feelings, particularly if confronted by the person targeted for discrimination. If you are a manager, and an employee is second-guessing you or double-checking your directives with others, discuss this with him or her immediately. The last thing you need is a challenge to your credibility.

In addition, discuss the problem with colleagues, and even with your boss, to make them aware. If you're the only African American, or one of two at your level, you must reach out to peers and superiors who are in the majority. Didn't get a memo or e-mail? Be aware that you may be mistakenly left out of important meetings or given partial information that can affect your performance. To counter any deliberate omission, try to align with someone in the company who can be trusted to provide you with the right information. Keep in mind that you may not be able to change a person's prejudice, but you can and should correct his or her behavior.

Q: When do I need an employment attorney?

A: You should build a relationship with an employment attorney as early in your career as possible, says "CB" Bowman, president and CEO of Career Strategies Inc., a New York job search and career management firm. One of the main reasons is that, "in many states, our legal system favors employers due to `termination at will' laws, and employees need to ensure a level playing field," she warns. Outside of litigious matters, employment attorneys can advise you on offer letters, performance reviews, release letters, particularly those containing employee rights waivers, noncompete clauses and confidentiality agreements.

The burden of proof in most discrimination cases lies on the employee. It can be very difficult to prove employer intent without proper guidance. Many employees wait until they are terminated before they look for an employment attorney. Seeking one beforehand can ensure that you'll learn how to document evidence and keep the appropriate records, notes Bowman. Professional career coaches and personal referrals are two good avenues to finding an employment attorney. You could also contact the American Bar Association headquartered in Chicago, at 312-988-5000.

FIGHTING BACK: KEEPING DETAILED RECORDS ON DISCRIMINATION IS A START

The number of job discrimination cases has remained high during the past five years. In 2000, the Equal Employment Opportunity Commission[6] received close to 80,000 charges of discrimination. Many of those charges were race-based, but American employees filed record numbers of sexual, ethnic, age, and religion discrimination cases as well during the past decade.

Unfortunately, many employees who go to courts for justice lose their cases because they failed to write down all the facts. Without proper documentation, the success rate of most discrimination cases is less than 30 percent. Consider taking the following steps if you find yourself faced with discrimination in the workplace:

- *Try to resolve your problems internally.* Your attorney will want to know that you have gone through the proper channels before deciding to file suit.
- *Keep a diary of your daily work activities.* Document your actions, accomplishments, and work activities. If a court case evolves, your employer will have kept dibs on you, so be sure that you know what actions were taken, and on what dates.

CAREER AT A GLANCE—ON THE CASE

Occupation: Intelligence analyst

Job Description: Research, analyze, and develop cases on illegal international import/export threats. Areas of concentration include commercial fraud, terrorism, narcotics smuggling, child pornography, and money laundering.

Salary range: $20,000 to $58,000 (U.S. Government GS5 to GS12 status). Depending on the city, include a $3,000 to $5,000 locality pay.

Training: Bachelor's degree and six weeks of intelligence and technical training are required.

For more information about intelligence analysts, contact the U.S. Customs Service, Office of Human Resources Enforcement Division, 2121 L Street, NW, Second Floor, Washington, DC, or contact your local Office of Personnel Management, Federal Job Information Center.

- *Review your personnel file.* In many states, employees are legally entitled to an annual review of their files.

- *Obtain a written job description.* It is the guideline for what is expected of you, and the barometer used during performance evaluations.

- *Correct false information immediately.* If left uncorrected, it could suggest that you had performance or behavioral problems in the past.

- *Don't build a case on the words of coworkers.* When it comes time to testify, they probably won't be willing to risk their jobs for you.

AN INSIDE HIT: SUCCESS IN TODAY'S WORKPLACE REQUIRES SELLING YOUR IDEAS TO COLLEAGUES

Do you have what it takes to implement your ideas in the face of fierce corporate competition? Of course you do—it's just a matter of developing the right sales pitch. Karen Smith, a sales manager for a major New York commercial bank, realized, very early in her career, that her sharp selling skills would play a key role in her advancement. Although she started out as a branch teller in 1988, Smith was determined to move into other areas of the bank that offered greater employment opportunities.

Her first sales pitch was to her boss. Smith convinced him that she could handle additional responsibilities by showing her creativity on a daily basis. "While some of my fellow coworkers did only what was required, I knew I had to go above and beyond my job description to get noticed," Smith explains. "While moving from teller to a sales position was very rare in my company, I was convinced that I could do the job well, and I made others believe in me too."

Part of her strategy was to make herself visible. She built a partnership with her supervisor by volunteering for projects and making herself a resource for him to bounce ideas off of. She then familiarized herself with bank products and services and made suggestions to customers as she handled their daily banking transactions. She monitored company job postings and applied for a sales associate position, which eventually led to a sales manager post.

In her current position, she uses her selling skills to gain the support of her staff. "I'm not a one-woman show," says Smith. "I try

---

DID YOU KNOW?

Richard Parsons, President and COO at Time Warner Inc. skipped two elementary school grades to enter the University of Hawaii at 16.— *Black Enterprise*, February 2000

---

to enroll everyone in my vision by showing each person what special talents they can contribute to the project." It's not altruism that drives most people to work every day. Besides income, people want to know how an organizational change or new idea will benefit them individually.

Last quarter, when Smith told her sales staff that they would have to increase their sales goals by 20 percent, the idea was met with discontent. "I had to sell them on their strong points and go to each person and tell them in what areas they could improve," recalls Smith. As a result, all quotas were met.

How can you convince your colleagues that your ideas are worth their investment?

- *Know your company.* Whom should you pitch your ideas to first? Who would care about your idea? Understanding your company's history, political climate, and culture can help you evaluate when and how to pitch your next idea. Determine the success of employees who've tried to implement new business strategies or operations in the past, and follow their lead. After you've determined what your company's needs are, honestly assess whether your idea can be viable.

- *Do your research.* Has your idea been tried before? If so, what were the results? Bosses generally appreciate employees who provide fresh innovative ideas, but they have little confidence in employees who offer ideas that have already been implemented. Find a way to make your idea unique.

- *Make the pitch.* Just do it! After you've convinced yourself that your idea provides your company with a competitive advantage, pass your passion along to your colleagues. Be enthusiastic and confident. Make them feel that this is an opportunity that can't be missed.

SURVIVING A MERGER

In the 1980s and 1990s, companies scuttling about for funds prompted many mergers. Today, corporate marriages are being driven by a search for new customers, markets, and talented employees. Yet, however promising these deals may be for shareholders and customers, all this corporate gyration is leaving employees in a lurch.

The workers most threatened by mergers are in human resources, accounting, and data processing—areas that may overlap when the two companies come together, says Dave Jones,[7] vice president of Career Management Services at Personnel Decisions International, in Minneapolis, Minnesota. But, he adds, there is hope for employees in areas such as sales and information systems. Employ the following tips if the threat of a merger looms:

- *Understand your emotions and uncertainty.* Know that you are going to have fears. You will go into a self-preservation mode, but keep it in perspective.

- *Watch your attitude.* Stay positive, and look for new and exciting opportunities in the reconstituted company.

- *Be open to change.* Uttering the phrase, "This is how we have always done it" is the kiss of death. Don't assume that the acquiring company wants to maintain your status quo. If you are rhapsodizing about the old company, what good will you be to the new organization?

- *Keep your ear to the ground, and stay visible.* It's a natural tendency to recede into the woodwork during times of chaos. Wrong move. Cancel your vacation plans. Communicate with your manager in a nonconfrontational way, and ask, "What's next?"

- *"Company people" are survivors.* Attend all meetings and functions. Introduce yourself to all members of the new team. Your help on a project, no matter how trivial, will go a long way toward raising your workplace visibility.

- *Control your own career and develop a plan.* You can't rely on an immediate supervisor to remember all your contributions. Often, the acquiring company will evaluate your worth. Write a summary of your accomplishments at the mere hint of a merger, and update it weekly. Be sure to highlight newfound or untapped skills that can be transferred.

- *If you are part of the acquisition team, be encouraging to the new staff.* Let them know that they are important and you won't run roughshod over them.

HOW TO LAND A JOB IN A TIGHT ECONOMY

What goes up must come down and the job market is no different. After several robust years of low unemployment rates and jobs abound, the market is experiencing a deceleration. Hiring freezes became evident at the start of the year as the economy slowed and the dot-com fallout left many highly talented professionals in its wake. No doubt, as the U.S. economy continues putting on the brakes, those companies that are hiring will be very selective. With the playing field now getting crowded, how can you stand out from the rest and land the job you want?

First, you must change your mindset about the job search. Traditionally, most managers or executives seek positions of more responsibility and loftier titles. "However, if you are looking for a position in today's market, you must be willing to come in at a manager or director level," says Dawn Rivera,[8] director of human resources at Media Solution Services in New York. "Don't be title hungry because responsibilities vary: A vice president at one place could be the equivalent of a director at another." Try to get a copy of the job description from human resources or the executive recruiter and compare, advises Rivera. "If the job does not fulfill all your expectations, then look at it as a foot in the door and bargain for the benefits or salary that will make the job worth it."

You should also not rule out the possibility of relocating. Often, a move out of state or even the country can offer better career opportunities. For example, low to no corporate taxes has made Las Vegas attractive to many companies seeking to relocate, but it's not so popular with job seekers, particularly those already established in the Northeast or South.

Networking should be ongoing throughout your career track whether you're seeking a job or not. That means attending conferences, doing volunteer work, and not being to big to mingle with subordinates or those outside your department who may have leads or a heads-up on internal or outside job opportunities, adds Rivera. You should also stay in touch with recruiting managers at companies you've interviewed with as well as executive recruiters. If your name is fresh in his or her head, then you stand a good chance of being tapped when an opportunity arises.

UPGRADING YOUR SKILLS

Sometimes a career move may involve looking on the inside rather than only on the outside. "Reflect on what you majored in at college," says Rivera. "Perhaps you were an accounting major, but you've spent most of your career in marketing. It might be time for a career change." If you need to advance your education, now is the time to do it! It can be as little as upgrading your technical skills to earning an executive MBA. "Most mid-level professionals had secretaries and are not familiar with programs that can increase their value such as Word, PowerPoint, or Adobe Illustrator. When asked in an interview why you don't have the requisite technical skills, offer to learn them after hours, adds Rivera. It shows the recruiter your flexibility and that you're serious about getting the job.

Depending on your career pursuits, an executive MBA program—a part-time but intensive version of the traditional MBA—might be the ticket. An executive MBA allows busy professionals who must juggle work and family with their studies the opportunity to earn a degree on the weekends or after work. The main difference between a traditional and an executive MBA is that the latter prepares professionals for senior-level positions. Students in executive programs—who are generally older (often in their late 30s and 40s)—get a broad view of management issues and situations where they can apply and share their own experiences. Most executive MBA programs require five to 10 years of practical business experience.

Beyond the spread of executive MBA programs, the greatest boom has been in the area of executive education. Many corporations are willing to invest $1,500 to $25,000 to upgrade their managers' business and leadership skills. These increasingly popular training courses, which can range from a few weeks to several months, are designed to offer managers a quick way to gain the skills necessary to compete in today's ever-changing workplace. Certificate- rather than degree-based, they are, once again, developed to fit the schedule of a busy professional.

All in all, the road to a new job is paved with steadfast rules: continually upgrade your skills, craft a blockbuster resume, network with determination, dress professionally, and ace the interview. However, it's the fortitude, foresight, and finesse you apply in paving that road that makes the difference.

Just because you have the job doesn't mean you should hole up in your office or cubicle and devote yourself solely to your prescribed job description. It is important that you get to know the organization and the your fellow associates—peers, superiors, and subordinates! You don't need to be the company social director, but you should make sure that you know the corporate culture, protocol, and who the movers and shakers are. Most importantly, a good attitude, professionalism, finesse, and foresight will go a long way in making your job better in order to have a fulfilling career.

12

PREPARING FOR THE JOB OF YOUR DREAMS

You're educated and successful, and you have been exposed to a diverse lot of experiences and situations. You may even consider yourself a very sophisticated, career-minded individual. With a new job, you will be called upon to act in new and different ways. You'll want to be at your best because your performance will be evaluated and closely tied to your success or failure at the company. Fall short of expectations and you might soon be replaced. This rule applies not only to your tangible work skills, but also to your knowledge of business etiquette.

Even astute and polished individuals can forget some of the most obvious, and often subtle, rules of etiquette. A command of business etiquette—knowing what is correct and how to act in all situations—will give you a sense of confidence that can help you get ahead.

ON YOUR BEST BEHAVIOR

From black-tie events to office parties, the spirit of the holidays returns each year, but remember: Professionalism doesn't end just because you let your hair down. Inappropriate behavior at company functions can

---

**EVERYDAY BUSINESS ETIQUETTE BY MARILYN PINCUS
(BARRON'S EDUCATIONAL SERIES)**

This book tells how to deal gracefully and effectively with every aspect of a career, from job searches for recent college graduates to doing international business.

---

lead to suspension, ostracism, or even dismissal. Some people avoid these events because of anxiety; others feel compelled to attend. And, of course, some firms make attendance mandatory. Even if you are one of the few African Americans at your firm, a party can turn out to be a beneficial career opportunity by providing exposure and creating a comfort level among your peers. It may be your one opportunity to meet senior executives, or individuals from other departments who can later be very helpful in your current position or can clue you about other career opportunities within the company.

Being visible at these events is important, but having social grace is of the essence. Employers and employees alike should take into account that not everyone celebrates the calendar holidays. People of various religious backgrounds shouldn't be made to feel distanced, or forced to participate, if celebrating would mean going against their beliefs. Following these simple guidelines can ensure a pleasant and memorable holiday season:

- Above all, if you drink, don't drink too much. Nothing is more embarrassing than loose lips—saying the wrong thing because your inhibitions have been lessened with libation.

- Don't overdress or look too provocative. Depending on the venue where the party is being held, your best bet would be to dress as you do for work, enhancing the look with a dressier shirt or blouse. If you change completely, then stay clear of New Year's Eve or formal wear unless the location or invitation says "black tie."

- If your office is doing a "Secret Santa" or grab-bag gift, don't give personal items such as toiletries or lingerie. Instead, give work-related gifts such as stationary, pens, or calendars. The

---

DID YOU KNOW?

Stacey J. Mobley, Senior Vice President and Chief Administrative Officer at Dupont Foundation, is also a registered pharmacist.—*Black Enterprise*, February 2000

---

more generic, the better. Do not make the mistake of a wrong gift (a male gift for a woman, or vice versa) or one that insults.

- Don't tell jokes that will offend others, especially the boss, and remember that sexual harassment laws still apply in anything work-related.

- Mingle with others. Nothing is worse than a party where the same people who work together, every day, congregate together during the whole evening.

- Relax and enjoy yourself.

ON THE ROAD WITH YOUR BOSS: EVEN THOUGH YOU'RE OUT OF THE OFFICE, IT'S STILL STRICTLY BUSINESS

You're about to embark on a three-day business trip with your boss. To make it a success, keep in mind that "the business trip is an extension of the office, and professionalism is key," advises Sandra Morisset, founder and president of Protocol Training Services, in New York. "You are still being observed and evaluated. Therefore, carry your manners with you," she says. To remain in the good graces of your superiors:

- *Arrive early.* Whether you're sharing a ride by taxi or corporate jet, attending a meeting, or going to dinner, don't make your boss wait.

- *Mr., Ms., or Mrs.?* If she is "Ms. Smith" in the office, she does not become "Fran" during the trip. Unless told otherwise, stick to protocol.

- *Dress professionally.* Your attire should be the same as it would be if you were in the office. Take it up a notch if your office wardrobe is more casual.

- *Limit the conversation.* Follow your boss's lead. Resist gossiping or asking about personal or confidential company business.

- *Say "Yes."* If your superior invites you to dinner, accept. Brush up on your dining etiquette, and quickly decide what you want from the menu. The host or hostess picks up the tab.

- *Be kind.* Practice common courtesy, and don't try to throw your weight around. Treat sky caps, flight attendants, hotel personnel, and waiters with respect. The words "Hello," "Thank you," and "Please" can have amazing results.

CAREER AT A GLANCE—
DETERMINING PROBABILITY

Occupation: Actuary

Job description: Assembles and analyzes facts, and estimates the risks and returns on financial planning decisions in a specific area of expertise. Employed mostly in the insurance industry, but increasingly in government, education, finance, and health care.

Salary range: $34,000 to over $100,000 (commensurate with each exam).

Training: A bachelor's degree in actuarial science, business, mathematics, or statistics. Interpersonal and communication skills are musts. Completion of all exams takes five to 10 years.

Throughout their careers, actuaries must take exams that can require up to five months of study. Practitioners say the career offers a high level of satisfaction and challenge. Creative thinking and problem-solving skills are key. For more information, contact the Casualty Actuarial Society at 703-276-3100, or the International Association of Black Actuaries at 313-556-1643.

- *Yin and yang.* Okay, so your boss is just inherently rude. Send him or her a subliminal message by maintaining your composure and being polite. You're also representing the company, so set an example.

Q: Can the message on my home voice mail or answering machine hinder my job prospects?

A: It can. Communication is an integral part of the interviewing process, and it includes your personal telephone, says Verba Edwards,[1] president of Wing Tips & Pumps, an executive recruitment firm in Troy, Michigan. Rap music, long jazz intros, a singing child, or religious statements may be forms of self-expression, she says, but they don't work with some employers.

"I have had employers tell me they refused to call back a candidate because of a two- to three-minute presentation on their answering machine," says Edwards. Ask yourself if the message on your machine is one you wouldn't mind your new boss hearing. If you use music, make sure it's not overbearing, and don't let background vocals compete with your voice. Have a friend listen to your message and judge whether it puts you in a professional light. After you've landed the job, you can go back to being creative.

DID YOU GET THE MESSAGE? BUSINESS ETIQUETTE IN THE AGE OF TECHNOLOGY

Admit it. You sometimes read the faxes addressed to colleagues as you wait for yours to be transmitted. Your secretary might be retrieving your voice-mail messages, unbeknownst to callers.

In today's business environment, e-mail, voice-mail, and faxes have become commonplace. Despite the quick pace that has electronic communication revolutionizing the workplace, the rules of "netiquette" lag behind. With face-to-face meetings a distant memory, it's easy to forget that there is a real person on the other end. Be conscientious. Respect the rights and space of your colleagues. Another point to consider: Your company e-mail may not be as secure as you think. With the growth of network systems, be mindful that any information you submit is insecure and can be viewed by a third party while in transit. Here are five tips for maneuvering through today's office communication channels:

1. In your voice-mail greeting, inform callers who will be listening to their messages; for example, "After the beep, you may leave a confidential message," or "Your message may be retrieved by my assistant."

2. Faxes are mail. Don't read them unless they're for you. If you must print a confidential document, send it to a private printer or retrieve it immediately.

3. It is disrespectful for your cellular phone or beeper to go off during a seminar or meeting. When necessary, be incommunicado.

4. Don't use a birth date or a child's name as your password. Use the first letters of the words in a sentence, for example, The end of the day = TEOTD.

5. Keep in mind that "unlisted" phone numbers may be a thing of the past as more companies—particularly those in customer service—employ Caller ID.

HOW TO DRESS WHEN MOVING UP THE LADDER

Your appearance plays a greater role than you might think. For your flight up the corporate ladder, dress like the leader you are.

Look in the mirror. What do you see? Perhaps you're one of those women who still wears tennis shoes with your "power suit." Do you still iron your dress shirts, or worse, your suits? If so, you've made strides along the management track but, sadly, your image is still entry-level.

Many mid-level managers, and even some executives, remain trapped in a fashion abyss for years. The very same suits, hairstyles, and makeup that helped launch their career years ago are sabotaging their image today. "Often, we don't want to change because we don't know where it's going to take us," says Gloria Respress-Churchwell,[2] president of Churchwell Fashion Consulting, in Nashville, Tennessee. "But a modern, upgraded look is going to add to your credibility."

The same amount of time you devote to enhancing your public speaking skills and upgrading your technical know-how should also be spent on bolstering your looks. Allowing your appearance to take a back seat for too long may, in fact, derail your career. Keep in mind that the image you project must reflect not only where you are but where you want to go in your career.

"In 30 seconds, people make judgments about you, based on how you look," says Charmaine McClarie,[3] president of Image Design, an executive development and communications consulting firm in San Francisco. "Observe how your colleagues dress, not only in your company but in your industry. Ask yourself, 'What does a leader look like?' Then study those leaders at networking events and in business and industry publications."

Go for quality, not quantity. Those who have been in senior-level positions for years can spot quality immediately. Natural fibers such as cotton, wool, silk, and blends of these fabrics last longer and fit and wear better.

There's no question that custom-made clothing is the form for the executive suite, says McClarie, who consults with many Fortune 500 company executives and prominent attorneys. Deep, finished hems, hand-stitching, and generously cut fine fabrics are the mark of quality clothing.

Fit is also essential. Few people can buy something off-the-rack that fits perfectly. If you purchase a suit from a retail store, make sure you have it altered accordingly. "It makes a subtle, yet powerful difference. Nothing looks worse than a man or woman moving up the ladder in a cheap, ill-fitting suit," insists McClarie. For men, suit sleeves should have bound button holes, not faux ones with buttons sewn on top. Buttons should also be metal or bone, not plastic. You'll be surprised at how a simple change of the buttons can make a dramatic difference.

How many clothes should an executive have? According to McClarie, your wardrobe should be 60 percent accessories: ties, pocket squares, scarves, jewelry, and shoes; and 40 percent major pieces: suits, blazers, and dresses. An array of accessories offers different looks.

For example, a man should have three shirts and six ties for every suit. Put those ties on the hanger with a suit and remove them after each wear, to avoid the "safe look"—that same outfit that everyone compliments you on every time you wear it. It's also wise to keep an extra suit, shirt, or blouse, and a pair of shoes, tucked away at the office for emergencies. Men should include a couple of ties with these items, and women, at least two changes of accessories.

YOUR SIGNATURE

A leader is a risk taker. If you're going for a high profile, you've got to have a signature style—something that allows you to subtly stand out while still fitting in. "Don't play it safe," advises McClarie. "It says nothing about you except that you're safe." Yet African Americans, known for being vibrant and fashion-conscious, should keep that signature statement low-key and avoid anything too flamboyant.

As Robert T. Ross[4] made gallant career strides along Merrill Lynch's management track, he witnessed an interesting trend. Many at the top of the financial services industry shunned the bold colors and tapered cuts of Italian designers, and opted instead for a more conservative button-down American or British style. Ross, now a vice president and sales manager at Merrill Lynch's Grand Central Financial Complex in New York, was quick to take the cue. "I had a wide selection of nontraditional colored suits in taupe, browns, and greens, and switched to navy suits, white shirts, and red-toned ties," he says. Despite adopting "the uniform," Ross didn't lose his style, which he accentuated with quality fabrics and cufflinks etched with his initials or the logo of his company or of Morehouse College, his alma mater. "People expect a certain image, and you must maintain it if you want to look like the guy in charge," says Ross, who regularly conducts public seminars and has some 100 brokers under his charge. "I believe your first impression must be a success, otherwise you're just behind the eight ball."

For Pam Cross,[5] weekend anchor and reporter at News Center 5, WCVB-TV in Boston, scarves and pins became her signature piece. "Since I'm seen mostly from the waist up, it was important that I find one item that could be my trademark." Cross, who has been in the business for 20 years, knew that the way she looked had to have as much impact as the news she delivered.

By employing the services of Respress-Churchwell, Cross got more than fashion advice; she got more free time, something foreign to today's fast-paced professionals. "She went to the store ahead of me and laid items aside. I got an honest opinion about how I looked without the pressure of a salesperson," adds Cross. The relationship didn't stop there. Respress-Churchwell periodically called Cross to offer suggestions and give feedback about her on-camera appearance. "A personal shopper was something that I never thought of, but the cost was well worth it." At $35 to $175 an hour, depending on the consultant and where you live, investing in a personal shopper and image consultant can be a wise move. It may also be a tax-deductible business expense. If you're a high-profile executive, your company may absorb the cost.

Whether you get help from professionals or do it on your own, be open to change. Each season, assess what's in your closet and determine whether it's representative of your position as well as your goals. A little wardrobe building, updating, or upgrading may do a lot for your career and your personal life.

You might have the skills and credentials, but possessing the proper etiquette in manner and dress will round out the package. The job search is a little bit like traveling in a foreign country. You are depending on the locals to get you where you want to go; it's very easy for the locals to talk behind your back; and there are certain customs that are good to know if you want to get anywhere at all. So always show respect and courtesy to all. Don't be the "ugly American" and unload your baggage on unsuspecting bystanders with anger and complaining and observe the rules. Putting your best foot forward all the time will pay off greatly in the long run.

NOTES

Introduction

1. U.S. Bureau of Labor Statistics
2. U.S. Census Bureau
3. Cassandra Hayes, "Riding the Wave," *Black Enterprise* magazine (February 1999), p. 84.
4. *Ibid.*
5. *Workforce 2020.*
6. Cassandra Hayes, "The Calm After the Storm," *Black Enterprise* magazine (February 1998), p. 86.
7. *Ibid.*, p. 84.
8. *Ibid.*
9. *Ibid.*

Chapter 1: Planning Your Career

1. Survey: George Mason University/Potomac Knowledge Way.
2. Live interview; Cassandra Hayes, *Black Enterprise* magazine (April 2001), p. 108.
3. Cassandra Hayes, "Merger Maestro," *Black Enterprise* magazine (September 1998), p. 84.
4. Cassandra Hayes, "Sowing a New World Harvest," *Black Enterprise* magazine (September 1997), pp. 106–108.
5. Cassandra Hayes, "The Making of a Corporate Executive," *Black Enterprise* magazine (June 1996), p. 84.
6. Cassandra Hayes, "Choosing the Right Path," *Black Enterprise* magazine (April 2001), p. 110.
7. Cassandra Hayes, "Deeds Over Dollars," *Black Enterprise* magazine (November 1995), pp. 112–119.
8. *Ibid.*, p. 116.
9. Coopers & Lybrand salary survey.
10. Live interview (not her real name, and identifying elements have been changed).
11. Cassandra Hayes, "Women Dynamos," *Black Enterprise* magazine (August 1998), p. 60.
12. Cassandra Hayes, "Selling into the Stratospere," *Black Enterprise* magazine (June 1997), pp. 172–181.

Chapter 3: Building a Network

1. Cassandra Hayes, "Choosing the Right Path," *Black Enterprise* magazine (April 2001), p. 113.
2. Live interview.
3. Cassandra Hayes, "Reap College Rewards for Life," *Black Enterprise* magazine (February 1995), p. 66.
4. Society for Human Resource Management (Mentors).
5. Dexter Bridgeman, Diversified Communications Group. Live interview.
6. Cassandra Hayes, "Line Up Those Mentors Now," *Black Enterprise* magazine (December 1994), p. 51.

Chapter 4: Hunting for the Right Job

1. Cassandra Hayes, "From Temp to Permanent," *Black Enterprise* magazine (September 1997), p. 71.
2. Cassandra Hayes and Charlene Solomon, "The Lure of Temping," *Black Enterprise* magazine (February 1996), pp. 119–120.
3. *Ibid.*, p. 122.
4. Cassandra Hayes, "Temporary Work Is an Asset," *Black Enterprise* magazine (May 1995), p. 53; "The Lure of Temping," *Black Enterprise* magazine (February 1996), p. 122.
5. Survey: Virginia Tech & ITAA.
6. Cassandra Hayes and Tariq Muhammad, "Tech Careers 2001," *Black Enterprise* magazine (December 1998), p. 135.
7. U.S. Bureau of Labor Statistics.
8. Cassandra Hayes and Tariq Muhammad, "Tech Careers 2001," *Black Enterprise* magazine (November 1998), p. 140.
9. Cassandra Hayes, "The Calm After the Storm," *Black Enterprise* magazine (February 1998), p. 92.
10. *Ibid.*, p. 90; "Prescription for Career Success," *Black Enterprise* magazine (January 1997), p. 69; "Perfecting Your Sales Pitch," *Black Enterprise* magazine (September 1996), p. 203.
11. Donnette Dunbar and Cassandra Hayes, "Perscription for Career Success," *Black Enterprise* magazine (January 1997), p. 69.
12. *Ibid.*, p. 71.
13. *Ibid.*, p. 70.

Chapter 5: Preparing for an Interview

1. Cassandra Hayes, "Feel Like You're Filling a Quota," *Black Enterprise* magazine (February 1995), p. 65.
2. Cassandra Hayes, "Reverse Selection," *Black Enterprise* magazine (April 1998), p. 46.
3. *Ibid.*
4. *Ibid.*
5. Cassandra Hayes, "Your Credit Can Affect Your Job Prospects," *Black Enterprise* magazine (October 1995), p. 61.
6. Cassandra Hayes, "Is That Legal," *Black Enterprise* magazine (February 1995), p. 65.

Chapter 6: Gathering Experience

1. The Council of Graduate Schools.
2. Survey: The Council of Graduate Schools.

3. Cassandra Hayes, "World Class Learning," *Black Enterprise* magazine (May 1998), p. 86.
4. *Ibid.*
5. *Ibid.*, p. 87.
6. *Ibid.*, p. 88.
7. *Ibid.*, p. 90.

Chapter 7: Negotiating Your Salary

1. Cassandra Hayes, "What to Know about the Counteroffer," *Black Enterprise* magazine (March 1996), p. 55.
2. Cassandra Hayes, "Alternatives to a Pay Raise," *Black Enterprise* magazine (November 1994), p. 71.
3. Cassandra Hayes, "Separation Pay," *Black Enterprise* magazine (October 1997), p. 55.

Chapter 8: Mining the Workplace

1. Cassandra Hayes, "Deskilled but Not Defeated," *Black Enterprise* magazine (December 1994), p. 51.
2. U.S. Census Bureau.
3. Federal Glass Ceiling Commission.
4. Cassandra Hayes, "Life Atop the Crystal Stair," *Black Enterprise* magazine (February 1998), p. 108.
5. *Ibid.*, p. 110.
6. Study: Kimbro Institute.
7. Cassandra Hayes, "Life Atop the Crystal Stair," *Black Enterprise* magazine (February 1998), p. 110.
8. *Ibid.*, p. 114.
9. *Ibid.*

Chapter 10: Making a Career Switch

1. Cassandra Hayes and Robyn D. Clarke, "The Long and Winding Work Road," *Black Enterprise* magazine (May 2001), p. 68.
2. Cassandra Hayes, "Presto Change-O," *Black Enterprise* magazine (June 1999), pp. 269–272.
3. Cassandra Hayes, "Didn't Know I Had It in Me," *Black Enterprise* magazine (May 1998), p. 55.
4. Cassandra Hayes, "The Verdict, Jones & Jury," *Black Enterprise* magazine (December 1994), p. 233.
5. Survey: American Management Association.
6. Cassandra Hayes, "Presto Change-O," *Black Enterprise* magazine (June 1999), pp. 269–272.
7. Cassandra Hayes, "Ackward Positions," *Black Enterprise* magazine (June 1996), p. 79.
8. Cassandra Hayes, "How Accountable Are You for Your Success?" *Black Enterprise* magazine (July 1997), pp. 111–112.
9. Cassandra Hayes, "Can't Move Up? Then Consider Shipping Out," *Black Enterprise* magazine (June 1996), p. 79.
10. Cassandra Hayes, "Insuring All Goes Well," *Black Enterprise* magazine (March 1996), p. 56.
11. Cassandra Hayes, "The Career Path Less Traveled," *Black Enterprise* magazine (December 1998), p. 55.

12. Cassandra Hayes, "You Can Go Home Again," *Black Enterprise* magazine (July 1998), p. 52.
13. *Ibid.*
14. *Ibid.*
15. *Ibid.*
16. Cassandra Hayes, "From Job-to-Job," *Black Enterprise* magazine (April 1998), p. 45.
17. Study: Presented at the Academy of Management Meeting Frieda Reitman and Joy Schneer.
18. Cassandra Hayes, "Go For It," *Black Enterprise* magazine (February 1997), p. 73.
19. *Ibid.*
20. *Ibid.*, p. 74.
21. *Ibid.*, p. 78.
22. *Ibid.*, p. 80.
23. *Ibid.*, pp. 100–105.
24. Cassandra Hayes, "The Intrigue of International Assignments," *Black Enterprise* magazine (May 1996), p. 98.
25. *Ibid.*, p. 104.
26. Study: Business Horizons.
27. Cassandra Hayes, "What's Yours Is Mine," *Black Enterprise* magazine (June 1997), p. 75.
28. Cassandra Hayes, "Think Before You Leave It Off Your Resume," *Black Enterprise* magazine (April 1997), p. 53; (July 1996), p. 51.

Chapter 11: Succeeding at Work

1. Cassandra Hayes, *Black Enterprise* magazine (December 1994), p. 52.
2. Cassandra Hayes, *Black Enterprise* magazine (December 1994), p. 52.
3. Cassandra Hayes, "Passing on the Baton," *Black Enterprise* magazine (September 1996), p. 52.
4. *Ibid.*
5. Cassandra Hayes, "You Left, Now They Want You Back," *Black Enterprise* magazine (April 1995), p. 53.
6. Equal Opportunity Commission.
7. Cassandra Hayes, "Surviving a Merger," *Black Enterprise* magazine (June 1997), p. 76.
8. Cassandra Hayes, "How to Land a Job in a Tight Economy," *Black Enterprise* magazine (October 2001), special advertising section.

Chapter 12: Preparing for the Job of Your Dreams

1. Cassandra Hayes, "Alternatives to a Pay Raise," *Black Enterprise* magazine (November 1994), p. 74.
2. Cassandra Hayes, "How to Dress When Moving Up the Ladder," *Black Enterprise* magazine (October 1996), pp. 131–133.
3. *Ibid.*, p. 132.
4. *Ibid.*
5. *Ibid.*

INDEX

SUBSCRIBE TO YOUR GUIDE TO FINANCIAL EMPOWERMENT

Yes! ☐ $17.95

Please enter my personal subscription for 1 Year at $17.95
That is 12 issues including our special issue—**B.E. 100s** and MORE!
You save 51%
off the single copy rate.

BLACK ENTERPRISE

YOUR ULTIMATE GUIDE TO FINANCIAL EMPOWERMENT

G12K

Save 51%

Name _____

Address _____

City _____

State _____

Zip _____

E-mail _____

Send to:
BLACK ENTERPRISE
Subscription Service Center
PO Box 3009
Harlan, IA 51593-2100

Basic annual rate is $21.95. Foreign rate $36.95.

For faster service, call 1-800-727-7777 or
for *EVEN FASTER* service, go to blackenterprise.com
and click on the SUBSCRIBE button.

blackenterprise.com The Virtual Desktop For African Americans

Empower Yourself

We don't claim to be the best site for African American wealth building. WE ARE.

Visit blackenterprise.com where you'll find:

- Easier navigation
- Online investing services
- Exclusive surveys
- Downloadable Wealth Building Kits
- Financial Fitness Contests
- Personalized home pages
- Up-to-date news and information
- **blackenterprise.com's** exclusive Black Stock Index
- Weekly columns from **blackenterprise.com** editors
- Over 150 industry specific news categories

Visit the NEW blackenterprise.com today!

Unlimited Opportunities Await You

BLACK ENTERPRISE
CONFERENCES AND SPECIAL EVENTS

Be Inspired
Black Enterprise/Bank of America Entrepreneurs Conference
(May, Opryland Hotel, Nashville, TN)
An exclusive gathering of entrepreneurs, this important conference brings together the country's leading CEOs and key executives for stimulating sessions, exhibits, receptions, and golf—with plenty of time to meet old contacts and establish new ones.

Be Challenged
Black Enterprise/Pepsi Golf & Tennis Challenge
(Labor Day Weekend, La Quinta Resort & Club, Palm Springs, CA)
Mix and mingle with the nation's top business minds for a weekend of golf, tennis, spa—and just plain fun. Share ideas, discuss business strategies and meet other executives in business and finance. Enjoy receptions and entertainment in a beautiful setting filled with networking opportunities.

Be Energized
Black Enterprise/AXA Advisors Ski Challenge
(Presidents' Day Weekend, Vail Cascade Resort & Spa, Vail, CO)
From slopes to seminars, snowshoeing to snowboarding, this winter networking event offers something for everyone — with ski, spa, and kids club packages to meet every need.

For details and more information about these exciting events, call 800-543-6786 (Entrepreneurs Conference)
800-209-7229 (Golf & Tennis/Ski Challenges)
or visit our website at **www.blackenterprise.com**

TAKE ONE STEP CLOSER TO FINANCIAL EMPOWERMENT

Introducing the BLACK ENTERPRISE **Wealth Building Kit**, a step-by-step guide to financial empowerment from the nation's No. 1 authority on black business. To get your free kit, log on to blackenterprise.com and visit our personal finance section or call toll free **1-877-WEALTHY**

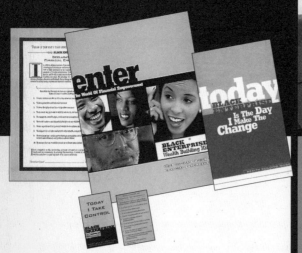

BLACK ENTERPRISE

YOUR ULTIMATE GUIDE TO FINANCIAL EMPOWERMENT